D0530212

LONDON
by **PUB**

Dedicated to the regulars and staff
at the Sir Richard Steele, Hampstead –
a cheerier and more helpful bunch
I could not have wished to find.

LONDON
by **PUB**

PUB WALKS AROUND
HISTORIC LONDON

Ted Bruning

PRION

First published in 2001 by
Prion Books Limited, Imperial Works,
Perren Street, London NW5 3ED

Text Copyright © 2001 Ted Bruning
Design © 2001 Prion Books Ltd

All rights reserved

No part of this book may be reproduced, stored in a retrieval system,
or transmitted in any form or by any means, electronic, mechanical,
photocopying, recording or otherwise, without the prior written
permission of the publisher.

A catalogue record of this book can be obtained from the British Library

ISBN 1-85375-431-5

Photography by Ted Bruning and Mick Slaughter
Printed and bound in Singapore
Cover pictures by Mark Turner
Cover Design by Bob Eames

CONTENTS

INTRODUCTION

"You must not be satisfied with seeing its great streets and squares, but must survey the innumerable little lanes and courts."

Dr. Johnson

LONDON, so the cliché goes, is as much a collection of villages as a city; and in a way that's true.

Until the 1660s, London was still quite compact. But the rebuilding that followed the Great Fire of 1666 didn't stop at the old city limits; instead, London went on growing, street by street, field by field, farm by farm. The ancient settlements to the east were soon swallowed up and are still recalled in the name Tower Hamlets. A great wave of speculative building broke over the old royal hunting-ground to the west, still called Soho after the huntsman's cry. Swamps were drained; rivers were culverted; great beds of clay were excavated and fired to make the brown bricks that still characterise the city.

During this process, which lasted three centuries, many long-established villages and small towns were absorbed into the swelling city. But the saying that London is a collection of villages isn't based on the survival of the old nuclei of these settlements, for they were not only swallowed up but also razed. If you look for, say, a medieval church or an ancient inn in one of London's countless high streets, you'll be disappointed. Road-widening and redevelopment over the years have accounted for pretty well all of them, and London's so-called villages retain none of their original rural character.

But the sporadic nature of London's expansion, often carried out by speculative builders who might have developed anything from a single street to a huge estate, has created a city of enclaves, each with its landmarks, its history, its character. The diversity of this mosaic is compounded by London's topography: the crowded boroughs of the floodplain are markedly different from the more expansive hillside quarters such as Hampstead, Highgate or Dulwich.

There is only one way to experience and enjoy this diversity to the full, and that's on foot. Forget the open-topped double-decker tour bus: if you want to delve into promising side-streets, or take in some unexpected vista, or pause to inspect a particular building that catches your eye, you need the freedom to move at your own pace and to choose your own route. In short, you have to walk.

For London is marvellous walking country. The air, it's true, is none too clean, certainly not in the main thoroughfares; but you never have to depart too far from the principal routes to shake off the traffic and its fumes.

And London offers the walker delights not to be had in the countryside. For one thing, you can go pretty well wherever you choose. I live in a village which has two or three public footpaths skirting the huge prairies of wheat that surround it, and once you've walked them, you've no choice but to walk them again. But in London you need never take the same route twice, for no street is barred to you.

There's always something different to see, too. It can take hours to struggle across a Yorkshire moor, under the same sky, with only the same flock of sheep and a handful of stunted thorns in view. In London the scene changes minute by minute. Every street is different, and every street has something to see, provided you know how to look.

London has its riverside walks, for the Thames provides not one walk, but many: it's hard to believe that the South Bank and Chiswick Mall front the same river. London has its views: the panorama from Alexandra Palace or Suicide Bridge, where Hornsey Lane crosses Archway Road, is the equal of anything in the Malverns or the Peaks. London has its open spaces, and what's more, you can roam all over Wimbledon Common or Hampstead Heath without some irate son of the soil chasing you off. And London has its wildlife: there are jays in Clissold Park, as well as herons, and I've heard owls hooting more often along the railway cutting through Manor House than in the degraded agri-desert where I live now.

And there's one special delight that walkers in London can enjoy and walkers in the country can't: pubs. Not that the country has no pubs, although it has fewer every year. And not that there's anything wrong with country pubs – the best of them are the best in the world. But in the country, they're so far apart you can die of thirst as you toil from one to another. In London, they're everywhere. At the slightest excuse – a minor inclemency in the weather, an incipient call of nature, the earliest apprehension of impending thirst – you can dive into the nearest pub, where you will find the answer to whatever ails you. Not that you need an excuse, of course; a whim will do perfectly well.

London pubs of real antiquity are few and far between. There are a handful of 16th and 17th-century survivals, and a larger smattering of 18th-century pubs in enclaves such as Hampstead. But just as most of London is late Georgian and Victorian, so are most of its finest pubs. It does not follow, however, that there is any lack of variety. In this book you will encounter tiny mews pubs, built in the narrow streets and yards behind the mansions of the nobility, and catering for the huge population of servants who ran the aristocratic households. You will visit huge, garish gin-palaces, competing brashly with their neighbours in the capital's main thoroughfares. You will be invited into the hidden haunts of off-duty City types, tucked away in the maze of courts and alleys that in many cases still follow the medieval street-plan. In an afternoon you can move between centuries, between worlds.

And these pubs are not only worthy of a visit for themselves, for their architecture, for their history, for their atmosphere: they are also a key to recreating London as it was. So much of London has changed beyond recognition even in the last 20 years that it seems sometimes to have no history. Only its pubs survive, like Hansel's pebbles, to mark out a way through the wilderness.

BELGRAVIA
MASTERS & SERVANTS

LENGTH OF WALK: THREE MILES

ONE of the most opulent quarters of London – and hence the world – is Belgravia, a diamond shape bounded by Knightsbridge, Sloane Street, Buckingham Palace Road, and on the east by the gardens of Buckingham Palace itself.

Within its limits there are no great public institutions, no landmark art galleries or museums, no world-renowned universities or hospitals. For this is the private domain of the rich, where every house is a mansion. Once the London homes of imperial Britain's movers and shakers, many of them are now embassies, the headquarters of multinational corporations, or discreetly luxurious hotels. But Belgravia has not lost its character: it is still opulent, it is still very private ... and plenty of very, very rich people still live here.

The development of Belgravia by the Grosvenors, ancestors of today's Duke of Westminster, began in the 1820s. The land that the engineer Thomas Cubitt was given to work with was far from promising. Much of it was a virtually uninhabited swamp, the Five Fields, through which the polluted River Westbourne oozed a dreary course. The two main crossings of the Westbourne, Knightsbridge at what is now Albert Gate, and the Bloody Bridge where Cliveden Place is now, both had frightening reputations for ambushes by gangs of highwaymen.

Cubitt tackled the task with characteristic energy, draining the Five Fields, channelling the Westbourne, and stripping off the surface clay, which was used to make the bricks to build the houses and then replaced with soil from St Katherine's Dock, then under construction. In 1827, five years after the work began, the architect George Basevi, Disraeli's uncle, designed and built Belgrave Square, the quarter's heart, facing Cubitt's bricks with gleaming stucco. The Westbourne had a brief moment of revenge in 1865, when Cubitt's masonry was breached during the cutting of the District Line and the works were briefly flooded.

But not all the inhabitants of Belgravia were so elevated. In fact, most of them were not aristocrats or diplomats or politicians or merchant princes at all: most of them were servants. In every mansion there was the butler, the housekeeper, the gardener, the footmen, the grooms, the coachmen, the nursemaids, the parlour-maids, the kitchen maids, the poor put-upon between-floors maids – a whole society, in fact. And overworked and underpaid as they were, they had to have their leisure.

Their few free hours might be spent strolling in St James's Park, but they were more likely to be whiled away in the innumerable small pubs in the warrens of service alleys and mews courtyards behind the mansions. These were not the great elaborate gin-palaces of the commercial districts and high streets: like the area itself, they were discreet and restrained. And they were not only places where servants could shake off the regimentation of their working lives for a few precious hours: they were also places of business.

For the great households of Belgravia spent an awful lot of money, on everything from game to saddle soap, from pots and pans to bed-linen; and the butler and the housekeeper had the spending of it. One can only guess at what bribes and inducements changed hands in the parlours of these discreet pubs, but if a tradesman wanted to do business with a butler, this was the place to do it.

Now, as then, Belgravia's mansions may be closed to us, but its pubs are open. We can gawp as much as we like at the suave exteriors of the great houses, but in its pubs, many of them remarkably well-preserved, we can get a genuine sense of what everyday life was really like for most of the quarter's inhabitants.

START: HYDE PARK CORNER.

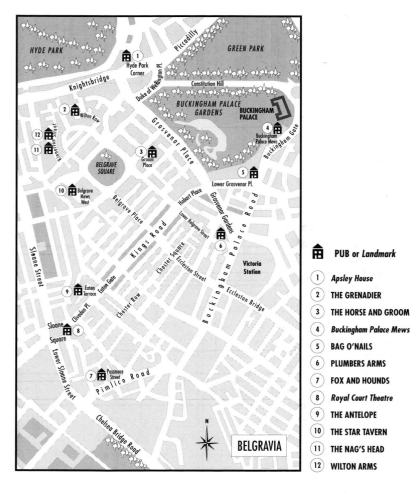

BELGRAVIA

APSLEY HOUSE.

Number One London, Apsley House's old postal address, was designed by Robert Adam in the 1770s and bought by the Duke of Wellington in 1817. Hyde Park Corner was presumably less busy then than it is now.

The house was given to the nation in 1947 and is now the Wellington Museum, housing a fabulous collection of china and silverware together with paintings – appropriately, bearing in mind that Spain was the scene of Wellington's most important campaigns -

by Velasquez, Goya and Murillo. Wellington also chose to remind himself of his fallen adversary by installing a 12-foot statue of Napoleon, stark naked, on the stairs.

THE MUSEUM IS OPEN 11–5 TUESDAY–SUNDAY.

Walk west along the south side of Knightsbridge and turn left into Old Barrack Yard. Follow Old Barrack Yard through the courtyard and under the arch until you come to the corner of Wilton Row.

THE GRENADIER
18 WILTON ROW

Once the unofficial officers' mess for the Duke of Wellington's Regiment, the Grenadier claims a date of origin of 1827 and is undoubtedly one of the pearls of the quarter.

From the outside, this tall, tree-framed late Georgian cottage is plain in itself but beautifully set – stone steps, with a sentry-box at the bottom, lead up to the front door. Two enormous carriage-lanterns are still lit by gas.

Inside, the tiny front bar is smothered in Guards memorabilia: crossed sabres, racks of bayonets, prints of regimental dinners, World War I flare pistols, an ornate brass cuirass – even a bearskin busby, which a genuine guardsman occasionally comes to groom. An unusual, perhaps unique, survival is a pewter bar-top, a little patched, but lovingly polished. Through an archway beside the bar is the pub's dining-room, which is rather grander but no less intimate.

It is claimed that Wellington himself came here from time to time to carouse with his officers, although what one knows of Wellington suggests that he wasn't much of a carouser. Those officers who did frequent the Grenadier were ferocious gamblers; one of them, caught cheating at cards, either did the decent thing or had it done for him (stories vary): his ghost still haunts the place today.

A more modern tradition occurs every Sunday, when the pub runs a Bloody Mary bar, with the Bloody Maries made to its own secret recipe. They claim to have sold nearly 300 on a record Sunday, and at £4.50 a shot they're not doing too badly.

Open noon–11.30 Monday–Saturday; noon–10.30 Sunday. Bar food 12–2.30 and 6–9.30 Monday–Saturday. Restaurant open noon–1.30 (last sitting), 6–9.30. Real ales: Courage Best & Directors, Marston's Pedigree, Morland Old Speckled Hen.

Turn left out of the pub and follow Wilton Row round to Wilton Crescent. Turn left again and follow Wilton Crescent into Belgrave Square. Walk down the east side of Belgrave Square and turn left again into Chapel Street. Cross Chapel Street and follow a little alley on your right down to Groom Place.

HORSE & GROOM
GROOM PLACE

Cobbled, narrow Groom Place, its horizons hemmed in by the towering roof lines of Belgravia's great houses, is as perfect an evocation of the district as you could wish. The mews cottages that once housed the servants who gave the little street its name, however, are now the London pieds-à-terre for the very rich – even the little corner shop is a good-quality Italian deli.

The Horse & Groom has succeeded in retaining its character perfectly, even though it has recently been "done up", with a new stripped-pine floor and comfortable upholstery. Other than that it's still the tiny one-room, wood-panelled pub it was when it opened in

1864, taking advantage of the Beer Act which abolished beer duty and allowed any householder to sell beer on payment of two guineas a year to the justices.

This perfect mews pub had its moment in the spotlight in the 1960s, when mews dwelling became very chic among the nouveaux-riches of the pop, film and art world. A regular was Beatles manager Brian Epstein who lived in Chester Street, and tradition has it that as much mescalin and LSD was consumed here as beer. The pub is still a place of pilgrimage for dedicated Beatles fans.

OPEN 11–11 MONDAY–FRIDAY. CLOSED WEEKENDS, BUT AVAILABLE FOR HIRE. HOME-COOKED FOOD AND BAR SNACKS ALL DAY. REAL ALES: SHEPHERD NEAME MASTER BREW AND SPITFIRE.

Leaving the pub, go straight ahead down Groom Place, crossing Chester Street into Wilton Mews. At the end, turn left into Wilton Street and then right down Grosvenor Place. Turn left at the crossroads, taking your life in your hands to cross into Lower Grosvenor Place. Walk along Lower Grosvenor Place to its junction with Buckingham Palace Road.

BUCKINGHAM PALACE
BUCKINGHAM PALACE MEWS

Originally built as a modestly grand country mansion on what was then the edge of town, Buckingham House was bought by George III in 1761 as a family home within convenient distance of the monarchy's business headquarters, St James's Palace. Its name was changed to the Queen's House, and 14 of George III and Queen Charlotte's 15 children were born in it.

It was only turned into a palace proper 65 years later, when George IV commissioned Nash to start work on a massive and extremely expensive transformation, partly paid for by the sale of the Brighton Pavilion. The work was taken over by the architect Edward Blore on George IV's death, and it will come as no surprise to learn that Thomas Cubitt was also heavily involved. The project, which more than doubled the palace's size, was not completed until 1847.

Queen Victoria was the first monarch to reside officially at Buckingham Palace: Kensington Palace, the official residence throughout the 18th century, was turned into apartments for minor and retired royals.

The east front of Buckingham Palace is probably one of the best-known facades in the world, but Queen Victoria herself wouldn't recognise it. After her death, the soft French sandstone used by Blore was found to be rotting away, and in 1913–14 the whole front was replaced with Portland stone.

Eighteen of the Palace's 660 rooms are open to the public, if only sporadically, with Queen Victoria's Picture Gallery and the Throne Room the highlights of the tour. Telephone 020 7321 2233 for details.

Easier of access are the Royal Mews on the corner of Buckingham Palace Road and Lower Grosvenor Place. In the Nash-designed stable yards are displayed the Queen's state carriages, including the Gold State Coach and the Glass Coach. It's usually open 12–4 Monday–Thursday, but this is subject to change. Telephone 020 7839 1377 or 7799 2331. The same number will provide opening times for the Queen's Gallery just up the road, also designed by Nash and originally a conservatory.

BAG O' NAILS
6 BUCKINGHAM PALACE ROAD

Opposite the Royal Mews, the Bag O' Nails was once the local for Buckingham Palace's enormous complement of grooms, coachmen and stableboys.

It was supposedly first licensed in 1774, shortly after George III had bought Buckingham House. However it was rebuilt in the 1830s as the Grosvenor Estate expanded, and is today a biggish single-bar pub with a vaguely Victorian feel – lots of dark wood panelling and pressed paper, with framed sepia prints of no-one in particular and odd shelves of sundry bric-à-brac – whereas the strictly hierarchical servants of an earlier period would have preferred a lot of small rooms segregated according to status.

Location is perhaps the biggest selling-point for the Bag O' Nails, but the origin of its unusual (though by no means unique) name gives rise to an interesting – and, thankfully, inconclusive – argument. Tradition has it that the word is a corruption of "Bacchanals", a classical allusion to the Dionysian rites surrounding the grape harvest

and, by extension, drunken revelry and revellers in general. And indeed the Oxford English Dictionary does give an 18th-century origin for Bacchanals as an English word.

Dunkling & Wright in their scholarly Dictionary of Pub Names, however, maintain that there is not a shred of evidence for this, and that the name derives from nothing grander than a sign in the form of a nail-studded sack, denoting an ironmonger's shop and in common use in the 17th and 18th centuries.

You pays your money ...

OPEN 11–11 MONDAY–FRIDAY, NOON–10.30 SUNDAY. BAR FOOD SERVED FROM OPENING TO 9.30. REAL ALES: COURAGE BEST & DIRECTORS, GREEN KING ABBOT, MORLAND OLD SPECKLED HEN, THEAKSTON'S BEST, PLUS UP TO THREE GUEST ALES.

Turn right out of the pub down Buckingham Palace Road. Cross Grosvenor Gardens and turn right into Lower Belgrave Street.

THE PLUMBERS ARMS
14 LOWER BELGRAVE STREET

The name of this cheerful, slightly scruffy boozer provides an insight into a fascinating slice of 19th-century social history.

Pubs named after a particular trade are not at all uncommon. Often this reflects a calling peculiar to the locality – the Miner's Arms is an obvious example. But many publicans in the 19th century would try to market themselves to a particular trade. "Houses of call", as such pubs were known, functioned as lodging houses and labour exchanges for particular crafts, even hiring out the tools of the trade to workers who couldn't afford their own.

It was an arrangement which suited everybody: an itinerant craftsman arriving in a strange town knew exactly where to go to get work; a contractor seeking particular trades knew exactly where to find them; and the publican, hopefully, cornered a juicy little market.

It seems likely that this pub served as just such a house of call for itinerant plumbers seeking work on the fast-expanding Grosvenor Estate in the mid-19th century. The sign bears the arms of the Plumber's Company, established in 1588: many of the plumbers of the 1820s and '30s would have been near-illiterate but would recognise the arms of their calling.

Later in the century, once Belgravia was built, the Plumbers Arms reinvented itself as a superior establishment for the servants of the surrounding mansions. In the 1880s it was rebuilt, and would originally have been divided into three or four rooms, segregated according to status. Now, alas, it is all one big room, although much of the Victorian decor, including a pressed paper or Lincrusta ceiling, survives.

But none of this is the reason for the Plumbers Arms's fame – or infamy. On the night of 7 November 1974, the bar fell silent as a wild blood-stained woman burst in, babbling a tale of horrible murder. She was Lady Lucan, and her husband had just beaten their nanny, Sandra Rivett, to death in the darkened family home in Chester Square opposite, and had tried to do the same to her. He fled before he could be caught, and has never been seen since ...

OPEN 11–11 MONDAY–FRIDAY, 12–3 SATURDAY. CLOSED SATURDAY NIGHT AND SUNDAY. BAR FOOD ALL DAY. REAL ALES: COURAGE BEST & DIRECTORS, CHARLES WELLS BOMBARDIER.

Cross Lower Belgrave Street and turn right. Turn left into Chester Square and walk all the way down, crossing Elizabeth Street, as far as Bourne Street. Cross Bourne Street and turn left. Turn right into Graham Terrace.

FOX & HOUNDS
29 PASSMORE STREET

Blink and you'll miss this tiny pub on the corner of Graham Terrace and Passmore Street, which originally served the working-class families who lived in this humble corner of Belgravia.

This southern extremity, which borders Pimlico, has never been part of Belgravia proper; but the great mansions further north were always a source of employment for tradesmen – glaziers, plumbers, chimney-sweeps – and this is where they lived.

Until a couple of years ago, when Diane Harvey retired after 25 years as tenant, the Fox & Hounds had the distinction of being London's last beer-only pub. This dates it firmly to the years between 1830, when the Beer Act was passed, and 1869, when it was repealed – and indeed, the pub claims a date of origin of 1860.

The Beer Act was an attempt to break the power of the big

brewers, who were busily buying up all the pubs they could get. It allowed any householder, on payment of a two-guinea annual fee, to set up as a beerhouse; and within a couple of years of its passage thousands of small householders had done precisely that.

The Act caused exactly the same sort of tension between licensed victuallers and beerhouse-keepers as exists today between licensed taxis and minicabs, and when it was repealed the licensed victuallers successfully opposed the applications of many beerhouses for licences. Others, like the Fox & Hounds, managed to get licences, but were not at first allowed to sell spirits. Over the years these beerhouses either fell by the wayside or succeeded in getting permission to sell spirits; the Fox & Hounds was the last of its kind until 1998, when its new tenants successfully applied for the beer-only condition to be revoked.

The restricted licence was not the only survival of old tradition at the Fox & Hounds – until 1980 it had only a single (outdoor) loo, which the landlady shared with her customers. But such was its atmosphere and character that it had become a favourite with actors and staff at the Royal Court Theatre just round the corner, who were perfectly happy to forgo their G&T and didn't mind peeing under the stars.

OPEN 12–3 AND 5.30–11 MONDAY–FRIDAY, 12–3 AND 6–11 SATURDAY, 12–3 AND 6.30–10.30 SUNDAY. BAR FOOD LUNCHTIME. REAL ALES: YOUNG'S BITTER AND SPECIAL.

Turn left along Graham Terrace and right along Holbein Place into Sloane Square.

ROYAL COURT THEATRE

The Royal Court is only included in this tour on a technicality: in spirit it belongs to literary Chelsea, but its location on the east side of Sloane Square puts it just inside Belgravia – albeit at the scruffy end.

The Royal Court is also probably a bit too liberal for the liking of most Belgravians: built in 1888, its first successes were the social dramas of Sir Arthur Wing Pinero in the '90s and, later, the even more subversive works of George Bernard Shaw, produced under the management of Harley Granville Barker.

The theatre closed down in 1932 and, except for a brief spell as a cinema, remained so for 20 years. Then came the English Stage Company, with its yet more shocking and radical productions - *Look Back In Anger*, *Chips With Everything*, *The Entertainer*, and *Early Morning*, in which Queen Victoria enjoys a lesbian affair with Florence Nightingale – a tradition of innovation which continues to this day.

In 1980 a rehearsal room was adapted to form an 80-seater auditorium, the Theatre Upstairs. More recently, a huge tranche of lottery money has gone into restoring and updating the Royal Court in a four-year project during which the company operated from other theatres. Telephone 020 7565 5000.

Turn right along Cliveden Place and left into Eaton Terrace.

THE ANTELOPE
22 EATON TERRACE

The genteel, discreet Antelope stands only 100 yards from the Bloody Bridge where, before the Five Fields were drained and Belgravia was built, the Kings Road crossed the noxious River Westbourne. This was a notorious spot for footpads and highwaymen and got its name from their practice of taking no chances and silencing the victims as a matter of course by murdering them.

Some say the Antelope was already standing before Cubitt and his gangs moved in in the 1820s, and that it was an isolated and villainous country pub whose main source of custom was the bandits themselves. Others maintain that, like many Belgravia pubs, it was purpose-built to serve first the navvies and builders who created Belgravia and then the servants who came after them.

Certainly it served long and well in the latter capacity. Its restrained decor and fittings of wooden settles, stripped floors, matchboard ceiling and panelled dados are still sober enough to please the stuffiest and most status-conscious of butlers. Most of the internal partitions

24

which would have created separate rooms for the various strata of staff are gone; but the snug reserved for the higher echelons of domestic service is still intact.

OPEN 11.30–11 MONDAY–SATURDAY. CLOSED SUNDAY. BAR FOOD 11.30–2.30. REAL ALES: DRAUGHT BASS, TETLEY BITTER, GUESTS.

Turn left along Eaton Terrace and right into West Eaton Place, then left again into Chesham Street and right into Chesham Place. Cross Chesham Place at the German Embassy and walk up Belgrave Mews West.

STAR TAVERN
6 BELGRAVE MEWS WEST

Another of Belgravia's tucked-away gems is the Star Tavern, like so many others a late-Georgian pub intended for the servants of the great houses and the tradesman who sought their business.

The Star became a focal point, during the 1960s, for a well-heeled demi-monde of gangsters, slumming aristocrats and the rest of the brittle glitterati of the time. Under the eye of long-serving landlord Paddy Kennedy – a character renowned for refusing to serve anyone he didn't like the look of – the likes of Billy Hill and the Great Train Robbers rubbed shoulders with pop stars, models, actors, and the Gaekwar of Baroda.

In those days the pub still had its original theme of separate rooms, including a secluded snug at the back and a private room upstairs. Since then it has been opened out into two big, airy, rather dignified rooms, which recapture the sedate nature of the original without being too self-consciously traditional.

OPEN 11.30–11 MONDAY–FRIDAY, 11.30–3 AND 6.30–11 SATURDAY, 12–3 AND 7–10.30 SUNDAY. BAR FOOD 12–2.30 AND 6–9 MONDAY–SATURDAY, 12–2.30 AND 7–9 SUNDAYS. REAL ALES: FULLER'S CHISWICK, LONDON PRIDE, ESB.

Turn left through the arch into West Halkin Street; turn left into Wilton Terrace and right into Motcomb Street; cross Motcomb Street into Kinnerton Street.

THE NAG'S HEAD
53 KINNERTON STREET

Kinnerton Street was built in the 1820s as cottages for the artisans and tradespeople who served the great chasms of masonry then being thrown up as palaces for the wealthy. Today you have to be wealthy to own one: a glance at an estate agent's window will tell you that you need access to £500,000 or thereabouts for the privilege of living in one of the charming but tiny houses which make up what locals call "the village".

The Nag's Head was the smallest pub in London until the 1970s, when a room at the back was opened up. In its early years it had a double life: the first landlords also hired out horses.

In the century to 1960 the Nag's Head had only five landlords, but in the 1970s it fell on hard times and went through a succession of owners, eventually closing down altogether. Happily, it did not remain boarded up for too long before the present owners arrived in 1979 to breathe new life into it.

As well as being Belgravia's only genuine free house, it is also one of its most characterful pubs. The first thing you notice is that the bar is the right height for persons of restricted growth, and that the stools are similarly stumpy. Then you realise that the pub is built on several levels, and the floor behind the bar is a good couple of feet lower than the floor you are standing on.

The next thing you notice, as you lower yourself to the level of the bar, is the antique beer engine with its little Chelsea pottery hand-pulls. As you look around you, take in a veritable curiosity shop of bric-à-brac, cartoons, and all sorts of odds and ends including two 1930s penny-in-the-slot machines. Underlying this haphazard collection is a very proper Victorian bar-room with a big cast-iron fireplace and range, wood-panelled walls and brown pressed-paper ceiling.

OPEN 11–11 MONDAY–FRIDAY, 12–11 SATURDAY, 12–10.30 SUNDAY. BAR FOOD UNTIL 9.30. REAL ALES: ADNAM'S, TETLEY.

Turn left along Wilton Place and right along Knightsbridge; return to Hyde Park Corner.

FINISH: HYDE PARK CORNER

KENSINGTON
WELL-BORN ARTISTS

LENGTH OF WALK: THREE MILES

MENTION Kensington and most people instantly think of the Albert Hall opposite Kensington Gardens with the Albert Memorial opposite, and the Science Museum, the Natural History Museum, and the Victoria & Albert Museum just to the south. But this area – "Albertopolis", as it used to be known after Queen Victoria's Prince Consort – is not strictly Kensington at all but South Kensington; and its character – huge Victorian mansion blocks laid out in regimental lines along broad, straight avenues and geometric squares – is very different from that of old Kensington, and on this walk it's to old Kensington we're going.

It's an area with many different aspects and characteristics, determined partly by its geography and partly by its history. The ground rises sharply upwards towards Notting Hill, creating an open, airy feel in the streets and squares on the upper slopes to the north. And, unlike the great building projects of Notting Hill to the north and Albertopolis to the south-east, it grew piecemeal in a series of small speculative developments over the whole course of the 19th century, during which its population jumped from 8,000 to 175,000.

As a quiet, relatively modest suburb with a great deal of charm, Kensington lured a galaxy of artists and writers in the late 19th and early 20th centuries. It was especially attractive to those who preferred a lifestyle rather more refined than that of Bohemian

Chelsea: Ford Madox Ford, who lived at South Lodge in Campden Hill Road from 1913 to 1919 and then moved to Campden Hill Square, described it as a high-class Greenwich Village for "wealthy, refined, delicate and well-born" artists. South Lodge was actually owned by the novelist Violet Hunt and was the headquarters of the English Review. Among the loose grouping of avant-garde writers associated with the English Review who lived in the surrounding streets were Wyndham Lewis, who decorated South Lodge, and Ezra Pound.

From 1909 to 1914, Pound lived in a tiny and very basic cottage without even running water in Kensington Church Walk. While living there he challenged the Georgian poet Lascelles Abercrombie to a duel and, as Pound was a skilled fencer, Abercrombie's choice of weapons was unsold books – Pound's and his own – to be flung at each other. Upjohn, the painter in Richard Aldington's 1929 novel *Death of a Hero*, is based on Pound in this period. In 1914 Pound married Dorothy Shakspear in St Mary Abbott's, Kensington Church Street, and moved to a more conventional home in Holland Place. There the Pounds lived until Ezra's decision to leave England in 1920: he only returned 45 years later to attend the memorial service of his friend and protégé T S Eliot, who spent his last years in Kensington Court Gardens and whose *Four Quartets* was originally entitled The Kensington Quartets.

Kensington Square, just south of Church Street, was also popular with writers and intellectuals: Richard Steele, Thomas Carlyle and John Stuart Mill all lived in it at various times, and William Makepeace Thackeray had the house on the corner of Young Street from 1843 to 1856. Thackeray's house is today overshadowed by the vast bulk of Barker's department store, but when it was free-standing, its two deep bays and parapet prompted him to attribute to it "the air of a feudal castle", where, he said: "I'll have a flagstaff put over the coping of the wall and hoist a standard when I'm home." Here he wrote *Vanity Fair, Pendennis*, and *The History of Henry Esmond*. Charlotte Brontë came to a ball here in 1848 but was too shy to speak; halfway through the evening the bored host went off to his club.

G K Chesterton is even more strongly associated with Kensington: he was a scion of the family which founded the eponymous estate agency, and was born in Sheffield Terrace in 1874, marrying Frances Blogg in St Mary Abbott's Church (designed by Sir Giles Gilbert Scott, with the highest spire in London at 278 feet) in 1901.

Campden Hill Square in the 1890s was the stamping-ground,

although not the home, of another of the biggest literary lions of the day: the Llewellyn Davies family, whose eldest son Jack was the inspiration for Peter Pan, lived there, and J M Barrie was a constant visitor. He actually became the children's guardian when they were orphaned in 1910.

Another children's writer whose work is tinged with tragedy and who lived in Kensington was Kenneth Graham. He lived in Phillimore Place from 1901 to 1908 while writing *The Wind In The Willows* for his pampered son Alistair, who later committed suicide by lying down in front of a train.

The pubs of Kensington reflect, for the most part, the district's suburban tranquillity. Notting Hill Gate and Kensington High Street may be full of hideous modern style-bars and restaurants where the food is as overpriced as it is overhyped; but away from the main roads are quiet residential enclaves, with unfussy pubs to match.

START: NOTTING HILL GATE.

From Notting Hill Gate tube, walk east along the southern side of Notting Hill Gate for a few yards, then turn right into Kensington Church Street.

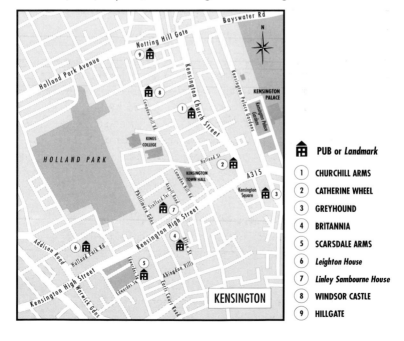

🏠 **PUB** or *Landmark*

1. CHURCHILL ARMS
2. CATHERINE WHEEL
3. GREYHOUND
4. BRITANNIA
5. SCARSDALE ARMS
6. *Leighton House*
7. *Linley Sambourne House*
8. WINDSOR CASTLE
9. HILLGATE

31

THE CHURCHILL ARMS
119 KENSINGTON CHURCH STREET

Originally called The Marlborough after John Churchill, Duke of Marlborough, who led Britain to victory in the War of the Spanish Succession, this pleasantly scruffy mid-Victorian pub was renamed after the celebrated member of a cadet branch of the family who did his country the same favour in World War II.

It's a large pub, with all the original partitions knocked out to create one big horseshoe-shaped lounge, which is all wood-panelled in the appropriate way. More about the decor it's hard to say, however; for at the Churchill bric-à-brac has run riot over the years.

Naturally enough, there are paintings, photographs and busts of Churchill himself; but whoever has amassed this astonishing collection of bits and pieces has not been able to stop there. There's a picture gallery boasting every Prime Minister from Robert Walpole to Harold Wilson (with, of course, a portrait of Churchill as a centrepiece); there are enough stoneware flagons, copper jugs, brass buckets and wicker creels hanging from the ceiling to revive the Old Curiosity Shop; there are, rather bizarrely, old legal documents done up in red ribbon also hanging from the ceiling; there are exotic butterflies mounted in glass cases – 1,600 of them, it's said, but who counted? - and Heaven knows what beside. At the back, however, the mood changes utterly. A recently added conservatory, hung with cool fronds of foliage, doubles as a restaurant where Thai food is an evening speciality.

OPEN 11–11 MONDAY–SATURDAY, NOON–10.30 SUNDAY. FOOD SERVED NOON–2.30, 6–9.30 MONDAY–SATURDAY, NOON–2.30 ONLY SUNDAY. THAI MENU AVAILABLE EVENINGS ONLY. REAL ALES: FULLER'S RANGE.

Turn right and continue down Church Street.

CATHERINE WHEEL
23 KENSINGTON CHURCH STREET

Designed in 1870 by the architect W E Williams, the Catherine Wheel dominates its corner site just off Kensington High Street, its wide ground-floor facade provided with a handsome brown marble fascia, and inside its ceiling, now painted bottle-green, is unusually high.

But it's not actually a very big pub at all, and it's hard to imagine what it must have been like when — as it undoubtedly originally was — it was partitioned into two or three rooms. Sadly, successive refurbishments have left few clues other than a single pleasant fireplace, of about the right size to heat a smallish snug, with a surround of red tiles and a fine cut-glass mirror above. Still, it's a pleasant and well-situated retreat from the hustle and bustle of Kensington High Street.

The name, incidentally, is usually taken as referring either to the Turner's Company, which uses a Catherine Wheel in its coat of arms, or to the Order of St Catherine, which protected pilgrims in Crusader times and whose symbol was therefore associated with travel in general. It wasn't an uncommon name among coaching inns and posting houses, so perhaps Williams's Catherine Wheel replaced an earlier posting house on the site.

OPEN NOON–11 MONDAY–SATURDAY, 12–10.30 SUNDAY. BAR MEALS NOON–6 MONDAY–SATURDAY, WITH TOASTED SANDWICHES AVAILABLE AFTER 6; ROASTS ALL DAY SUNDAY. REAL ALES: ADNAM'S BITTER, FULLER'S LONDON PRIDE, CHANGING GUESTS.

Proceed into Kensington High Street. Turn left, then cross the road opposite Barker's and turn right down Young Street alongside the store.

THE GREYHOUND
1 KENSINGTON SQUARE

Almost opposite Thackeray's house, the Greyhound the novelist knew was a humble working man's boozer where an old custom was carried on.

It was common, in the 19th century, for labourers to down tools at lunchtime and go and buy a chop or a steak, which a friendly publican would grill for them for nothing on condition that they bought a pot or two of beer to wash it down with. We know that this custom was observed at the Greyhound because Licensing World in 1898 recorded complaints that there would be no such facility when it was pulled down and rebuilt.

The new Greyhound, which opened in 1899, was a very much

smarter emporium, noted for its glasswork. When two full-sized billiard tables were installed (taking up much of the bar), it rapidly became a centre for the game where the stars of the day such as Joe and Fred Davies would often play. All this came to an end one night in 1979, when a gas explosion destroyed the pub in its entirety. (Luckily no-one was in at the time.)

The facade was rebuilt as before, but the interior is very different, comprising not much more than a single enormous room, comfortable enough if a trifle anonymous, with a low ceiling which makes the whole place appear rather gloomy. The location, however, could hardly be better: although not more than 200 yards from Kensington High Street, Kensington Square is a calm green oasis of modest but very pleasant 18th-century houses. It's no wonder that the philosopher John Stuart Mill, the actress Mrs Patrick Campbell and the Pre-Raphaelite painter Edward Burne-Jones all chose to live in it.

OPEN 11–11 MONDAY–FRIDAY, 12–11 SAT; 12–10.30 SUN. MEALS SERVED NOON-10. REAL ALES: THEAKSTON BEST BITTER, COURAGE DIRECTORS.

Stroll round Kensington Square, returning to Kensington High Street via Derry Street. Turn left into the High Street and follow it until you come to Allen Street on your left. Turn left into Allen Street.

THE BRITANNIA
1 ALLEN STREET

This charming and unpretentious little pub, with its little public bar partitioned off from the wood-panelled lounge, was once the tap for William Wells's Britannia Brewery — indeed, the old brewery stable yard is now the pub's conservatory.

The brewery and pub were built in 1834, shortly after the area, previously market gardens, had been developed largely as working men's cottages by a Bond Street tailor named Thomas Allen, who had made his fortune supplying uniforms to the Duke of Wellington's

army. The brewery never seems to have done well, however: it only ever had one other tied house, the Britannia Tap in Warwick Road, which was once London's smallest pub; and in 1902 it went bust. It was bought out of liquidation only to go bust again in 1924, upon which it was bought, along with its two pubs, by Young's.

The brewery was soon demolished – Allen Mansions now stands on the site – and in 1938 the pub, previously the Britannia Brewery Tap, was given its present shorter name. The existing frontage and interior panelling actually date only to 1960, when the pub was remodelled and extended, but such are their simplicity that they are effectively timeless – and proof that modern design can be as good as any, if only the vernacular is understood and respected.

It's still very much a locals' pub – although the locals today are very much grander than they were when the district was developed – with the emphasis on quality: it is one of only a couple of dozen or so pubs across the nation to have appeared in every single edition of the Campaign for Real Ale's *Good Beer Guide* since the first edition in 1974.

OPEN 11–11 MONDAY–SATURDAY; 12–10.30 SUNDAY. BAR FOOD SERVED ALL DAY; SEPARATE RESTAURANT. REAL ALES: YOUNG'S RANGE.

Continue south down Allen Street. Turn right into Abingdon Villas; cross Earl's Court Road and cut down Earl's Walk beside the Police Station. Turn right into Edwardes Square.

SCARSDALE ARMS
23A EDWARDES SQUARE

The Scarsdale Arms is a base deceiver. Its creeper-clad Georgian exterior leads you to expect an interior as antique and jealously preserved as that of the Grenadier in Belgravia. But it isn't. It's undergone a thorough revamp, apparently comparatively recently, and is none the worse for it.

All the original partitions have gone, leaving a square island bar projecting into a single large room. But skilful design has created three quite distinct spaces. On the left as you enter is a bistro-like dining area with walls of whitewashed brick; the lobby area retains its pubby feel thanks to a predominance of bare woodwork; while to the right is a second dining area with a more formal atmosphere created by a dark green and red colour scheme, with a few large, well-chosen paintings in heavy gilt frames and discreet wall lighting.

This is a pub which, with its imaginative selection of real ales, its fine wines, its Bloody Marys made to a secret house recipe and its excellent food, suits its neighbourhood very well. Edwardes Square, named after the second Lord Kensington, was laid out by a French speculative builder, Louis Changeur, between 1811 and 1820 and is extremely elegant and well-heeled. Leigh Hunt, who lived at No 32, described it as a French Arcadia. Kensington High Street is a mere 100 yards away, with all its noise, fumes, and traffic, but Edwardes Square remains leafy, tranquil and private. A famous resident of recent years was a very private man who must have appreciated its apparent seclusion: Frankie Howerd, the comedian, lived in the Square from 1966 until his death in 1992.

OPEN NOON–11 PM MONDAY–SATURDAY, 12 NOON–10.30 PM SUNDAY. FULL MENU NOON–3 PM AND 6–10 PM; BAR FOOD ALL DAY. REAL ALES: COURAGE DIRECTORS, MARSTON'S PEDIGREE, MORLAND OLD SPECKLED HEN, PLUS TWO GUEST ALES FROM MICRO BREWERIES.

Turn right out of the pub and immediately left. Walk round south and west sides of Edwardes Square and into Kensington High Street; cross; turn left, then right into Addison Road and immediately right into Holland Park Road.

LEIGHTON HOUSE

Tucked away down a side-street in what appears, from the outside, to be a modest red brick town house, is the delightful Leighton House Museum. Designed in 1866 by George Aitchison, it was for 30 years home to the Olympian Movement painter Lord Frederick Leighton, and became a private museum after his death in 1896. During his life there, Leighton, who was the leading society artist of his generation and was made a peer almost on his deathbed, packed the house with works of art, both his own and his contemporaries'. Indeed he saw his house as a palace of art, and the only bedroom in it (apart from the servants' quarters, of course) was his own. The domed Arab Hall, added in 1879, is entirely decorated with tiles and woodwork collected from all over the Levant – even the wooden gallery or zenana with its lattice screens comes from Damascus. Sadly, his personal collection, including his furniture, had to be sold on his death to endow a trust fund for art students; but over the years the house has been patiently restocked, and it is a wonderful surprise to find such a magnificent collection in such an unlikely location.

OPEN MONDAY–THURSDAY 11–5.30. TELEPHONE 0207 602 3316.

Continue along Holland Park Road. Turn right at the end, then left along Kensington High Street. Turn left into Phillimore Gardens, then right into Stafford Terrace.

LINLEY SAMBOURNE HOUSE
This tall Georgian terraced house was the home of cartoonist and illustrator Linley Sambourne until his death in 1910. After he died it was never modernised, and is now presented to the public as he left it, decorated in the Aesthetic manner complete with William Morris wallpaper, furnished with Sambourne' choice of late 19th-century pieces, and hung with works by well-known artists of the period. It also contains the photographic equipment and many of the photographs he worked from, as well as his collection of oriental ceramics. At the time of going to press, it is closed for restoration work, but should reopen early in 2002.

Continue along Stafford Terrace. Turn right at the end into Argyll Road, then left, then immediately left into Campden Hill Road. Continue north along Campden Hill Road and cross over.

WINDSOR CASTLE
114 CAMPDEN HILL ROAD

It's an old story, reminiscent of the music hall song about Hackney Marshes, that the Windsor Castle at the top of Campden Hill Road got its name because on a clear day you could see Windsor Castle from it, if it wasn't for the houses in between. Well, there are 16 pubs named the Windsor Castle in London, and it's a fair bet that you could never have seen Windsor Castle from many of them. Or from this one, probably.

In fact the 1840s, when the district was first developed and the pub was built, was a turbulent decade, with plenty of Chartists, Socialists and republicans about; those who were fervent monarchists liked to make a show of it, and one potent monarchist symbol was the royal residence itself. It became even more so in 1917, when George V changed the name of the dynasty from Saxe-Coburg-Gotha to Windsor. It is a pub to make a patriot and a nationalist of anyone, for it enshrines so many of the virtues we English like in our pubs.

The beer is well-kept; the food ranges from simple but excellent snacks up to full-blown gourmet extravagances; and the decor and the atmosphere, while utterly unspoilt and in some regards even basic, are the essence of pub distilled.

The front bar is divided into three well lived-in areas, all bare boards, wooden panels, and high-backed settles; while the only access to the other two bars is by midget hatchways through the partitions. Each of these snugs actually has its own street door, but these are evidently never used. (In one of them, the Sherry Bar, it used to be the custom to serve a house variant on the Bloody Mary, the Hunter, made with fino sherry instead of vodka. On my most recent visit I was told that the custom had died out: if so, I hope it is soon revived.) Beyond lies a large and pleasant stone-floored courtyard almost continental in feel, with a shady plane tree, gas heating, and plenty of tables and benches.

A sad story is told about the Windsor Castle. William Cobbett, the early 19th-century radical politician and journalist, had the bones of Thomas Paine shipped back from America, intending to make a memorial for them, but died before he could do so. Years later his son Richard, the adored companion of many of Cobbett's Rural Rides but a disappointing dissolute in adult life, sold Paine's skeleton to the landlord of the Windsor Castle to settle his slate. I have no idea if this is true. I hope it isn't.

OPEN NOON–11 PM MONDAY–SAT, NOON-10.30 SUN. FOOD NOON–10 PM. REAL ALES: DRAUGHT BASS, FULLER'S LONDON PRIDE.

Continue along Campden Hill Road. Turn right into Kensington Place and left into Hillgate Street.

THE HILLGATE
39 HILLGATE STREET

Further up Campden Hill Road, and literally within spitting distance of Notting Hill Gate, is Hillgate Village.

A greater contrast with the cosmopolitan hum of the main thoroughfare to the north and the large villas and town houses to the south could scarcely be imagined. For this is a working-class quarter of comparatively humble houses and cottages set in small, unassuming squares. It was laid out in the 1840s and '50s on the site of a notorious slum by a family of builders and local landowners called Johnson, one of whose members became Lord Mayor of London in 1846. Hillgate Street was originally Johnson Street, and the Hillgate was the Johnson Arms when it was built in 1854.

And although so much has changed – thanks to the London property boom in general, and the film *Notting Hill* in particular, as well as the village's own quiet charm, the larger houses here now sell for £1 million or thereabouts – this is still a discreet residential area, with small local shops and unpretentious restaurants.

The two-bar Hillgate is also still a genuinely local pub. Visit in the early afternoon, when the lunchtime trade has died down, and you'll even find elderly working-class drinkers here, villagers all their lives, gossiping in genuine working-class accents about nothing very much;

although how they can afford to hang on here is anybody's guess. (How much their homes, even unmodernised, will fetch when they finally pop their clogs is, on the other hand, the subject of intense and well-informed speculation on the part of doubtless impatient heirs.)

There's nothing particularly special about the Hillgate, it has to be said: it has no history to speak of, and the architecture is workaday; but therein lies its appeal. It's just a bloody good little boozer with plain food and excellent beer — if only there were more like it!

OPEN 11–11 MONDAY–SATURDAY, NOON–10.30 SUNDAY. BAR FOOD NOON–3 PM, 6–9 PM. REAL ALES; GREENE KING IPA AND ABBOT, SHEPHERD NEAME SPITFIRE; CHARLES WELLS BOMBARDIER.

Continue along Hillgate Road; turn right into Notting Hill Gate.

FINISH: NOTTING HILL GATE

BAYSWATER
THE FIRST SUBURB

LENGTH OF WALK: TWO MILES

THE monumental stuccoed terraces which line the north side of Bayswater Road resemble nothing so much as the seafront of a south-coast resort, but they look out over the green acres of Hyde Park and Kensington Gardens rather than the blue billows of the English Channel.

Perhaps because of this pleasant aspect, Bayswater and Paddington were among the first suburbs built expressly for people who worked in the City itself, with development starting in the 1820s and pretty much complete by the 1860s. As early as 1843, Paddington was so populous that it was proposed to connect it to London by rail; and in 1860 work finally started on the world's first underground railway, today's Metropolitan Line, connecting Paddington Station and Farringdon.

At 350 acres, Hyde Park to the south of Bayswater Road is central London's largest open space. Originally part of the estate of Westminster Abbey, it was appropriated by Henry VIII in 1536 and opened to the public by Charles I 100 years later. In the 18th century, after Kensington Palace had become a royal residence, the park was gradually landscaped, a key event being the damming of the Westbourne, which enters the park just to the west of Lancaster Gate, to form the Serpentine, in 1730.

The area to the north of Bayswater Road – then the main coach-road to Oxford, Bath, and Exeter, and haunted by highwaymen such as the gallant Claude Duval – remained open farmland right up to the Regency period. Bodysnatchers as well as highwaymen carried out their gruesome trade in safety in this unpopulous neighbourhood: the graveyard behind Hyde Park Place was a favourite target, and among the corpses resurrected was that of Laurence Sterne, who died in 1768. It was recognised by the doctor the "Abraham Men" sold it to, and reburied, being finally moved to the Yorkshire village of Coxwold, Sterne's home in life, in 1969.

A map of 1822 shows a thin crust of housing on the north side of the road, with denser development only in the immediate area of Lancaster Gate; as late as 1856 the Westbourne north of the park was still open, but it had become so polluted that William Blake, who used to fish in it, would not have recognised it, and finally it had to be covered over.

The part of Bayswater immediately fronting the park itself was, and remains, opulent and upper-crust, if not as opulent and upper-crust as Mayfair to the east of the park or Kensington to the south of it. But beauty here, as everywhere, is only skin-deep: venture northwards from Bayswater Road and you pass quickly through layers of successively less affluent housing.

"Wastes of compo mansions, terraces and squares", Percy Fitzgerald described Bayswater as in 1890. "There is a general pretentiousness, from the uniform stuccoed balustrades, the languid trees, and dusty foliage. Middle-class folk live in these would-be palaces and terraces." But Paddington was: "a world of another complexion; the tame yellow houses of Westbourne and other terraces being ... side by side with a huckstering neighbourhood of streets and shops of a poorer sort."

Paradoxically, last century, the grander streets and squares originally built for respectable City workers (who commuted their daily rail-fare for a cheaper season ticket) degenerated into a district of seedy hotels and poky multiple-occupancy flats and bedsits far slummier than the neighbouring terraces of labourers' cottages which had, at first, been the humbler. In the post-war decades Paddington was one of London's poorest and most crime-infested districts; now, of course, it's all coming up again. Terraced houses and the smaller villas here have been highly desirable for years; and while the bigger houses are still, in the main, used as hotels or divided into flats, a huge new development of luxury apartments and shops at Paddington Basin, currently under construction, coupled with London's perennial property-price inflation, will doubtless see them return to prosperity again. Could this be the Islington of the 2010s?

START: LANCASTER GATE

Turn right out of the station.

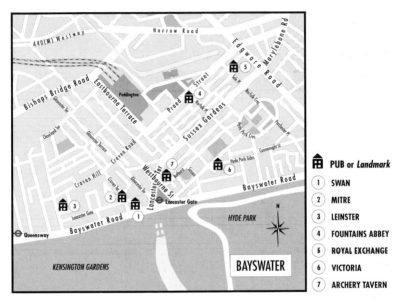

THE SWAN
66 BAYSWATER ROAD

The Swan's chief glory, despite the traffic, is its location facing Hyde Park across Bayswater Road. Its most visible asset is its large covered forecourt with dozens of tables and benches, and the area is heated on cold days – pretty effectively, it must be said – with big gas-fired contraptions. On a nice day it's a fine place to stop and watch the world go by, especially on a Sunday, when amateur artists turn the park railings into a huge open-air gallery.

The pub trades on a supposed association with Claude Duval, superstar highwayman, who was fêted for two centuries after his death for his gallantry. A Norman by birth, Duval ran away from home as a youth and joined the household of one of Charles II's retinue, then in exile. Coming to England on the Restoration in 1660, he survived for 10 years as a highway robber, swindler, card-sharp and lover. He was finally caught – dead drunk, as so often with highwaymen – in a pub near the Strand and was hanged at Tyburn in 1670, aged 27. His epitaph said of him:

Here lies Duval. Reader, if male thou art,
Look to thy purse; if female to thy heart.
Much havoc has he made of both: for all
Men he made stand; all women he made fall.

It's true that the old Uxbridge coach road was one of his haunts; but as the Swan is not recorded until 50 years after his death, it's unlikely he ever celebrated a particularly fine haul with a bumper of sack here. Nor did he stop for a last drink here en route to meet his maker: condemned men on their way from Newgate to Tyburn generally stopped halfway, in St Giles; not here, which is several hundred yards west of the fateful spot.

Nor should we make too much of the Swan's claim to have been a coaching inn: it's far too close to central London to have made a stage, or stopping-point for a change of horses.

First recorded in a list of licensed victuallers of 1721, from 1790 it served as the tavern for a pleasure garden, the Floral Tea Garden, where Londoners would come at weekends for a breath of country air and a few beers. The Floral was founded on the site of a physic garden established by an 18th-century apothecary and herbalist, Sir John Hill, a favourite of George III's on whose succession, said Horace Walpole, he "was made gardener of Kensington, a place worth £2,000 a year." In deeds of 1829 – from when the existing rather modest frontage appears to date – the Swan is still recorded as possessing a tea garden and skittle alley, but the last of the land (apart from the front garden) was built over in the 1860s.

Inside, the pub has been stripped out to form one large L-shaped room, with a formal air created by wooden panelling which looks to date from the 1930s, and a collection of rather sombre old prints in heavy gilt frames.

OPEN 10 AM–11 PM MONDAY–SAT; 10 AM–10.30 PM SUNDAYS. FOOD SERVED UNTIL 10.30 MONDAY–SAT, 9.30 SUN. REAL ALES: THEAKSTON BEST, COURAGE DIRECTORS.

Turn right out of the pub and right again into Craven terrace.

MITRE
24 CRAVEN TERRACE

What an incredible and unexpected find this Grade II listed pub is! Originally built in the 1850s for the servants and tradesmen who depended on the mansions fronting Hyde Park, its elegant black marble fascia stands out in a street which was never terribly salubrious and is even less so now.

Inside, a recent refurbishment has done remarkably little damage to an interior that still retains a remarkable collection of original features. The partitions which would once have divided the main bar into three (each of which had its own street door) have now gone all save stubs, some of which have fragments of their original etched glass. However a charming little snug, originally for women only, survives almost intact, complete with decorated glass and moulded timber door and window cases of the 1880s or '90s.

This snug shares a beautifully-tiled entrance lobby with a small but grandly-appointed billiard room, which has dignified wooden panelling, a marble fireplace, arched moulded timber door-cases fine enough to grace a small country house, and a stained-glass skylight.

Another grand marble fireplace graces a separate snug at the rear, which is distinguished from the rest of the building by having dignified Georgian-style square sash windows instead of gothic arched ones. This would originally have been, in the strictly hierarchical world of the late 19th century, the sanctum of the uppermost classes of servant and tradesman: butlers, certainly, and some of the higher-class grocers and others with whom they did business.

What's charming about the Mitre is that it is utterly unselfconscious. It's never been marked down as an architectural treasure, so it doesn't behave like one. There's nothing best-bib-and-tucker about it. It is what it has always been: a local. And as a result, you're welcome.

OPEN ALL PERMITTED HOURS. FOOD SERVED NOON–9.30. REAL ALES:
MARSTON'S PEDIGREE, BODDINGTON'S, WADWORTH 6X, GREENE KING
ABBOT ALE.

Return to Bayswater Road. Turn right. Continue to Leinster Terrace. Turn right.

THE LEINSTER ARMS
17 LEINSTER TERRACE

The Leinster Arms is another of those perfectly respectable taverns that feels the need to claim the status of former coaching inn. As with the Swan, it's so close to central London that by this stage in the journey the horses wouldn't even have worked up a sweat, let alone needed changing. It also suffers from the handicap of being set in a quiet side-street well back from Bayswater Road, so the coaches on the first stage of their route to Bath wouldn't even have seen it. Oh, and it also dates from the 1830s or 40s, by which time long-distance coaching was already dying.

The misconception may have arisen because it does possess a coach arch, but this leads on to a long mews where the well-to-do of the surrounding mansions once kept their private carriages and teams. This mews betrays the Leinster Arms's true origins as a servants' and tradesmen's pub, very much smaller than the Mitre (which also fronts a long mews), but equally respectable.

Don't let its claim to a false dignity put you off, though. Inside it has been knocked into one room, but it's a very cosy and pleasant room with bare floorboards and a low ceiling covered in pressed paper from the 1890s or thereabouts. A certain amount of USAAF memorabilia recalls the pub's wartime popularity with American aircrew.

The playwright J M Barrie may not have been conscious of the fact at the time, but this was his local. He lived at 100 Bayswater Road, on the corner of Leinster Terrace, from 1902–1909 and wrote *Peter Pan* in the summerhouse in 1904, having met Jack Llewellyn Davies, the model for Pan, while walking his dog in Kensington Gardens.

OPEN: ALL PERMITTED HOURS. FOOD SERVED TO 7.30 PM
MONDAY–THURSDAY, 7 PM FRIDAY-SUNDAY. REAL ALES: DRAUGHT BASS,
FULLER'S LONDON PRIDE, TETLEY BITTER.

Turn right. Take second right into Craven Hill. Continue along Craven Hill, Craven Road, and Praed Street to the corner of Norfolk Place.

FOUNTAINS ABBEY
109 PRAED STREET

Briefly Tavistock's, this big 1880s or '90s pub has now reverted to its original name, even though it seems ignorant of its origins.

You know and I know that the ruined Fountains Abbey, landscaped by Capability Brown, is one of the biggest tourist attractions in Yorkshire. Here, though, a notice board propounds some absurd conflation of a local spring and the area's past owner, Westminster Abbey. Mind you, quite why a pub hard by Paddington Station should call itself after an abbey in Yorkshire, whose London terminus would be King's Cross, is a mystery – but that's pub names for you.

But this is a pub that enjoys its myth.

In 1928 the physician Alexander Fleming had a laboratory in St Mary's Hospital, whose window was exactly opposite the pub. The story goes that Fleming discovered penicillin by accident. He apparently left some Petri dishes cultured with lethal bacteria beside an open window while he went on holiday, and on his return found they had been

colonised by a strange fungus that had totally destroyed the bacteria. The fungus (they like to tell you at the Fountains Abbey) originated in the pub's cellars and proves the curative power of beer. Well, it might be true – but if I were the manager of the Fountains Abbey and my cellar was full of fungus, therapeutic or otherwise, I wouldn't want to boast about it.

The present pub replaces an original on the site that was recorded in 1824, when the district was first being developed. The original internal partitions have, of course, long been knocked out; but in buzzy, cosmopolitan Praed Street a big, lively, one-room pub is somehow more appropriate than a warren of tiny dens.

Some traces of the 1890s fittings survive, though, notably a huge fireplace and overmantel in tiles of a green lurid enough to prove that not all Victorian craftsmen and designers had taste. A curious feature of this fireplace

is a set of three roundels bearing portraits of grave late-Victorian gentlemen, one of whom has his head turned away to show a balding pate. There are arguments in the pub as to whom these portraits represent – a variation on the three monkeys theme, perhaps?

OPEN: ALL PERMITTED HOURS. FOOD SERVED 11–10 MONDAY-SATURDAY, 12–9.30 SUN. REAL ALES: OLD SPECKLED HEN, COURAGE DIRECTORS, THEAKSTON BEST, COURAGE BEST, CHARLES WELLS BOMBARDIER.

Continue along Praed Street and turn right into Sale Place.

ROYAL EXCHANGE
26 SALE PLACE

Any visitor to London who doesn't know what a London local could and should be mustn't miss this cosy little free house.

Tucked away down a side street, the single bar of this family-run pub could be a million miles from the roar of the Praed Street traffic and the constant barrage of noise from a huge prestige redevelopment project which, when finished, will undoubtedly ruin the area.

There's nothing exceptional about the humble exterior of the Royal Exchange, which was built probably in the 1820s or 30s along with the rest of the district. The Grand Junction Canal came through the fields here in the 1790s and Richard Sale, the canal company's solicitor in the 1820s, was responsible for the development of all the adjoining land that had been bought to make way for it. It's possible — for it was certainly common practice — that the pub was the first of the new buildings, and served as a builders' canteen while the surrounding houses were under construction.

Inside there's nothing exceptional, either, which is what's so wonderful about it. It's comfortably and cosily decorated, with no pretension to anything but comfort and cosiness. The upholstery is very slightly – just comfortably and cosily, in fact, worn. The food seems to consist mainly of enormous bowls of hefty-looking sausages and a pile of mash, all patiently awaiting their destiny in a hot cabinet behind the bar.

And everybody seems to know each other. This is an attribute of the London pub that's common in TV soaps but rare in reality; but at the Royal Exchange almost every entrance and exit is greeted with a chorus of cheery and evidently familiar greetings and farewells. Perhaps it's because the same family has owned and run the pub for over 20 years – another rarity in these troubled times, and one to be celebrated when found.

Like the Fountains Abbey, the Royal Exchange doesn't seem to know quite where it got its name. One theory is that it's called after the great City institution founded in the reign of Elizabeth I – but why should it be? Another is that it commemorates the way mail-coach guards would hurl bags of mail for delivery at the postmaster while simultaneously swiping bags for collection off hooks mounted by the road, all without slowing the coach. The third suggestion, and the one chosen for the sign, is a king – presumably Richard III, although the sign doesn't make it look much like him — exchanging his crown for a horse. As is so often the case, yer pays yer money.

OPEN 11–11 MONDAY–FRI; 11–4, 7–11 SAT, 12–4, 7–10.30 SUN. FOOD UNTIL 10 PM. REAL ALES: BODDINGTON BITTER, BRAKSPEAR BITTER.

Carry on down Sale Place, Norfolk Crescent, and Porchester Place. Turn right into Kendal Street and carry on down Connaught Street. Circumnavigate Hyde Park Square on the south side, and carry on into Strathearn Place.

VICTORIA
10A STRATHEARN PLACE

The Victoria is one of those Tardis-in-reverse pubs which looks enormous from the outside but is actually quite small once you get in. It's just as well the original partitions which divided it in two have long

been taken out: there would hardly have been room to breathe if they'd made the bars any smaller.

But taking out the partitions seems to be just about all they've done to the pub since 1864 which is when, if you can trust the date on the face of the clock mounted in the bar-back, it was fitted out (it was probably built 30-odd years earlier).

The original features include open fires (now converted to gas, and none the worse for that) at each end, one small and rather delicate, with bands of marquetry and a mirror painted in the French manner, one large and moulded, with a huge plain mirror now obscured by a giant roll-up satellite TV screen.

The walls are panelled to dado height, with a frieze of painted

56

panels above showing somewhat faded British army redcoats in glorious action against some natives or other. Above that is a rather good reproduction of hand-printed 1860s wallpaper.

But the pub's chief glory are the mirrors mounted in the bar-back and down one wall of the front bar. These are, quite simply, fantastic: a gothic mass of intertwining and endlessly repeating patterns of fleurs-de-lys (or, more likely, Prince of Wales plumes) in a glorious Puginesque riot of gold, ruby red and deepest blue, with a band of roundels loosely based on Tudor roses above. It's said the glass was imported from Germany, although there must have been British firms capable of the work at the time; and one of the panels is actually a post-war replacement – the staff will challenge you to tell which.

Up the steep and twisting stairs are two more rooms. One is a superbly comfortable, rather clubby Library, with green leather armchairs, gilt-framed oils of venerable Victorian gents, a fine marble fireplace, panelled walls, and even a few books in niche cases built into the corners. Children are allowed in here - although presumably they're not allowed to speak.

The other is the Theatre Bar, a small function room which is not usually open. Its design is of a different inspiration than the downstairs bars, having been copied from a bar which opened in the Gaiety Theatre, Strand, in the 1860s – although staff will tell you it actually used to be a theatre, in which case it would have had room for a single performer and an audience of four.

OPEN 11–11 MONDAY-FRIDAY, NOON–11 SATURDAY, NOON–10.30 SUNDAY. FOOD SERVED NOON–2.30 AND 6–9.45 MONDAY-SATURDAY, NOON–3.30 AND 6–9.15 SUN. REAL ALES: FULLER'S RANGE.

Continue along Strathearn Place into Stanhope Terrace. Turn right in Sussex Square, then left into Bathurst Street.

THE ARCHERY TAVERN
4 BATHURST STREET

Given its name, and the amount of toxophilogical memorabilia that decorate its walls, the Archery Tavern has surprisingly little connection with actual bows and arrows. True, the site was briefly occupied by archery butts, but the local for all the would-be Robin Hoods (and Maid Marions – archery was a sport popular with women, since it could be indulged in even while wearing crinolines, multiple petticoats and stays) was actually the Crown, which stood at the corner of Lancaster Terrace and Bayswater Road and was demolished in 1933.

The archery connection started in 1818 when Thomas Waring, a manufacturer of bows, arrows and toxophilite sundries based in

58

Bloomsbury, rented four acres of land here from the Bishop of London and, under the auspices of the Royal Toxophilite Society with which he was closely connected, established the butts. The lease was renewed in 1828 and the butts are marked on a map of 1832.

By 1834, however, the lease had been transferred to the landlord of the Crown, Thomas Bott, who first sold off part of the land for building, and then converted the rest into the Bayswater Tea Gardens. In 1839 the Gardens were in their turn built over, and the Archery Tavern was built as part of the quiet, villagey Regency side-street which went up on the site.

The upshot of this speculative development is a rather rustic and very pleasant town tavern of the servants-and-tradesman type, with a horseshoe-shaped front bar and a quiet snug at the back. Of course, the original partitions have long gone, and the wooden panelling and bar-back look suspiciously modern; but a pretty little fireplace, the pressed-paper ceiling, and a moulded plaster cornice survive from earlier times.

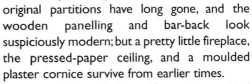

A living link with the pub's past is provided by one section of the clientele. Although the traffic of Bayswater Road hurtles past scarcely 100 yards away, you mustn't be surprised by the succession of stable girls in straining jodhpurs and riding boots coming in and out of the pub. Equestrianism remains, as it has always been, a big leisure activity in Hyde Park, and the girls work in a stable in the mews behind the pub which is still fulfilling the function it was built for 160-odd years ago.

OPEN ALL PERMITTED HOURS. FOOD SERVED NOON–3 AND 6–9.30, INCLUDING SUN. REAL ALES: BADGER AND KING & BARNES RANGES.

Turn right out of pub and cross Westbourne Street.

FINISH: LANCASTER GATE

FLEET STREET
BETWEEN CITY AND PALACE

LENGTH OF WALK: TWO MILES

IT WAS always crazy to maintain huge factories – which is, in effect, what the printing-presses of Fleet Street were – on such expensive real estate. But it was still a great pity when, one by one, the national newspapers moved out to Wapping in the 1980s, for with them went five centuries of history.

Long before there was printing, there was Fleet Street. Along with the Strand and Ludgate Hill, it was known to the Saxons as Akeman Street; St Bride's Church is probably of Saxon origin; and St Clement Danes was founded for or by the Danes converted to Christianity by Alfred the Great. Once Edward the Confessor had made Westminster the seat of royal power, Akeman Street became the main thoroughfare between the City and the Palace: a busy suburb quickly sprang up outside the City gates at Temple Bar, while the area between Akeman Street and the Thames was soon filled with great houses.

Where Essex Street is today there stood the Bishop of Exeter's House, which after the Dissolution became the London home of the Earls of Essex and was demolished and built over by one of London's first commercial property developers, Nicholas Barbon, son of Praise-God Barebone, speaker of the eponymous Barebones Parliament. Immediately to the east was the Temple which, after the suppression of the Templars in the 14th century, proved an ideal base for lawyers with

business both in the City and at Westminster. To the east again was the Carmelite convent of Whitefriars, which remained a legal sanctuary for 160 years after the Dissolution. The River Fleet next formed the moat of the Fleet Prison, established some time before 1155; and across the Fleet were the Dominicans, or Blackfriars.

When William Caxton set up England's first printing press in 1476, he saw his books as luxuries for the privileged few. He therefore established himself where the privileged few were to be found, in Westminster, where he published around 80 books pandering shamelessly to aristocratic tastes: romances of courtly love, poetry, handbooks of etiquette.

His successor, the aptly-named Wynkyn de Worde, inherited the business in 1491 and saw the potential of a wider market. So in 1500 he moved to St Bride's to exploit the mercantile patronage of the City; and when de Worde died in 1535, he had published more than 800 books. He had also founded an industry which took its tone more from the robustly independent character of the City than from the established ruling class at Westminster: Bishop Tunstall, crusading against Protestantism in the 1520s, was right when he said: "We must root out printing or printing will root us out."

Thanks perhaps to the presence of the printing industry, Fleet Street – and especially its taverns – became the centre of London's flourishing intellectual life. The Devil at number 2 and the Mitre at number 37, among others, were home from home for Shakespeare, Jonson, Beaumont and Fletcher in the 16th century, and for Johnson, Goldsmith, Addison and Steele in the 18th. The Mitre was, indeed, that very "throne of human felicity" where Johnson and Boswell went for their first drink together after meeting in a Covent Garden bookseller's in 1763.

By then the newspaper industry was well-established: the first Fleet Street daily, the *Courant*, was founded in 1702, taking advantage of a strategic location halfway between the two best sources of news in the land – Court and Parliament less than a mile away in one direction, the City no further off in the other.

"The man must have a rare recipe for melancholy who can be dull in Fleet Street," wrote Charles Lamb; and Dudley Barker's biography of G K Chesterton evokes the buzz of the place: "It was a life of taverns, of roaring discussions that went on for hour after hour, of articles scribbled on odd sheets of paper wedged on the pub table beside the tankard of beer, the printer's boy waiting patiently for the copy; and the gas-lamps flaring over the presses bringing out the issues for that night."

The demand for space in Fleet Street was such that it often left no room for the old taverns, however venerable: the Devil was demolished in 1787, and the Mitre followed 42 years later: both made way for banks. But the thirst of Fleet Street's topers meant that new establishments always sprang up: the Quill Club occupied Goldsmith's old house in Wine Office Court; and the Wig & Pen Club at 229–300 Strand was founded for lawyers and journalists in two houses knocked together, one of which, 229, had been built in 1625 for the gatekeeper of Temple Bar.

Fleet Street is very different now. Perhaps it would be kindest to remember it as H M Tomlinson described it in 1900, and as it was right up to the end: "Fleet Street was waking up to its usual crisis. Midnight was coming. It was growing tense with the knowledge of important things which 24 hours had engendered ... Each narrow side-turning was filled with ranks of newspaper carts, waiting for the hour ... From basements and walls came the rumble of machinery, already beginning with the first revolutions of its heavy load of rumours and alarums to communicate a tremor to the earth."

START: TEMPLE

Turn left out of the station. Cross Temple Place and turn right. Turn left into Milford Lane and climb Essex Steps into Essex Street. Turn left into Little Essex Street.

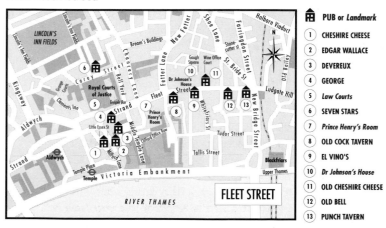

🏠	**PUB** or *Landmark*
①	CHESHIRE CHEESE
②	EDGAR WALLACE
③	DEVEREUX
④	GEORGE
⑤	*Law Courts*
⑥	SEVEN STARS
⑦	*Prince Henry's Room*
⑧	OLD COCK TAVERN
⑨	EL VINO'S
⑩	*Dr Johnson's House*
⑪	OLD CHESHIRE CHEESE
⑫	OLD BELL
⑬	PUNCH TAVERN

CHESHIRE CHEESE
5 LITTLE ESSEX STREET

Before plunging into the hubbub of Fleet Street itself, it might be as well to pause a while in a small, intimate, back-street pub where, as far as I know, no great men have opined, no literary giants have caroused, and no history has been made. It's always good to have a reminder that pubs are not necessarily about poets and playwrights: they are, primarily, ordinary places for ordinary folk, where poets and playwrights are welcome as long as they don't give themselves airs.

There are certainly no airs or graces about the Cheshire Cheese, a handsome brick-built mid-Victorian pub in the Olde English style, not to be confused with the much grander Olde Cheshire Cheese. A single bar is divided by dark wood settles; there are panelled walls and black beams overhead; and the natural light is gently diffused by the frosted glass in the Jacobean-style leaded windows.

Around the walls are framed police shoulder-flashes from America and Canada as well as England, all collected by the landlord over many years. It started when a visiting delegation of New York policemen called in at his previous pub in Great Portland Street in the 1970s and struck up a friendship; they gave him their badges as mementos, and it built up from there. And that's how traditions start.

OPEN 11–11 MONDAY–FRIDAY. FOOD 11–3, 5–9. REAL ALE: COURAGE BEST AND DIRECTORS.

Return along Little Essex Street.

EDGAR WALLACE
40 ESSEX STREET

Until 1975 the Edgar Wallace was the Essex Head, standing as it does on the site of Essex House.

The big open-plan bar is rather anonymous, with a couple of slender iron columns and some scraps of engraved glass as sole survivors of the original late-Victorian scheme. But the much older pub it replaced was well-known to Dr Johnson, who was a member of Sam's Club which started meeting on the premises in 1783.

Clubs like Sam's, defined by Johnson as "an assembly of good fellows, meeting under certain conditions", were once extremely common. They had no premises of their own, and were really no more than circles of drinkers, united by an interest in anything from radical politics to caged birds, meeting regularly and

gradually evolving constitutions and customs. Probably the most famous of them was one of the very first: the Apollo Club at the Devil, founded by Ben Jonson.

The Essex Head was run by a former servant of Johnson's great friends the Thrales, and Johnson agreed to support him by patronising his club. It was one of three or four which boasted the convivial Johnson as a member, and he wrote: "The terms are lax and the expenses light. We meet thrice a week, and he who misses forfeits twopence."

In 1975 the pub was renamed to mark the centenary of the birth of journalist and mystery writer Edgar Wallace, who in his 57 prolific years wrote 23 plays, 957 short stories, and 165 films as well as novels such as *The Four Just Men*. Why the brewery chose Wallace for such an honour I don't know: perhaps it was trying to repeat the success of the Sherlock Holmes off Trafalgar Square, but maybe I'm being unkind. At any rate, memorabilia were donated by Wallace's daughter, and the Edgar Wallace Society holds its annual lunch upstairs.

OPEN 11–11 MONDAY–FRIDAY. FOOD SERVED 12–3. UP TO SIX REAL ALES.

Leave the pub by the back door and turn left into Devereux Court.

DEVEREUX
20 DEVEREUX COURT

This handsome neo-classical building with its pink stucco, rusticated quoins, and square sash windows would be a fine pub even if it had no history. But history is something it's got lots of.

Essex House, which once occupied the site, was until 1646 the home of the Earls of Essex, the second of whom was executed by Elizabeth I in 1601, while the third (whose bust is over the front door) led the Parliamentary army in the early years of the Civil War. It then stood empty for nearly 30 years until Nicholas Barbon bought it, along with several other grand properties in the area, for demolition and redevelopment.

Essex House and its gardens made way for Essex Street, Little Essex Street, Essex Court and Devereux Court, which were described in 1720 as "well inhabited by the gentry" and were well provided with taverns and coffee houses. The spot occupied by the Devereux was then the best-known coffee house of the day, the Grecian.

Coffee houses came to London in the middle of the 17th century. Much of the business of the time was done in taverns; and businessmen were quick to realise that by basing oneself in a coffee house rather than a tavern one could get through a day's work without alcohol. Not surprisingly, coffee houses spread rapidly, and by the turn of the century there were 480 of them.

The Grecian quickly became the favourite of Addison, the radical journalist and editor of the Spectator, and also of Sir Isaac Newton. A century later Goldsmith was also to be found here, when he had money. By that time, however, the great age of the coffee house was

ebbing: the Grecian finally closed in 1842, to be pulled down and replaced by Eldon Chambers in 1844.

However, there was a tavern on the ground floor of the new building from the very start, ensuring some continuity of use; and today's Devereux is a very handsome pub indeed, with its chintz curtains and print wallpaper creating – rather curiously, in a London pub – something of the feeling of a comfortable country house.

OPEN 11–11 MONDAY–FRIDAY. RESTAURANT OPEN 12–3; BAR FOOD ALL DAY. REAL ALES: COURAGE BEST AND DIRECTORS, JOHN SMITH'S, THEAKSTON BEST, GUEST ALE.

Turn left out of the pub.

THE GEORGE
213 STRAND

With the Temple just behind and the Law Courts immediately opposite, this is the place to come and watch the legal profession at play, either in full fig during breaks in court proceedings or unwinding after a hard day's arguing.

The George was originally a coffee house, founded in 1723 and named, supposedly, not after the reigning monarch but after its proprietor. With a long bar running all down one side of the narrow room, and dim alcoves and benches opposite, it still has something of the atmosphere of the 18th century; but in fact it is entirely late-Victorian, of the school described by Mark Girouard as "back to the inn", characterised by "half-timbered gables, leaded lights, bottle glass, lanterns, wooden barrels, carved black oak, and artificially smoked ceilings between artificially warped beams."

The George, with its tall, imposing, half-timbered facade, is something of a landmark, being situated where the City ends and Westminster begins. The half-timbering is, of course, fake, if that isn't too harsh a word for such an elaborate and delightful pastiche. Of particular charm are the carved monks, one with a blue cat and one with a blue dog.

The work was commissioned in the late 1890s by an entrepreneur called Frederick Stanley, who also owned a pub called the Windsor. The Windsor made him a handsome profit of some £700 a year; but

the George, on which he had spent heavily, lost twice as much, and like so many others in the business, Stanley soon went bust.

OPEN 11–11 MONDAY–SATURDAY, 12–10.30 SUNDAY. FOOD 11–3, 5.30–8.30. REAL ALES: DRAUGHT BASS, SHEPHERD NEAME MASTERBREW.

Cross the Strand.

Law Courts

Built in 1882 to hear the civil cases previously held at Westminster Hall and Lincoln's Inn, this is one of London's great examples of Victorian Gothic and covers an astounding eight acres. It was described by Henry James as "in a good stage of that dusky silvering which is the best that London buildings can look for in the ... tormenting air."

Great hall open Monday–Saturday 10.30–4.30.

Go through Clement's Inn to the left of the Law Courts. Turn right through Grange Court into Carey Street.

Seven Stars
53a Carey Street

London has precious few really old unspoilt pubs, and this is one of them. Built in 1602, 14 years before Shakespeare died, it's a real woodman's axe – the head and the haft have both been changed God knows how many times, but somehow it's still the same axe.

Its long, low, rustic exterior sticks out like a sore thumb against the background of a giant 1950s office block, and once you get through the doors – one marked "Private Counter", the other marked "General Counter" – the impression of incongruity doesn't fade.

Although it's stuffed with lawyers – the back door of the Law Courts is directly opposite, and the shop next door is called The Wig Box – the Seven Stars is no Rumpole of the Bailey-style city tavern; it feels much more like an old-fashioned country pub. Apart from a tiny snug, there's just one very plain bar with bare floorboards, oak beams, crazy walls, ancient scrubbed tables and rickety chairs that a man of more than modest weight wouldn't trust too far (although everybody here seems to drink standing up anyway). To add to the rustic character, most of the clientele seem to know one another.

The pub's name is sometimes explained as a reference to the naval flag of the United Provinces of the Netherlands at the time of the Glorious Revolution, and therefore a Whiggish sign of loyalty to William III. However there are pubs elsewhere in the country called the Plough and the Bear which show seven stars on their signs (even though the Plough has only six), so maybe the name has astronomical rather than political significance.

Carey Street, incidentally, used to be the location of the bankruptcy courts, and "in Carey Street" is a now obsolete expression meaning broke.

OPEN 11–11 MONDAY-FRIDAY, 12–8 SATURDAY. BAR FOOD 12–2.30. REAL ALES: ADNAM'S RANGE.

Continue along Carey Street and turn right into Bell Yard. Cross Fleet Street at the Temple Bar and turn left.

PRINCE HENRY'S ROOM

Housed in a rare survival of the Great Fire, Prince Henry's Room at 17 Fleet Street had been an inn called the Hand since the beginning of the 16th century, but was rebuilt in 1610, and renamed the Prince's Arms to celebrate the investiture of the first Prince of Wales for nearly a century. The upstairs room, now open to the public, has an amazing plaster ceiling – the best of its kind in London – which includes a Prince of Wales plume and the initials P H. Various stories have been concocted to connect the Prince with the inn, but none of them stand up to scrutiny.

The inn was later renamed the Fountain, and the front part was let to a celebrated exhibition, Mrs Salmon's Waxworks. The building was bought and restored by the Corporation of London in 1900, and since 1975 has housed a permanent exhibition dedicated to Samuel Pepys, who was born in nearby Salisbury Court.

OPEN 11–2 MONDAY–SATURDAY.

Continue along Fleet Street.

OLD COCK TAVERN
22 FLEET STREET

Don't be fooled by the apparent solidity of the Old Cock: it has an unnerving habit of moving. The original Old Cock was first recorded at 190 Fleet Street, just opposite, in 1549, and was one of those celebrated Fleet Street taverns which entertained the Elizabethan and Jacobean literati. It must have been a grand place: it was prosperous enough for the landlord to issue his own trade tokens when coinage was in short supply in the 1650s, and a fireplace and overmantel are always said to be by the hand of Grinling Gibbons himself.

The fireplace and overmantel, alas, were all that survived the Great Fire, but the Cock – then the Cock & Bottle – was soon rebuilt and was a favourite haunt of Pepys, perhaps because the landlady, Mrs Knipps, was one of his many lovers. Here he "drank, and ate a lobster, and sang, and mightily merry."

Dickens knew the place well, as did Tennyson, who celebrated it in one of the worst stanzas in the language:

Oh plump head waiter at the Cock
To which I most resort,
How goes the time? 'Tis five o'clock.
Go fetch a pint of port.

A warning, surely, not to try writing poetry after a pint of port – although, to be fair, the rest of Will Waterproof's Lyrical Monologue is not quite as bad.

In 1887 the same fate befell the Cock as had already befallen the Devil and the Mitre: it was demolished to make way for a bank. The licence, however, was transferred to the new site, and a thoroughgoing Olde English tavern was built, with the maybe-Gibbons fireplace and overmantel intact. Those celebrated fixtures survived a second fire in 1990, so most of what you see today is not Cock Mark I, Mark II, nor even Mark III, for the interior had to be extensively reconstructed.

It has to be said that they didn't make a bad job of it: it's appropriately dim and oaky, with settles and booths and all that sort of thing; but it also has a more contemporary mezzanine with comfortable-looking leather sofas as well as a restaurant and a function room.

OPEN 11–11 MONDAY–FRIDAY. FOOD SERVED NOON–9 PM. REAL ALES: COURAGE BEST AND DIRECTORS, MARSTON'S PEDIGREE, MORLAND OLD SPECKLED HEN.

Turn right out of the pub.

EL VINO'S
47 FLEET STREET

As a young reporter I was always too scared to venture into El Vino's: it was, after all, the bibulous headquarters of my profession, where senior journalists of doughty repute, the high priests of my craft, foregathered to drink themselves insensible, uttering weighty, if slurred, pronouncements on the state of the nation as they did so. All in all, it was far too intimidating for a tyro like me.

It still has that atmosphere, although the journalists have all now been spirited away to the glass fortresses of Wapping. But there are plenty of lawyers still about, and lawyers recreating en masse can be just as formidable as journalists.

It is not, however, one of the most ancient institutions in Fleet Street, for it was founded only in 1879 by Arthur Bower, a wine-shipper. Originally it was not a bar at all; but customers would be invited to free samplings in the hope that they would buy. When few did (for journalists then, as now, loved a freebie), Bower started charging. Eventually he added a restaurant to the bar, changing the name to El Vino's in 1922 to further his ambitions to the Lord Mayoralty, it having been made clear to him that having one's name over the door of a celebrated place of inebriation, however classy, was hardly consonant with the dignity of the office. Bower duly achieved the mayoralty in 1924.

One of those celebrated inebriates was G K Chesterton, who used to come here to do some "hard drinking and hard thinking". So hard did Chesterton think that he would always hail a cab immediately on leaving, even though his office was no more than a few yards away; well, its best to be sure, isn't it?

Chesterton's biographer, Dudley Barker, recalls him "in a haze of talk and uproarious laughter", adding: "Sometimes he would break off for a while to cross the street, quite often stopping in mid-traffic, holding it all up for several minutes of oblivious pondering, or a chance meeting and an argument with his brother. Sometimes on his way down the street he would pull from his pocket a penny exercise book and pencil and write an essay against the support of the nearest wall. An American visitor noted that he had seen Chesterton standing in a shop doorway ... composing a poem, jotting it on a piece of paper and reading it aloud as he wrote."

These working practices would not go down well in today's Wapping.

Now I am older, and El Vino's is rather less intimidating. A jacket and tie are still essential, but women are now allowed to buy drinks at the bar, although they have to wear a skirt while doing so.

As for the look of the place, it can't have changed since Chesterton knew it, for it can't be said to have decor at all. It just has bottles in racks, and a few chairs and tables, and odd bits of wine-trade impedimenta scattered about. It's all very functional and masculine, but in a reassuringly cosy sort of way, like the senior common room of a very traditional public school.

OPEN 11–10 MONDAY-FRIDAY. RESTAURANT OPEN 12–3. BAR SNACKS AVAILABLE EVENINGS. NO REAL ALE – BUT A FRIGHTENING CHOICE OF FINE WINES.

Cross Fleet Street and turn right, then left into Bolt Court. Follow Bolt Court into Gough Square.

DR JOHNSON'S HOUSE

Number 17 Gough Square is a fine, four-square Queen Anne or early Georgian house, the last of its kind in a labyrinth of courts, yards and alleys which ought to be a wonderfully rambling maze of ancient dwellings but is in fact a disappointingly characterless complex of modern office buildings.

Johnson lived here from 1748–59, where he and his six Scottish copyists – who worked in the attic, standing up – completed his Dictionary in 1755. Johnson also published his twice-weekly periodical,

The Rambler, here from 1750, but neither enterprise made him much money and his bitterness on the subject of patronage is well-attested.

This is the only one of Johnson's many addresses in the area which is still standing. From 1759–65 he lived in Inner Temple Lane, in total idleness on a royal pension in a house that was demolished to make way for Johnson's Buildings. From 1765–76 he lived at 7 Johnson's Court, also now demolished, writing *A Journey to the Western Isles of Scotland* there. In 1776 he moved to his last address, 8 Bolt Court, where he died in 1784. It burnt down in 1819.

Six years after Johnson's death, 17 Gough Square became a hotel. It went steadily downhill, however, and was near collapse when Lord Harmsworth rescued it in 1911 and turned it into a museum. As many original features as could be preserved, notably a fine staircase and much American pine panelling, have been, and the house is stuffed with contemporary furniture and Johnson memorabilia including the Dictionary itself.

OPEN 11–5 MONDAY–SATURDAY, TELEPHONE 0207 353 3745.

Go through the archway opposite the house and Gunpowder Square. Turn right into Wine Office Court.

OLDE CHESHIRE CHEESE
WINE OFFICE COURT

It's easy to be cynical about a pub which has become so famous and such a tourist trap, but the Olde Cheshire Cheese, it has to be admitted, is the real McCoy.

It's claimed that the original building on the site was the guest-house of Whitefriars, sold off in 1538 as an inn after the convent was suppressed. And it's an entirely reasonable claim: there are plenty of examples of the same thing happening elsewhere.

It was rebuilt over the original medieval cellars as a tavern and chop-house after the Great Fire and still retains, at least in part, the characteristic layout of one large room and several smaller private chambers, rather like the surviving wing of the George in Borough High Street. On the ground floor are the small, cosy front bar; the Chop Room, which is the pub's showpiece, with its ancient black oak

panelling and furniture, low, oak-beamed ceilings, old prints, benches, and stuffed body of Polly, the pub parrot whose death in 1926 after 40 years' service merited a BBC obituary; and two more recent bars, the Cheshire Bar and the courtyard. Downstairs (not surprisingly) is the Cellar Bar, and on the first floor are two dining rooms and a function room. It's all incredibly atmospheric – even if it isn't all original – and its popularity is proof that, given a choice, most people prefer pubs that ramble to today's great impersonal barns.

The Cheese plays strongly on its connection with Dr Johnson, none of whose various addresses is more than a stone's throw away and whose protégé, Oliver Goldsmith, actually lived next door. In fact the pub isn't mentioned by Boswell at all, and "His" chair was imported from the Mitre when it was demolished in 1819. But the Doctor must have used the Cheese – and a slightly later resident of Gough Square testified that he knew people who had declared that indeed he had.

Real or not, the Johnson connection put the Olde Cheshire Cheese on the literary map. It's the setting, although not named, for a scene in *A Tale of Two Cities*; Thackeray knew the pub well; and G K

Chesterton used to dress up as Johnson for costume dinners held at the Cheese in the Doctor's memory. In the 1890s the upstairs room was home to the Rhymers Club, which included W B Yeats and a (rather unwilling) Oscar Wilde, as well as contemporary writers including John Davidson, author of *The Fleet Street Eclogues*, who wrote the following tribute:

This modern world so stiff and pale
You leave behind you when you please
For long clay pipes and great old ale
And beefsteaks at the Cheshire Cheese.

Trite, maybe; but it hits the spot. Another tradition at the Cheese was the cooking of a huge pudding on the first Monday of every October, to be cut by a celebrity of the day. The pudding weighed 50–80lbs and contained steak, kidneys, oysters and mushrooms, and Stanley Baldwin, Jack Dempsey and Conan Doyle are among those to whom the honour has fallen.

OPEN 11.30–11 MONDAY–FRIDAY, 12–3, 5.30–11 SATURDAY, 12–3 SUNDAY. BAR FOOD SERVED 12–9 MONDAY-FRIDAY. RESTAURANTS OPEN 12–9.30 MONDAY–FRIDAY, 6–9 SATURDAY, 12–2.30 SUNDAY. REAL ALE: SAM SMITH'S OLD BREWERY BITTER.

Continue down Wine Office Court into Fleet Street. Cross the road and turn left.

OLD BELL
FLEET STREET

The Olde English-style Old Bell is said to stand on the very site where Wynkyn de Worde set up the press he had inherited from Caxton: it's believed that at the time the tavern was called the Swan, and de Worde's imprimatur was "emprynted at the sign of the Swan in Fletestrete".

Not that the Swan is the only other name associated with the site: indeed, before it settled down to being the Old Bell it changed names with confusing regularity, being called at different times the 10 Bells, the 12 Bells, the Golden Bell, and the Great Tom of Oxford – from

Wren's Tom Tower at Christ Church, Oxford.

Whatever it was called at the time, it was razed to the ground in the Great Fire but was swiftly rebuilt as a canteen and hostel for builders engaged in reconstruction work. This is a claim made by several City taverns, and could well be true: later developers often built a pub before anything else, to cater for their workers, to create a cash flow while building work was going on, and to have a going concern to sell if the project went pear-shaped.

Builders were not the only patrons of the reborn Bell, however: another was the short-tempered (and, indeed, short) poet Pope, who poured half a pint of canary into a critic's hat during a fierce row here.

In the 1860s, when changes in the law made it profitable to retail wine by the bottle, the front portion of the 17th-century tavern was turned into what we would call an off-licence. In 1897 the property was bought by a couple of private entrepreneurs, the Baker Brothers, who planned to demolish it and replace it with a glitteringly opulent new pub as they had already done at the Punch Tavern, almost next door. Fortunately for us, the Bakers went spectacularly bust, along with many others of their kind, in the great collapse of 1899, and the Old Bell was taken over by the gin distillers Nicholson's, to whom the Bakers owed rather a lot of money.

Redevelopment plans were quickly shelved, and Nicholson's did nothing to the pub except appoint a landlady they could trust. Nellie Bear acquired a formidable reputation in Fleet Street and kept the Old Bell open right through the Blitz, even when a German bomb half-demolished St Bride's in 1940. She retired in 1946 after 40 years at the helm.

Not much has changed since: the shop at the front has been reabsorbed into the pub, to create an attractive entrance lobby with a semi-private little snug to the side of it; and inevitably the internal partitions have at some stage been removed. What's left is a cosy bareboards boozer, with a plain horseshoe bar counter, plenty of beams and dark woodwork, and a cheerful little fireplace – the good prototype, if you like, of so much bad modern pub design.

OPEN 11.30–11 MONDAY–FRIDAY, 12–4 SATURDAY. FOOD SERVED 12–3. REAL ALES: TETLEY, BRAKSPEAR BITTER, DRAUGHT BASS, TIMOTHY TAYLOR'S LANDLORD.

Turn right out of the pub.

PUNCH TAVERN
99 FLEET STREET

The glittering Punch Tavern is a very different proposition from the understated Old Bell. Its opulently glazed and tiled lobby almost seems to want to drag you in physically – so why resist?

The opulence is continued inside the big front bar. Under an ornate skylight are painted panels, elaborately moulded plasterwork, bright lights, huge mirrors, glass panels etched with birds on branches –

every hallmark, in fact, of a luxurious saloon of the 1890s; and once you know that the pub was bought in 1893 by the Baker Brothers, whose taste ran to the gaudy, you know that your analysis is correct.

Except that it isn't, quite. Three or four years ago, entirely fortuitously, the Punch Tavern was bought from Bass by a new company called ... Punch Taverns. The new owners subjected the old pub to an almost total refit, and it has to be said that they did a brilliant job, although they have gone rather over the top, perhaps understandably, with Punch & Judy artwork and memorabilia.

Actually, the pub's name derives from Punch & Judy only at one remove. It used to be the Crown & Sugarloaf; but in the 1880s it became the recreational HQ of the staff of *Punch* magazine, then at the height of its popularity. When the Baker Brothers rebuilt the place, therefore, they decided to rename it in honour of the magazine.

A curious dispute has literally torn the Punch in two. At some time, the ownership of the premises somehow became divided, one half belonging to Bass, the other to the Yorkshire brewer Sam Smith. Sam's, for some reason, closed and boarded its half a few years ago; and closed and boarded it remains. What treasure-trove of original 1890s fittings it might contain is a mystery known only to Sam's.

Punch Taverns soon gave up trying to negotiate the reunion of the two halves, and instead took over a shop behind the pub, which has now been incorporated as a separate bar. The conversion job has been as faultless as the refitting of the saloon. Still, it would be nice to see the pub made whole again. Perhaps one day.

OPEN 11.30–11 MONDAY–FRIDAY. FOOD SERVED 11.30–3. REAL ALES:
FULLER'S LONDON PRIDE, ADNAM'S BITTER, GREENE KING ABBOT.

Turn right out of the pub, cross New Bridge Street and turn right again.

FINISH: BLACKFRIARS

THE CITY
AFTER THE FIRE

LENGTH OF WALK: TWO-AND-A-HALF MILES

THE FIRE that broke out in a baker's shop in Pudding Lane, near the end of London Bridge, in the early hours of Sunday 2 September 1666 was not the first of its kind that had swept London; nor was it to be the last. It was not even the worst – not, at least, in terms of loss of life. But by daylight it was obvious to observers that it was going to be by far the most extensive.

All the conditions were right. That quarter of the city was one of packed alleys and courts, whose densely-clustered houses were built largely of timber and thatch which had been thoroughly prepared for their role in history by a long, hot, dry summer. The time of day was critical on two counts: individual citizens woke to the fire in a panic, and were more inclined to save what they could and flee than to stand and fight; while the authorities who might have done something to contain it were roused to action too late to be effective.

Still, the fire spread slowly. By Sunday evening Pepys, having buried his Parmesan cheese in his back garden for safety, had escaped to the South Bank, where the fire seemed to him "one entire arch from this to the other side of the bridge and in a bow up the hill, above a mile long." On Monday the flames reached Cornhill, swallowing up the Royal Exchange, and roaring westward into Cheapside. On Tuesday, the worst day, it was the turn of Old St Paul's, whose heat-shattered stones, wrote Evelyn, "flew like grenades, the melting lead running down the streets in a stream, and the very pavements glowing with fiery redness." That evening the Tower of London was saved by the blowing up of all the surrounding buildings, but in the west, where the King and the Duke of York had taken personal charge of operations, the flames vaulted the Fleet valley and consumed Fleet Street as far as Temple Bar.

On the following day the wind dropped, and with the use of gunpowder the fire was cordoned off. At Fetter Lane and Smithfield it was held, and by Friday it was all but out. On Highbury Fields there were 200,000 refugees; 450 acres of old London had been levelled; 87 churches including St Paul's, 44 Livery Company halls, 13,000 houses and Newgate Prison were smoking cinders; but only nine deaths were recorded.

What is therefore remarkable is that the area of the City we are about to walk through is not a smartly laid-out grid of broad boulevards, processional avenues and grand plazas, but a higgledy-piggledy ramshackle rat-run of old alleyways, narrow courtyards and twisting lanes, much as it was before the fire.

This is not because no-one wanted to reinvent a London of a grander geometry; indeed, every visionary there was submitted variations on the theme of grids and vistas, and the authorities would dearly have loved to have had a tabula rasa on which to rewrite London without congestion, without slums, without sewers, without disease. But they didn't, and for a strangely heartening reason: London wouldn't sell.

Every square foot of gently-smoking cinders belonged to someone; and to those who had lost their possessions, their meagre footprint of London soil was all the wealth they had. They would willingly sell it to King or Corporation for redevelopment according to some grand plan, if King or Corporation wanted it badly enough to stump up. Otherwise – and subject to new regulations governing the scale of rebuilding and the materials to be used – they would keep their property and build their new homes themselves.

The skeleton of the City, then, is a legal one of title deeds and leases, copyholds and charters which the authorities couldn't afford to buy out. The fire swept away brick and stone and wood and metal, but it couldn't destroy paper and parchment, which dictated that the new city should retain the shape, if not the substance, of the old. On this walk we will have the bizarre experience of passing between gleaming new towers of the 21st century whose ground plan was determined by the allocation of building plots in the 11th. You will see little that is truly old; yet away from the Victorian thoroughfares, which were blasted through the old pre-Fire street plan, you will be pacing lines laid out for you 1,000 years ago.

START: BLACKFRIARS

Cross Queen Victoria Street. The Blackfriar is immediately opposite the station.

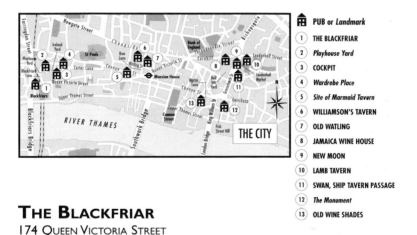

	PUB or *Landmark*
(1)	THE BLACKFRIAR
(2)	*Playhouse Yard*
(3)	COCKPIT
(4)	*Wardrobe Place*
(5)	*Site of Marmaid Tavern*
(6)	WILLIAMSON'S TAVERN
(7)	OLD WATLING
(8)	JAMAICA WINE HOUSE
(9)	NEW MOON
(10)	LAMB TAVERN
(11)	SWAN, SHIP TAVERN PASSAGE
(12)	*The Monument*
(13)	OLD WINE SHADES

THE BLACKFRIAR
174 QUEEN VICTORIA STREET

The wedge-shaped Blackfriar is unique. Built in 1875 and remodelled 25 or so years later, it would be a fairly straightforward Olde English pub with the usual black oak beams and small-paned leaded windows if it weren't for the astounding decorative scheme superimposed in 1902 by Henry Poole.

Poole was a leading figure in the Arts & Crafts movement inspired by William Morris, and was master of the movement's governing body, the Art Workers' Guild, in 1906. He took as his theme the Dominican friary which had occupied the site in the Middle Ages, and decorated the whole place inside and out with the most incredible copper bas-reliefs of fat, jolly and distinctly unspiritual friars engaged in various labours connected, in one way or another, with the pleasures of drink, all illustrated with trite aphorisms such as "Silence is Golden",

"Wisdom is Rare", and "Industry is All".

If that was all Poole had done, it would have been extraordinary enough; but he didn't stop there. Surely testing the depths of his client's pocket to the limit, he smothered the interior in marble. The walls are covered in plaques of it. The mullions of the windows are sheathed with it. There are columns of it and carvings in it; and the whole ceiling of the secluded little snug at the back is vaulted with it, as if it were a side-chapel in some Byzantine basilica. (Check out the four light fittings in this snug: labelled Morn, Noon, Even and Night, each has a marble figure including the devil hanging upside down like a sleeping bat at Noon; but each also has its little bronze monk.)

Then there are mirrors, mosaics, bronze gargoyles, stained-glass window-panes – every decorative trick conceivable in an explosion of exuberant, ebullient, effervescent, extravagant craftsmanship. It's a truly amazing feat, almost too good a thing for a mere pub. Indeed, the flippant tone of the decorations suggests that Poole might have thought as much himself. For all that, the Blackfriar is a major achievement and a landmark in the history of English decorative art.

OPEN 11.30–11 MONDAY-FRIDAY, 12–3 (5 IN SUMMER) SATURDAY, CLOSED SUNDAY. BAR FOOD 12–2.30. REAL ALES: ADNAM'S BITTER, FULLER'S LONDON PRIDE, DRAUGHT BASS.

Turn left out of the pub into Queen Victoria Street, immediately left up Blackfriars Lane, and right into Playhouse Yard. Continue along Ireland Yard.

PLAYHOUSE YARD

As you stand at the bottom of Blackfriars Lane, look up St Andrew's Hill at the dome of St Paul's rising majestically above the jumbled roofs of the surrounding houses. This is St Paul's as Wren meant it to be seen: Order as Divine, triumphant over the chaos of the merely human. You won't be able to see it like that for long though: a huge new development called Times Square, on the site of the former offices of *The Times*, is set to take over the whole north side of Queen Victoria Street between Blackfriars Lane and St Andrew's Hill, and what it will do to one of the few decent vistas of St Paul's is anyone's guess.

Another result of the development is that Playhouse Yard and Ireland Yard, halfway up the hill, have had their character entirely destroyed. Playhouse Yard was the site of Richard Burbage's Playhouse, which occupied some of the surviving buildings of the Blackfriars convent from about 1580. Burbage took it over in 1608; and *Cymbeline* had its premiere there in 1611. The Playhouse was closed in 1642 and demolished in 1655, but there's another Shakespeare connection here: Ireland Yard, where he bought a house in 1613 for £140, is his only known London address. The character of both yards, once narrow closed-in alleys, has been ruined by the demolition of their entire south sides. It is hardly to be expected that it will be restored when Times Square is completed.

THE COCKPIT
7 ST ANDREW'S HILL

There are rather self-conscious late-Victorian echoes of Burbage and Shakespeare at the Cockpit which, although it claims a date of 1787, actually dates from the 1830s and had its own cockpit until the sport was outlawed in 1846.

Its present character, however, dates to a complete remodelling of the 1890s, when it was turned into an Olde English extravaganza. The modest exterior with its theatrical black and gold fascia, lead-light windows, and big carriage lamps, does not hint at the mock-Tudor kitsch of the interior, which despite recent alterations (the inner partitions are gone, and the red plush and heavy drapes are rather out of character with the original intention) still includes a minstrels' gallery. It's not exactly a full-sized gallery, though: in fact you'd have to be a Minstrel of Restricted Growth to be able to use it.

OPEN 11–11 MONDAY-FRIDAY, 11–9 SATURDAY, 12–3, 7.30–10.30 SUNDAY. FOOD SERVED 11–2.30, 6–8.30 MONDAY–FRIDAY. REAL ALES: COURAGE BEST AND DIRECTORS, MARSTON'S PEDIGREE.

Turn left out of the pub and right into Carter Lane.

WARDROBE PLACE

Off Carter Lane to the right is a leafy, sequestered little courtyard of early 18th-century town houses some of which, almost uniquely in this part of town, haven't been converted to offices and still have people living in them. From the reign of Edward III to the Great Fire, this was the Royal Wardrobe, which was the depository not only of the King's robes of state but also of many treasures and antiquities.

ST PAUL'S CATHEDRAL

Emerging from the narrows of Carter Lane, one is suddenly treated to a vision of the south side of St Paul's, and the scale not only of Wren's masterpiece but also of his entire artistic vision is dramatically revealed. It makes you wonder what the City would have been like if he and the other Italian-influenced architects of the Stuart period had had their way with it. Would we have preferred the grand avenues, the noble vistas and the broad piazzas to the rat-runs, crooked alleys, and narrow courts we have?

Skirt St Paul's to the south and enjoy another vista of the Cathedral, which has been opened up with the construction of the Millennium footbridge. Ignore, however, the big pub called the Centre Page. This used to be the Horn Tavern and was very well-known to Dickens, who put it into *The Pickwick Papers*. It was going to form part of this itinerary, but recent remodellings have rendered it utterly devoid either of history or character.

Continue down Cannon Street.

SITE OF MERMAID TAVERN

On the south-western corner of the crossroads with Bread Street stood the Mermaid Tavern, frequent scene of the frolics of that little freemasonry of Elizabethan and Jacobean dramatists. "What things have we seen done at the Mermaid!" wrote Francis Beaumont to Ben Jonson in 1610. It was burnt down in the Great Fire, but in 1818 Keats wrote a hymn of praise to it anyway – "Souls of poets dead and gone/What Elysium have ye known/Happy field or mossy cavern/choicer than the Mermaid Tavern?" – proving that poetry about pubs, even by poets of the first rank, is always terrible.

Continue down Cannon Street. Turn left into Bow Lane, cross Watling Street, and turn immediately left into Grovelands Court.

WILLIAMSON'S TAVERN
GROVELANDS COURT, BOW LANE

Grovelands Court, a tiny alley off bustling Bow Lane, is reckoned by some to be the geographical dead centre of the City, although for my money it's a shade too far south. But as the whole of one side of it, as well as one end, is taken up by a rather good pub, it's probably a better place to spend time than the actual dead centre – wherever that is.

This was the site of the new Lord Mayor's house after the Great Fire; the wrought-iron gates, originally at the mouth of the court, were donated by William and Mary and include their initials. The house was not considered grand enough, however, and in 1739 it was sold to one Robert Williamson to convert into a hotel, although the new Mansion House took so long to build that the Mayors remained in residence at Grovelands Court until 1753.

Williamson's, despite its past, was never an especially grand hotel: its plaster ceilings were actually of whitewashed sailcloth, so inflammable that guests were not trusted to light their own cigars but had to ring for a maid with a taper. This rather cheapskate attitude persisted down the years: a flyer of 1916 addressed customers "who do not wish to pay for the glitter of gilt and brass buttons", and generations of poor maintenance meant that the whole place had to be pulled down in the 1930s.

Its replacement is a fine and extremely popular example of '30s

design: its two ground-floor bars are spacious, airy, and elegant, with a fine plaster ceiling and a Jacobean-style fireplace incorporating supposedly Roman tiles in the front bar.

OPEN 11.30–11 MONDAY–FRIDAY; CLOSED WEEKENDS. FOOD SERVED 11.30–3, 5–8.30. REAL ALES: BRAKSPEAR'S BITTER, GREENE KING IPA, ADNAM'S BITTER, FULLER'S LONDON PRIDE, DRAUGHT BASS.

Return to Watling Street.

YE OLDE WATLING
WATLING STREET

The Olde Watling always claims to have been built in 1668 to house the workers who built St Paul's – a claim shared with the Old Bell in Fleet Street on the other side of the Cathedral. It has to be said, though, that the pub doesn't look terribly – or even remotely – Carolean: it looks like what it is, which is a fine example of the style Mark Girouard describes as "back to the inn". And to be fair, it also proclaims itself as having been "restored" in 1901, which is when the "back to the inn" style was at its peak.

It's all very stern and mannish. There are oak posts and beams, supposedly old ships' timbers – which may be true, as the timbers of ships being broken up provided good straight lengths of brine-pickled lumber at rock-bottom prices, always popular with builders – there are crucks, there are ties, there are early English-style flat-headed archways, there is matchboard panelling. There aren't even that many tables and chairs: drinking is done either standing up, or perched on tall stools. It may not be a 17th-century city tavern. But it's an Edwardian Englishman's idea of what a 17th-century city tavern ought to be, which is the next best thing.

OPEN 11–10 MONDAY–TUESDAY, 11–11 WEDNESDAY–FRIDAY. CLOSED WEEKENDS. FOOD SERVED 12–2.30. REAL ALES: ADNAM'S BITTER, HARVEY'S SUSSEX BITTER, FULLER'S LONDON PRIDE, GUEST.

Turn left out of pub. Continue down Watling Street to Queen Victoria Street and fork right into Cornhill. Turn right into St Michael's Alley.

JAMAICA WINE HOUSE
ST MICHAEL'S ALLEY

Take only a few steps down St Michael's Alley and you are in a different world. It is, quite literally, Dickensian. Scrooge's counting-house was in a court just like this, facing "the ancient tower of a church, whose gruff old bell was always peeping down ... out of a Gothic window"; Mr Pickwick took up quarters in the George & Vulture, now a restaurant; and the shady lawyers of *The Pickwick Papers*, Dodson & Fogg, had chambers in Newman Court, thinly disguised as Freeman's Court, just across Cornhill.

So it's an absolute certainty that Dickens knew the Jamaica, which was already old in his day. It was founded in 1652 as London's first coffee house by a "Levantine" (that incurious generalisation for all Eastern Mediterraneans) named Pasqua Rosee, who had arrived in London as the servant of a Smyrna merchant, a Mr Edwards; and was re-established after the fire in the 1670s.

Coffee was a huge success among professional people and merchants of the 17th century for the simple reason that most of their business was done in taverns, and coffee provided an alternative and immensely preferable lubricant to wine or beer. As a handbill of Rosee's explains: "It prevents drowsiness, and makes one fit for business" – in other words, instead of making them drunk, it kept them sharp. By the end of the century there were about 500 coffee houses in London.

Rosee's, for some reason, started attracting merchants and others engaged in the West Indies trade and soon became known as the Jamaica. In 1750 it was described as "having been used for 60 years past

as the place at which letters should be left for Jamaica", and trade directories throughout the latter half of the century list "ship insurance brokers, owners and commanders of ships trading with the West Indies and Leeward Islands, also brokers and dealers in the produce of those places" as based at the Jamaica. A report compiled for Lloyd's in 1810 recorded a number of underwriters still writing policies at the Jamaica, but as the century wore on, less and less business was done in taverns, which became places of pure refreshment.

In 1869 the Jamaica was renamed the Jamaica Wine House; in 1892 it was bought by the Shoreditch wine merchants E J Rose and rebuilt in contemporary tavern style. It's still a totally unspoilt and magnificent example of its period, divided into little compartments by polished mahogany partitions, with an oak bar and plain pine-plank bar-back, dark lino underfoot and tobacco-glazed pressed paper between big beams overhead. It's far too masculine for such a softening influence as upholstery to be permitted: I swear there's not a scrap of cloth in the place.

It's in the same ownership as Simpson's in Ball Court, the next alleyway off Cornhill. Simpson's dates from 1757 and has what looks like its original shopfront; it's more of a dining house than the Jamaica, but does have a separate bar.

OPEN 11.30–11 MONDAY–FRIDAY; CLOSED WEEKENDS. FOOD SERVED 12–2.30. REAL ALES: ST PETER'S BEST AND GOLDEN, DRAUGHT BASS.

Turn left out of the pub, through St Michael's Churchyard into Bell Inn Yard. Down Bell Inn Yard, cross Gracechurch Street, turn left and right into Leadenhall Market.

LEADENHALL MARKET

The market, which stands on the site of a medieval manor called Leaden Hall (itself on the site of a huge Roman basilica) grew up in the 14th century on land belonging to Dick Whittington. It specialised in fish, game and poultry – a gander which escaped from a mass slaughter of 34,000 geese in 1797 lived for 38 years, fattened on titbits, and was christened Old Tom. The existing market was designed by the City Corporation's architect, Horace Jones – the same Horace Jones who built the markets at Smithfield and Billingsgate and Tower Bridge – and went up in 1881. It is the most glorious confection of decorative cast iron imaginable, and although it is now given over almost entirely to bars and restaurants, there are still two butchers and one fishmonger left.

NEW MOON

88 GRACECHURCH STREET

Of the two pubs inside the market, the New Moon, on the corner of the Gracechurch Street entrance, is the less well-known. And yet it's a magnificent pub, well worth a visit.

The ground-floor bar is long and narrow, with a counter stretching down most of its length and a fine carved wooden bar-back behind. Overhead is a high, sombre ceiling, heavily beamed in the Jacobean style, dwarfing the City folk who throng the bar talking loudly of gilts and securities in accents that range from Eton to East Ham. The impression is of formality and grandeur, as opposed to the cosier ambience of the Lamb in the centre of the market.

A bill found during a recent refurbishment and dated 18 August 1900 reveals that the pub was originally called the Half Moon. Steak and chips then would have set you back one and threepence.

OPEN 11–10.30 MONDAY–FRIDAY, CLOSED WEEKENDS. FOOD SERVED 11.30–2.30. REAL ALES: BRAKSPEAR'S BITTER, BODDINGTON'S, FLOWERS IPA, FULLER'S LONDON PRIDE.

Turn right out of the pub.

LAMB TAVERN
LEADENHALL MARKET

The Lamb is by far the better-known of Leadenhall Markets two pubs and is a very different proposition from the cavernous New Moon.

The first Lamb on the site was built in 1780 by a wine and spirits merchant named Pardy and was a proper inn. It was rebuilt, minus its letting rooms and outbuildings, along with the rest of the market and was a fine, ornate Victorian pub: Geoffrey Fletcher in *The London Nobody Knows* (1962) records its "windows with sprays of corn, as well as fine pub lamps", and its snob-screens decorated with birds and foliage.

The Lamb was always run as a free house, leased from the Corporation, but was taken over by Young's of Wandsworth in 1985 and substantially remodelled in 1987. A good deal of original work remains – the tiling in the dive bar, for instance, and the ceramic depiction in the lobby of Wren inspecting his plans – and Young's made pub history by turning the upstairs lounge into the City's first smoke-free bar. But the decision to insert a mezzanine, reached by a spiral iron stair, into the ground-floor saloon bar must have altered the character of the Lamb immensely. Instead of the grand bar with lofty ceiling that we still see in the New Moon, the Lamb is cosy and intimate.

OPEN 11–9 MONDAY–FRIDAY; CLOSED WEEKENDS. FOOD SERVED ALL DAY. REAL ALES: YOUNG'S RANGE.

Return to Gracechurch Street exit and turn left.

SWAN
SHIP TAVERN PASSAGE, 77–80 GRACECHURCH STREET

For such a small pub, the Swan has a very big address. It really is tiny, too, a narrow sliver of a pub lining one side of an alleyway off Gracechurch Street: one deep at the bar and the place is pretty well full, although there's a slightly larger area at the far end of the mahogany-panelled bar where three or four biggish people or half-a-dozen normal ones can at least breathe freely, if not gesticulate too animatedly. Up the stairs with their green marble tiles, though, it's a different story. The lounge spans the alleyway and is therefore twice as wide as the tiny saloon; and even though this room isn't exactly cavernous, 30-40 have been known to squeeze in at a time.

The upstairs lounge, though, really is a lovely room: with its heavy tasselled drapes, red printed wallpaper, and big gilt-framed mirror, it could be the drawing-room of an Edwardian parsonage – albeit one from which someone had removed all the armchairs. Well, you don't get both armchairs and 30 sociable brokers into a room this size, do you?

The Swan is one of the few outlets in the City for Fuller's excellent Chiswick Bitter, a former Champion Beer of Britain with an extremely sensible alcohol content of 3.5 per cent. This is not nearly as big a seller as the brewery's better-known and rather stronger London Pride, but regulars of the Swan will assure you that it's a far better lunchtime beer if you plan to do any work that afternoon.

OPEN 11–11 MONDAY–FRIDAY; CLOSED WEEKENDS. FOOD 12–3.
REAL ALES: FULLER'S RANGE.

THE MONUMENT

Built probably by Wren's assistant Hooke and completed in 1677, the Monument to the Great Fire of London is 202ft tall (this being the exact distance to the bakery in Pudding Lane where the fire started) and has a gallery reached by 311 steps, which was enclosed in 1842 after several suicides. Charles II refused to have his statue on top, saying: "I didn't start the fire." Originally there was an inscription blaming Catholics for the fire, condemning "Popish frenzy, which wrought such horrors." This accusation drew the condemnation of the poet Pope, who wrote of: "London's column pointing at the skies, Like a tall bully lifts its head and lies"; it was not removed until 1831.

OPEN DAILY 10–6.

Return to Eastcheap and turn left. Cross King William Street into Cannon Street and take first left, Martin Lane.

OLD WINE SHADES
6 MARTIN LANE

A lead cistern bearing the date 1663 makes the Old Wine Shades the sole verifiable survivor of the thousand City taverns recorded before the Great Fire – and it feels like it.

Known as Sprague's Shades in its early years and Henderson's Shades in the 1840s when Dickens was a regular, this is a proper City wine bar with ancient beams, high-backed settles, black oak panelling, and bare floorboards with a strip of runner almost as old as the place itself.

But was Dickens really a regular? Geoffrey Fletcher, who drew the pencil sketches for the Daily Telegraph's Peterborough column in the 1960s, wrote in *The London Dickens Knew* that it probably didn't matter: "Even if it had not been frequented by Dickens, it would be necessary for all students of Victorian and Dickens's London to see it, for the interior with its black panelling, dusty bottles, dim barometer, dark snug boxes and dusky mirrors – to say nothing of the hat-pegs, ancient oil landscapes and crumbling directories and old clocks – is a perfect period piece. Nothing seems to have been added since the old champagne advertisements were put up in the '90s. So used am I to the artificial insemination of Victoriana in drinking places I can never overcome my feeling of astonishment that everything is genuine."

Not much has changed since then – indeed, stability is guaranteed by the fact that the bar has been owned for many years by El Vino's, so wear a tie (if you're a man, that is). But the Old Shades (the "Wine" in the name is a recent addition) did survive a threat quite as terrifying as the Great Fire a few years ago when it was threatened with demolition to make way for yet another office-block. There was uproar among the City gents who drink here, so the developers proposed a compromise: they would incorporate it into the lobby of their planned new building. No way, said the gents – and for once, after a public inquiry held at the Guildhall, the objectors won.

OPEN 11–10 MONDAY–FRIDAY; CLOSED WEEKENDS. FOOD SERVED 11.30–3. NO REAL ALE.

Return to Cannon Street and turn left.

FINISH: MONUMENT

SMITHFIELD
BLOOD & MUCK

LENGTH OF WALK: ONE-AND-A-QUARTER MILES

THE JOURNEY by rail or tube from King's Cross to Farringdon is scarcely an edifying one. The lines pass deep between massive, grimy Victorian brick and stone buttresses, the soot-smirched backs of office buildings beetling down from above excluding any glimpse of sky. But for me it's made exciting by the knowledge that this is no ordinary cutting: it's carved out of the valley of the Fleet River.

The Fleet, also known as Turnmill Brook or the Holbourn, rises in Hampstead Ponds and, before it was all culverted and covered over, flowed down Haverstock Hill; through Camden Town to King's Cross; between King's Cross Road and Gray's Inn Road to Clerkenwell; then between Farringdon Road and Turnmill Street and past Smithfield into a deep ravine under what is now Holborn Viaduct. It crossed Fleet Lane where there was a bridge, now Sea Coal Lane; supplied the moat for the Fleet Prison; and finally joined the Thames at Blackfriars.

It was a filthy river. From medieval times it was a sewer for the households abutting it, and a drain for blood and guts from the slaughterhouses of Smithfield, it swept into the Fleet via Faggeswell Brook which oozed a slimy course through the market. As early as 1290 the monks of Whitefriars, which overlooked the Fleet, were protesting about the smell arising from the nefarious effluents and jetsam in its waters, and the Earl of Lincoln told Parliament in 1307 that

the previously navigable river had been entirely blocked by rubbish.

Four centuries later, little had changed. Pope wrote in *The Dunciad* of the Fleet's "large tribute of dead dogs to the Thames" and recorded children swimming in it: "Here strip, my children! Here at once leap in/Here prove who best can dash through thick and thin!" Swift was more descriptive still, writing in City Showers: "Now from all parts the swelling kennels flow/And bear their trophies with them as they go:/Filth of all hues and odours seem to tell/What streets they sailed from by their sight and smell... Seepings from Butchers' stalls, dung, guts, and blood;/Drowned puppies, stinking sprats, all dressed in mud,/Dead cats and turnip-tops come tumbling down the flood."

The river was culverted from Holborn to Fleet Street in 1732 and from Fleet Street to the Thames in 1765, becoming a sewer in which, according to myth, a race of wild pigs lived. The stretch up to King's Cross was covered in 1812, but blew up in 1846 when its gases were ignited: three poorhouses in Clerkenwell were swept away by the sewage, and a Thames steamer was thrown against Blackfriars Bridge and smashed. Twenty years later the Fleet was tamed at last, when its valley proved the line of least resistance for the engineers building the Metropolitan railway.

Immediately to the west of the Fleet was a small slum quarter known as Saffron Hill – there is still a street of that name – where, in medieval times, saffron crocuses had been grown and bull and bear-baiting had been staged, the latter continuing until at least 1700. It had been part of the Bishop of Ely's estate, which was given by Elizabeth I to a favourite of hers, Sir Christopher Hatton, and in the 17th century it was gradually built over. By the mid-18th century, law enforcement officials were noting with alarm the decay of old houses and yards into common lodging houses and crowded tenements, and by Dickens's day it was a mixed quarter of slum courts and light industry. Dickens located Fagin's den in Field Lane, a maze of courts and alleys at the southern end of Hatton Garden, eventually demolished to make way for the Holborn Viaduct; and the Three Cripples, Bill Sikes's local, was supposedly in Saffron Hill itself.

Smithfield itself, the smooth field, is an ancient space which may have been in use for as long as London has had walls. Lying just outside the fortifications and immediately before Newgate, it was a convenient journey's end for livestock destined for city folk to eat and, indeed, to ride, for there was a weekly horse fair here in medieval times. There was jousting, too, on what is now West Smithfield; and there were executions. For Tyburn was far from being London's only traditional place of sacrifice: amid the noise and turmoil of the great market, at a stake outside St Bartholomew the Great, heretics and martyrs met their fiery ends.

St Bartholomew is the name-saint not only of Smithfield's church, of course, but also of its hospital, Britain's oldest. This was part of the Augustinian Friary famously founded by Rahere, Henry I's court jester, after a vision in 1127. Hospitals in the sense that we understand them were rare in the middle ages, for although many monastic foundations described themselves as such, it was a word with several meanings. Commonly, it denoted an almshouse; but it could also be a pilgrims' hostel; only occasionally, as in this case, did it mean a foundation caring for the sick. There are a number of descriptions of such institutions, and most of them emphasize the same points: patients lucky enough to be admitted (and they were few) got decent nutrition; and both the patients and the hospitals themselves were kept scrupulously – religiously, if you like – clean. This alone gave the sick a better chance than they would have had anywhere else at the time.

In 1170 Bart's became an independent foundation, and survived the dissolution of its parent friary in 1537, Henry VIII presenting it with its charter in 1546 (his only surviving statue is to be seen in the gatehouse). William Harvey, who discovered the circulation of blood, was a doctor here in the late 17th century, and there are suitably pious Hogarth paintings, dated 1737, of the Good Samaritan and the Pool of Bethesda on the great stair.

Until 1855, however, the name of St Bartholomew was most associated not with church or hospital but with the greatest annual jamboree in the land: St Bartholomew's Fair, which was held on Smithfield for a fortnight starting every 24 August, and was a by-word for riot and revelry.

The Fair was first held in 1133 as an international gathering of textile merchants; but eventually the side-shows began to eclipse the main arena, and pleasure to come before business. There's a Ben Jonson play of the same name following the fortunes of characters at the Fair, and Pepys wrote about the wrestling competitions held there in his diary. Plays were staged there, too, with the great names of the London theatre taking a busman's holiday by indulging in a fortnight's street theatre; even a figure as August as Colley Cibber, manager of the Drury Lane theatre in the 1710s and '20s, acted in the booths. At St Bartholomew's Fair in 1722 Moll Flanders met "a gentleman extremely well dressed and very rich" who may well have been on the prowl for just such an encounter, since Cock Lane off Snow Hill was a notorious red light district. Wordsworth also knew the fair and wrote as much in wonder as disapproval of its "anarchy and din, Barbarian and infernal" in the *Preludes* of 1805, mentioning:

...Albinos, painted Indians, Dwarfs,
The Horse of Knowledge, and the learned Pig,
The Stone-eater, the man that swallows fire,
Giants, Ventriloquists, the Invisible Girl,
The Bust that speaks and moves its goggling eyes,
The Wax-work, Clock-work, all the marvellous craft
Of modern Merlins, Wild Beasts, Puppet-shows
All out-o'-the-way, far-fetched, perverted things.

St Bartholomew's Fair outlived its original function by centuries; but it could not outlive the closure of Smithfield Market, and the Stone-eater ate his last stone in 1855.

A weekly livestock market in Smithfield is described by the 13th-century writer William FitzStephen, and it hadn't changed much by the time Dickens knew it. *Oliver Twist* has it thus: "It was market morning. The ground was covered nearly ankle-deep with filth and mire and a thick steam perpetually rising from the reeking bodies of the cattle and mingling with the fog, which seemed to rest upon the chimney-tops ... Countrymen, butchers, drovers, hawkers, boys, thieves, idlers and vagabonds of every low grade were mingled together in a dense mass: the whistling of drovers, the barking of dogs, the bellowing and plunging of beasts, the bleating of sheep, and the grunting and squeaking of pigs; the cries of hawkers, the shouts, oaths and quarrelling on all sides, the ring of bells and the roar of voices that issued from every public house; the crowding, pushing, driving, beating, whooping and yelling; the hideous and discordant din that resounded from every corner ... and the unwashed, unshaven, squalid and dirty figures constantly running to and fro and bursting in and out of the throng rendered it a stunning and bewildering scene which quite confused the senses."

Smithfield in 1846 handled 200,000 cattle and 1.5 million sheep. The surrounding area was home to myriad processors – slaughtermen, knackers, sausage makers, tripe dressers, cat's-meat boilers, gut-spinners, bone-boilers, paunch-cookers, bladder blowers and, in an age when no commodity was too trivial to find a trade, God knows what else. Excrement and entrails piled the streets. Even though half of the 155 associated slaughterhouses had already gone by then, in 1850 a Royal Commission recommended closure.

Smithfield's owner, the City Corporation, held out until 1855, and when it bowed to the inevitable the market was moved to Copenhagen Fields, off the Caledonian Road. But in those days a successful market still needed a central location. So a new covered meat market was built on the old site by the same architect as Leadenhall Market, Horace Jones. It opened in 1869, dealing not in livestock on the hoof but in carcasses brought from the provinces by rail – an innovation which ended the London tradition of small insanitary back-alley slaughterhouses. The introduction of refrigerated transport made it possible for carcasses to be brought from even further afield, and by the 1880s two-thirds of Britain's meat imports came through Smithfield.

Over the years, Smithfield's national importance dwindled. But it remained the dominant centre of the meat trade for London and environs, and hung on to many of its traditions, too – the meat porters, who traditionally wore padded hats to help them balance boxes of meat on their heads, are still called "bummarees", and some of the pubs surrounding the market still open before dawn, as they have done for generations, so the bummarees can have beer for breakfast.

Smithfield survived when Covent Garden and Billingsgate moved out of central London and survived again when European hygiene regulations threatened to close it down. The older section at the eastern end has recently been restored, and you can see the market in action any weekday morning – provided you get up early enough.

START: FARRINGDON

Turn right out of station; cross Farringdon Road into Greville Street.

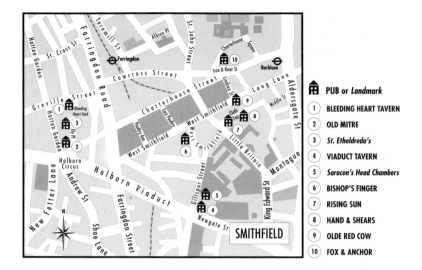

🏠	PUB or *Landmark*
①	BLEEDING HEART TAVERN
②	OLD MITRE
③	*St. Etheldreda's*
④	VIADUCT TAVERN
⑤	*Saracen's Head Chambers*
⑥	BISHOP'S FINGER
⑦	RISING SUN
⑧	HAND & SHEARS
⑨	OLDE RED COW
⑩	FOX & ANCHOR

BLEEDING HEART TAVERN
BLEEDING HEART YARD

This smart little dining-house has only been open for a couple of years; but it has a very much longer history than that.

It was first recorded in a register of licensed victuallers of 1746, when the Saffron Hill area was degenerating into a slum. Perhaps because of this, the landlords – the Hatton family – sold the whole area in 1785 in an auction held at Garraway's Coffee House in Change Alley. The Bleeding Heart and its yard were part of lot 71.

Three derivations are suggested for the Tavern's unique name. The most prosaic is that it comes from the arms of the Douglas family, which do indeed include a red heart; although what interest a Scottish border clan might have in this part of London I have no idea. The second is that there was a Church of the Bleeding Heart on or near the site, although I know of no bleeding heart in Christian iconography – a Sacred Heart, yes, but not a bleeding one. The third, and most romantic, is that it commemorates the murder at a ball held in the crypt of Hatton House in January 1626 of Sir Christopher Hatton's widow, Lady Elizabeth, by her jilted lover, the Spanish ambassador Gondemar.

There was nothing aristocratic about Bleeding Heart Yard by the time Dickens chose it for a location in *Little Dorrit*. Here Arthur

Clennam becomes a partner in the engineering firm of Doyce & Clennam, and here live the impecunious tenants, including the Plornishes, of the rent-collector Mr Pancks.

The area also figures in *Oliver Twist* as one of rotten houses, poverty-stricken Irish immigrants, and filthy shops. Fagin's den is not far away, in a court at the foot of Saffron Hill; and perhaps Dickens had the Bleeding Heart Tavern in mind when he described the Three Cripples: "In the obscure parlour of a low public house in the filthiest part of Little Saffron Hill, a dark and gloomy den where a flaring gas-light burnt all day in the winter-time and where no ray of sun ever shone in summer, there sat, brooding over a little pewter measure and a small glass strongly impregnated with the smell of liquor, a man in a velveteen coat, drab shorts, half-boots and stockings, who even by that dim light no experienced agent of police would have hesitated to recognise as Mr William Sikes."

Whether the Bleeding Heart was the model for the Three Cripples or not, it did not long survive the writing of the novel. The whole area was cleared and rebuilt in 1845-46 when Farringdon Road was built, and the existing pub dates from about that time. A century later, and two centuries after it was first recorded, it surrendered its licence and became the Windsor Grill. So it remained until 1998, when a local restaurateur relicensed it and created the smart, modern, airy, brick-lined dining pub it is today, as far removed from the Three Cripples and Mr William Sikes as you could possibly imagine.

OPEN 11-11 MONDAY-FRIDAY, CLOSED WEEKENDS.
RESTAURANT MENU 11.30-10.30. REAL ALES: ADNAMS RANGE.

Turn left up Greville Street, then left again into Hatton Garden. The tiny entrance to Ely Court is between two jewellers called Gedalovitch and Davril.

OLD MITRE

ELY COURT

"You must not be satisfied with seeing its great streets and squares, but must survey the innumerable little lanes and courts," Dr Johnson advised anyone who would truly know London; and surely he had little Ely Court and its solitary address, the Old Mitre, a tavern since 1546, in mind.

The graceful sweep of Ely Place was built in 1773 on a very ancient and historic site. Ely House had been the London palace and estate of the Bishops of Ely. It became the Spanish embassy in the 1620s; and when it was demolished the first building to go up in its place was almost certainly – if usual practice is anything to go by – the little mews pub which would first serve the builders as a canteen and would then become a modest place of refreshment for the servant population of the new houses.

It has to be said that nothing much has changed at the Old Mitre in all those years. Given the quarter's Elizabethan connections, it's not surprising that the pub proudly proclaims its Tudor past; but the chunk of timber exhibited as the maypole round which Sir Christopher Hatton and the Virgin Queen danced is surely one of those relics which are hugely enjoyable but utterly bogus. Instead, take the Old Mitre for what it really is: as near-perfect a little Georgian mews tavern as you could hope to find – plain but cosy; respectable but deeply relaxing – and one that no visitor to London should even dream of missing.

Its panelled main bar has a cheerful fireplace and a tiny little snug leading off, called the Closet; there's a front bar with its own separate street door; and upstairs there's an overspill bar with a narrow shelf running all the way round it and stools to perch on. None of the rooms are very big, and although they've all doubtless been redecorated time and time again in their 230-odd years, they still have the atmosphere of an older London – one that Dr Johnson might recognise and appreciate.

OPEN 11-11 MONDAY-FRIDAY; CLOSED WEEKENDS. BAR FOOD 11-9.30.
REAL ALES: IND COOPE BURTON ALE, FRIARY MEUX BITTER.

Turn left out of the pub and left into Ely Place.

St Etheldreda's

St Etheldreda's is all that is left of the old Bishop's palace, for it was his private chapel as long ago as the 13th century; and the dedication is to the Saxon queen who founded Ely Cathedral. It is also one of the few churches in London with much medieval fabric, although a thorough going restoration by Giles Gilbert Scott in 1874 rather sanitised it.

The interesting feature about the church, though, is that it was the first Roman Catholic church in London following the Reformation: James I gave it to the Spanish ambassador in the 1620s, and afterwards Charles I's French queen, Henrietta Maria, is said to have heard Mass here. It reverted to Anglican use soon after, but after was returned to Roman Catholic use in 1879 after the Emancipation.

Ely Place itself was used by Shakespeare as a setting for one of his most famous speeches, the "This sceptred isle ..." speech in *Richard II*, given by John of Gaunt, who lived here after his Savoy Palace was burnt down in the Peasants' Revolt in 1381 until his death in 1399.

Until quite recently, Ely Place was a unique administrative anomaly: although in the heart of London, it was actually part of Cambridgeshire. Its only pub kept Cambridgeshire licensing hours, and the Metropolitan Police had no jurisdiction within its wrought-iron gates, which were staffed by Cambridgeshire beadles.

Return down Ely Place. Cross Charterhouse Street and turn left into Holborn Viaduct.

The Viaduct Tavern
126 Newgate Street

It's a short walk but a long journey from the antiquarian's delight of Ely Place and the Dickensian echoes of Saffron Hill to the Viaduct Tavern, whose nature is announced by its name.

This is a pub with no pretensions to antiquity. It is, instead, a monument to modernity: a state-of-the-art, up-to-the-minute, cutting-edge pub built at a time when confidence in contemporary design and build standards was at its highest and when, indeed, the area's past was busily and resolutely being swept away. The building of the Holborn Viaduct in the late 1860s was the engineer's answer to the twin

problems of the Fleet Valley's stubborn geography and the decaying slum district that surrounded it: smash through the latter to bridge over the former. And at the same time that the span of the Viaduct was triumphantly completed in 1869, the Viaduct Tavern was, equally triumphantly if in a lower key, declared open.

And what a triumph it is. A heavily ornate plaster ceiling lowers down on a single horseshoe bar, its gantry supported on spindly mahogany barleysugar-twist pillars. There is much brilliant-cut glass, although not as much as formerly; there are stern faces in painted plaster roundels; there are huge mirrors in frames of marble and gilt; and there are three vast allegorical paintings of vaguely classical females in vaguely erotic dress, all doubtless representing some uplifting ideal and all actually painted on canvas, as the damage to one panel – allegedly caused by a soldier's bayonet in some drunken scuffle of World War 1 – clearly displays.

The construction of Holborn Viaduct necessitated the destruction of Newgate Prison: the Old Bailey, just across the way, occupies its site, and it's said that a small room in the Tavern's cellar was once a subterranean cell. The Viaduct itself, the Old Bailey, and in its humbler way the Tavern, all represented the victory of modern engineering, modern jurisprudence, modern design, over the barbaric brutalities and irrationalities of a medieval past.

But the actualities of steel and stone were necessarily preceded by an idea; and, rather neatly, the idea was made manifest in the year before the Viaduct was opened: the Capital Punishment Amendment Act of 1868 finally brought to an end the spectacle of public executions outside Newgate which had hitherto been the morbid chief attraction of the site.

OPEN 12-9 MONDAY-FRIDAY, 12-4 SATURDAY. CLOSED SUNDAY. FOOD 12-3. REAL ALES: ADNAMS BITTER, GREENE KING IPA, FULLER'S LONDON PRIDE.

Turn right out of the pub and walk up Giltspur Street. (Note Saracen's Head Chambers, on the site of the Saracen's Head where Nicholas Nickleby met Wackford Squeers who was based on a real Mr Simpson of Bowes.) Turn left along the western side of West Smithfield.

THE BISHOP'S FINGER

9-10 WEST SMITHFIELD

The Rutland Arms until 20 years ago, this is one of the Kent brewer Shepherd Neame's small estate of London pubs.

The new name referred to the brewery's strong ale, which was itself named after a type of road sign, carved to appear as if it had a digit. This type of sign was especially found on the Pilgrim's Way leading to Canterbury – thus the pointing digit was said to be the (Arch)bishop's. (Although a different derivation is suggested by the fact that the beer is colloquially known in its native county as "Nun's Delight".)

The pub's neat but fairly plain 1890s exterior is not matched by the interior, which consists of a small single bar on the ground floor with a second upstairs. When Shep's took over the Olde Red Cow on the other side of the market a few years ago, it decided that both pubs were more than merely grubby and needed not just a paint job but a complete refit.

As a result the Bishop's Finger is now a smart but understated modern pub, with bare but highly polished floorboards, plenty of light from big windows and pale yellow walls, and fresh flowers on every table. At the cost of drinking space, there is an open kitchen beside the bar which serves distinctive, upmarket, but reasonably-priced meals.

OPEN 11-11 MONDAY-FRIDAY. CLOSED WEEKENDS. FOOD 12-2.30 MONDAY-FRIDAY, 6PM-9 MONDAY-THURSDAY. REAL ALES: SHEPHERD NEAME RANGE.

Cross West Smithfield into Long Lane. Turn right into Rising Sun Court.

RISING SUN
38 CLOTH FAIR

All too many of the Victorian pubs on the main drag round Smithfield
have been aggressively and unsympathetically modernised; but dodge
down Rising Sun Court and you'll find a couple that haven't.

Brown in all its gradations, according to the 1950s architectural writers
Gorham & Dunnett, is the natural shade for a pub interior, and the Rising
Sun is a very brown pub indeed. Actually it's brown outside as well as in,
with a brown marble fascia at ground floor level and brown London brick
above; inside there are two rooms divided by brown wooden partitions;
the pressed paper ceiling is brown; the bare floorboards and the linoleum

that covers part of them are brown; and the plaster walls have acquired the pale brown patina that only years of cigarette-smoke can impart.

The pub was actually modernised not all that many years ago: previously it was tatty well beyond the point of picturesqueness. But the modernisation did not go too far, as it did at the Hope and the Castle, both in Cowcross Street: the best (apart, alas, from any trace of original glass) was rescued, and although the interior was opened out a little the original layout still more or less survives. As a result partly of Sam Smith's low-key approach and partly of its location down an alley, the Rising Sun has escaped the curse of trendiness and remains a straightforward, unpretentious, traditional, and charming London pub.

OPEN 11-11 MONDAY-SATURDAY, 12-3 AND 7-10.30 SUNDAY.
FOOD 12-2, 7-9. REAL ALE: SAM SMITH'S OBB.

Leave the pub by the back door, cross Cloth Fair, and turn left.

HAND & SHEARS
1 MIDDLE STREET

The charming Hand & Shears, huddled in a quiet backwater off Smithfield in the shadow of the gaunt grey towers of the Barbican, claims the longest pedigree of any of the market's pubs.

Although built only in 1849, it was built on the site of an alehouse which was originally within the precincts of Rahere's St Bartholomew's Priory itself, so in theory it could have been around since the 1120s. It was certainly in existence in Tudor times, when it derived its name from a close association with the Merchant Tailors' Guild (and not from the fact that it's traditionally a favourite with hospital staff!), and when it hosted the Court of Pie Powder which governed the conduct of the market.

In fact tradition has it that before the covered markets were built and the area was extensivley redeveloped, the old Hand & Shears used to front Smithfield, and it was from here that the Lord Mayor used to declare Bartholomew's Fair open every 24 August by cutting a ceremonial ribbon – except once, when a group of mischievous tailors hid in the pub overnight and rushed downstairs early in the morning to cut it first.

Today's Hand & Shears, unusually, retains its original layout of four cosy rooms, including a tiny private snug, all very much in the plain bareboard style, grouped round an oval bar. They say that Sir John Betjeman, who lived at 43 Cloth Fair from 1955 until he was finally driven out by the noise of early-morning juggernauts in 1977, was a regular; whether he was or not, it is certainly the kind of honest, simple, unspoilt London boozer he would have appreciated.

OPEN 11-11 MONDAY-FRIDAY. FOOD 11-3.
REAL ALES: COURAGE BEST AND DIRECTORS, PLUS A GUEST ALE.

Cross Middle Street.

YE OLDE RED COW
71 LONG LANE

"The Olde Red Cow gives good milk now; 'Tis such good liquor 'twould puzzle a vicar" goes the jingle, coined doubtless at some time in the 18th century to promote the pub's ale, possibly after a change of ownership.

Well, the Olde Red Cow has recently changed hands again, and since the Kent brewer Shepherd Neame bought it from Scottish & Newcastle it has certainly given good milk. Whether you appreciate the other changes is a matter of taste, for all trace of the original interior – the pub was built in 1854 – has disappeared completely.

However, it's a case of new need not equal bad; for while some other Victorian pubs in the vicinity have been reduced to utter soullessness, the small, modern, ground-floor bar of the Olde Red Cow is actually very smart and pleasant. It was completely refitted about four years ago, having been allowed to get very scruffy since its famous days under the showbiz landlord of the 1980s and earlier, Dick O'Shea.

The dining-room upstairs was O'Shea's stage, upon which he entertained showbusiness notables such as Bernard Miles and Peter Ustinov; he had not only a large Irish personality but also a secret recipe for a fiery hot toddy which included a lot of ginger. Proceedings could, by all accounts, get pretty riotous.

After his departure – as so often happens in the vacuum that follows the demise of a "personality" landlord – Scottish & Newcastle was uncertain how to handle the pub. It drifted for a number of years, first as a managed house, then as a tenancy, until S&N wisely decided to ditch the place and let someone with some fresh ideas have a go.

OPEN 12-11 MONDAY-FRIDAY. FOOD 12-3.
REAL ALES: SHEPHERD NEAME RANGE.

Cross Long Lane and walk up Lindsey Street. Cross Charterhouse Street and walk up Fox & Knot Street.

FOX & ANCHOR
115 CHARTERHOUSE.STREET

One of the few pubs which keeps the early-opening market licence, the Fox & Anchor is an incredible, if somewhat tatty, piece of Art Nouveau design.

Built in 1898, its narrow frontage is completely tiled – even the gargoyles on either side of the pub sign are ceramic. The entrance lobbies on either side of a little central bay window are decked out in gorgeous green tiles, with a fair quantity of etched and engraved glass.

Inside, there's a single long narrow room with the bar down one whole side. Under a heavily moulded plaster ceiling, the space is broken up somewhat by wood and glass partitions, with the walls a riot of William Morris-style wallpaper and Victorian sepia prints and photographs. The place was redecorated only a few years ago, but has already reacquired that slightly scruffy frowstiness which suits it best.

The only real change has been the removal of the ground-floor toilets – you have to go upstairs now, which effectively bars disabled visitors This was to make room for some new (but not too new-looking) booths at the back.

Like many pubs these days, the Fox & Anchor – the name may come from the combination of two earlier licences; or the anchor may originally have been a clumsy signwriter's attempt at the knot in Fox & Knot Street – opens for breakfast. The difference is that you can have a beer with your bacon and eggs, and before all-day opening was introduced in 1988 the pub was the first and last stop on a well-known 24-hour boozing circuit which took in a number of private drinking clubs to cover the gaps in pub licensing hours.

The Fox & Anchor is rather foody now: drinkers at the bar at busy lunchtimes aren't exactly made to feel welcome, so time your visit accordingly.

OPEN 7AM-11PM MONDAY-FRIDAY; FOOD TO 3PM.
REAL ALES: TETLEY, ADNAMS BITTER, FULLER'S LONDON PRIDE.

Turn right out of the pub and right again up Cowcross Street.

FINISH: FARRINGDON.

CLERKENWELL
REDS ON THE GREEN

LENGTH OF WALK: ONE-AND-A-HALF MILES

CLERKENWELL sprang up around two large religious institutions: the priory of the Hospitaller knights of St John, recalled in several street names, and a Benedictine convent just to its north. These stood on the far side of Smithfield from the City, and even after they were dissolved the City's authority here was at best shaky. As a result, Clerkenwell became a centre first of religious and later of political dissent.

In the 15th century Clerkenwell was a hive of heretical Lollards: in 1414 William the Parchmenter of Turnmill Street was hanged, drawn, and quartered for harbouring their fugitive leader, Sir John Oldcastle. After the Reformation, it hosted a community of Roman Catholics, three of whom suffered the same fate as William on Clerkenwell Green in the reign of Elizabeth I. Later, there was a cluster of leading Puritans in Clerkenwell: two of the judges in the trial of Charles I lived in Clerkenwell Close, and Oliver Cromwell himself was a neighbour. Later still there were communities of Quakers and other sects such as Brownists and Familists clustered round the Green.

In the 18th century, Clerkenwell became the epicentre of English radicalism, mainly as a result of the concentration of highly-skilled precision trades. Before there was mass transport, trades often clustered together to share access to skilled labour, to raw materials, and to markets. Hoxton, for instance, attracted the furniture-making trades; Spitalfields attracted the silk-weaving industry; and Clerkenwell attracted the clock and watchmaking trades. By the end of the 18th century 7,000 parishioners, divided into 100 different trades, were producing 200,000 watches a year. Thomas Tompion, inventor of the spiral spring, set up his workshop in Clerkenwell in the late 17th century; Daniel Quare, inventor of the repeating watch, also worked in Clerkenwell; and Joseph Bramah, inventor of the hydraulic press and the suction beer-engine and manufacturer of precision locks, was originally a Clerkenwell watchmaker. Clerkenwell was also the home of silversmiths, jewellers, manufacturers of surgical and navigation instruments, and locksmiths such as Dickens's Gabriel Vardy.

But most of these highly-skilled workers saw precious little return for their expertise, making prestige goods for the rich but living and working in slum conditions on miserly piecework rates; and in such a close community their natural dissatisfaction easily found a united voice. The dozens of taverns around the Green hosted meetings of early trade unions of silversmiths, cutlers and carpenters. A branch of the London Corresponding Society, which supported the French Revolution, was founded in the Bull's Head in Jerusalem Passage in 1794: three of Clerkenwell's "English Jacobins" were tried for high treason, but were acquitted. Even the better-off were strong for radicalism: in the 1768 election, 70 out of the parish's 100 electors voted for John Wilkes — a local boy, born in St John's Square — against the Court candidate.

Clerkenwell Green itself soon became a focus for all this political energy. The Chartist movement had its London rendezvous at Lunt's Coffee House facing the Green; William Cobbett addressed a mass rally on the Green against the Corn Laws in 1826; while in 1838 it was the scene of the triumphant mass welcome for the Tolpuddle Marytrs, returning home from transportation. In 1842 Peel sought to ban meetings on the Green, but it remained a convenient starting point for marchers of all persuasions. Alien radicals congregated in Clerkenwell, too: Garibaldi visited Mazzini while the latter was living in exile in Clerkenwell in the 1830s; Fenians blew up Clerkenwell's House of Detention in an attempt to rescue two of their number in 1867; and a red flag hung from a lamp-post on the Green during the Paris Commune in 1871s. Lenin we shall meet later.

Gradually, Clerkenwell's industries moved to less congested quarters, and the consequent ebbing away of the population, hastened by the Blitz, slowly changed the character of the area. It's now principally a district of legal and financial services overspilling from Holborn and the City, of PR companies and IT consultancies. But residents have moved back to some extent: not the watchmakers and cutlers of old, but loft-dwellers carving chic homes out of the hulks of old factories and workshops.

START: FARINGDON

Turn left out of the station and left again into Turnmill Street. Cross Turnmill Street into Benjamin Street, and at the end turn left up Britton Street.

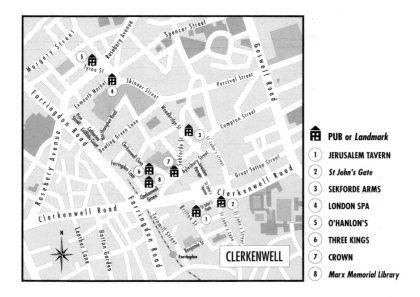

PUB or *Landmark*

1. JERUSALEM TAVERN
2. St John's Gate
3. SEKFORDE ARMS
4. LONDON SPA
5. O'HANLON'S
6. THREE KINGS
7. CROWN
8. *Marx Memorial Library*

THE JERUSALEM TAVERN
BRITTON STREET

Don't be misled by the date on the Jerusalem Tavern's Dickensian fascia: the building itself may be that old, but it's only been a pub since 1996.

When the tiny Suffolk-based St Peter's Brewery had to choose a name for its one London pub, it decided to revive one known in Clerkenwell as early as the 14th century, when there was a Jerusalem Tavern in the village at the Hospitallers' priory gates. A later Jerusalem Tavern that occupied part of St John's Gatehouse closed in 1754, and the name was transferred to the Red Lion in what had been Red Lion Street but was renamed Britton Street when it was rebuilt in 1723.

The new Jerusalem Tavern was a well-regarded house which was frequented by Dr Johnson and his circle and also provided a meeting place for many of the friendly societies and other working-class associations which sprang up in the heart of the watchmaking district. It was finally pulled down in 1878 to make way for Clerkenwell Road, which was driven straight through the middle of St John's Square to provide a new East-West route.

Red Lion Street took its new name from an extraordinary character, Thomas Britton, the musical small-coal man, who lived in the loft over his coal shed in Jerusalem Passage. By day he hawked coal in the streets; but every Thursday night from 1678 until his death in 1714 he would assemble the leading musicians of his day for a recital at his home, which was reached only by a ladder and trapdoor.

Britton played the viola, and among those who joined him at his soirées were the former Royal bandleader John Banister on violin, the composer Dr Pepuschi on virginals, and even, on occasion, the young Handel, playing a miniature organ. The audience – who paid a subscription of 10 shillings a year and could buy coffee at a shilling a cup – might include the Duke of Devonshire and the Earl of Oxford, who would also accompany Britton on book-buying sprees. Britton, although he never gave up his daytime calling, was a celebrity: Ned Ward wrote about him, and after his death, his elegy described him as:

Though doom'd to small coal, yet to art allied;
Rich without wealth, and famous without pride.
Music's best patron, judge of books and men,
Belov'd and honour'd by Apollo's train.

Red Lion Street was rebuilt as a wealthy one of fine houses, just like the building that is today the Jerusalem Tavern. In time, though, they were all let to small craftsmen and subdivided into shops, tenements and workshops: the Jerusalem Tavern's shopfront was inserted in about 1810. In this guise it went through many uses: before St Peter's bought it, it had been a café for many years.

The interior is a remarkable if rather masculine attempt to recreate an 18th-century tavern: the bare floorboards have been patched and replaced many times; the woodwork of benches and panels is painted a drab olive-green; and the walls are mostly bare plaster, with only a few faint frescoes and antique tiles for decoration. The space is broken up into intimate little alcoves and niches, one of which has a cheery little fireplace. Whether it really looks like the interior of an 18th-century tavern is hard to say, but it would be an enchanting place to assemble a coterie of sages.

OPEN 11–11 MONDAY–FRIDAY. CLOSED WEEKENDS. FOOD SERVED 12–3. REAL ALES: UP TO SIX FROM ST PETER'S RANGE.

Go down St John's Path next to the pub into St John's Square.

ST JOHN'S GATE

On your right as you emerge from St John's Path is the last remnant of the Hospitaller's priory: St John's Gate, built as a grand entrance in 1504 and left standing when the priory was demolished less than 40 years later. After the Dissolution, the gatehouse was divided up and had many different uses at different times. Part of it housed the Jerusalem Tavern for 200 years; another part was run as a coffee house by Hogarth's father in the reign of Queen Anne. The young Dr

Johnson was frequently to be found toiling here in the 1740s: the *Gentleman's Magazine,* for which he wrote, was printed in the gatehouse until 1781, when it moved to Fleet Street. The gatehouse was restored in the late 19th century. Inside is a free museum.

OPEN 9–5 MONDAY–FRIDAY AND 10–4 SATURDAY, WITH TOURS EVERY TUESDAY, FRIDAY AND SATURDAY LUNCHTIME.

Turn left into St John's Square, crossing Clerkenwell Road, and take Jerusalem Passage. Cross Aylesbury Street and turn right then left into Woodbridge Street.

SEKFORDE ARMS
34 SEKFORDE STREET

In the angle formed by Clerkenwell Road and St John Street lies one of those quiet residential quarters of late-Georgian and early Victorian terraces one often stumbles across only yards from the main thoroughfares, but seemingly a world away from the fumes and noise of the traffic. In the middle of this quarter, where Woodbridge Street and Sekforde Street cross, is exactly the right sort of pub for the area: bright, cheerful, comfortable, and inviting.

Thomas Sekforde, known as the Benefactor, was the second son of a Suffolk landowner, who came to London in the reign of Elizabeth I to make his fortune in the law. He did well in his profession, sitting on Royal Commissions on prison regulation and ecclesiastical law, and becoming first a senior judge and then MP for Ipswich.

Elizabeth rewarded him in 1573 with the grant of three acres in Clerkenwell, where he built himself a grand house to which he retired in 1581. He also managed to outlive his older brother, who died without issue, and so succeeded to the family estate in Suffolk as well. When he died in 1587, the rents of his estates went to found and support a school, a hospital, and almshouses in his native Woodbridge.

Over the years his London estate was let out and built over, with the rents still going back to his foundations in Suffolk. Part of it became the House of Detention; this part was developed in the 1830s as a residential quarter with a school, a chapel, a distillery, and this pub. And a very fine pub it is too.

Outside, it's a plain but handsome enough street-corner pub of its time, let down only by the rather grubby yellow tiling at ground-floor level. Inside, though, it's splendidly comfy, brightly lit, and divided by the chimney-breast with its tiled cast-iron fireplace into a large saloon and small snug. Unlike the sternly masculine Jerusalem Tavern, the Sekforde Arms is a much softer affair, with the carpets and upholstered banquettes you'd expect of a family local in a residential area.

One sign that you're still in Clerkenwell with its history of watchmaking is that the loft apartments just down the road are housed in what used to be the Ingersoll factory.

OPEN: 11–1 MONDAY-FRIDAY, 11–6 SATURDAY, 12–4 SUNDAY. BAR FOOD 12–9.30; UPSTAIRS RESTAURANT OPEN 12–2.30. REAL ALES: YOUNG'S RANGE.

Continue up Woodbridge Street and turn left into Skinner Street.

LONDON SPA
EXMOUTH MARKET

The name of this handsome late Victorian pub is a reminder that Clerkenwell was once a vital source of fresh water, and fresh air, for London.

The Clerks' Well sprang from the wall of the Benedictine convent, and its water was declared in the late 12th century by William FitzStephen, Thomas à Becket's secretary, to be "sweet, wholesome, and clear". The landowner in the late 17th century, the Earl of Northampton, donated it to the parish. Alas, the corrupt authorities soon leased it to a local brewer, who so polluted its stream that it became undrinkable. By the mid-19th century it had been built over and its site was lost; and so it remained until 1924, when it was accidentally uncovered again. It is now to be seen at the corner of Clerkenwell Green and Faringdon Lane.

All this time the area to the north of the convent was public open land, known at first as Coldbath Fields (showing perhaps that the spring was not only for drinking) and later as Spa Fields. Street names such as Coldbath Square, Spa Street, and Spa Fields Gardens recall those times. In 1832 Spa Fields was the scene of a rally by the National Union of the Working Classes which turned violent. A policeman was stabbed by a rioter he had hit with his truncheon; but the inquest jury, in true Clerkenwell style, ruled the killing lawful and criticised the police as "ferocious, brutal, and unprovoked".

The London Spa stands on the corner of Exmouth Market, which was the main thoroughfare until Rosebery Avenue was built in the 1890s. Like the Flasks in Highgate and Hampstead, it was a popular venue for Londoners seeking less polluted air. In the 1720s it was known for prize-fights, bear-baiting and cockfighting; and also for dances which were said to be a favourite night out with the legendary Islington dairymaids, single young women who worked the many large dairy farms just to the north.

An engraving of the early 1860s shows a sturdy three-storey late-Georgian building, with classical pediments over the first floor sash windows and a balustrade surmounted by Grecian urns along the roof line. It then belonged to an independent wine shipper named James Wilson, but in 1865 it became the first pub in the H H Finch chain which rebuilt it in the 1880s. Finch's was bought out by the Wandsworth brewer Young's in 1991.

The pub's interior has, sadly, all been knocked into one big room, but it retains some interesting cream and blue tiles from the 1880s, and also a vast Bass mirror.

OPEN: 11–9 MONDAY–FRIDAY; 11–3 SATURDAY. CLOSED SUNDAY. FOOD SERVED 12–3 MONDAY–FRIDAY. REAL ALES: YOUNG'S RANGE.

Turn left up Tysoe Street and cross Rosebery Avenue.

O'HANLON'S
8 TYSOE STREET

O'Hanlon's may not be O'Hanlon's by the time this book is published, but it will still be a pub well worth visiting.

The Three Crowns, as it had been since it was converted from a private house in 1939, was an unexceptional little street-corner pub until 1992, when John O'Hanlon bought it.

He set about transforming it into a genuine Irish pub – not one of those corporate abortions with no claim to Irishness beyond a daft name, but a genuine Irish pub run by an Irishman, whose Irish mother cooked Irish food, and who eventually, despairing of the poor quality

of the so-called Irish beers available in Britain, started brewing his own at a miniature plant in Vauxhall.

O'Hanlon's was always a great pub, a very basic bare-boards boozer with two big plain rooms somehow concealed behind the narrowest of frontages, and a TV turned on only for rugby. But as time wore on, John found the brewing side of the business was running away with him. Other pubs were queuing up to stock his beers; and when he started putting them into bottles as well as casks, supermarkets started clamouring for them too. Eventually, in summer 2000, he and his wife Liz upped sticks and decamped to Devon, taking their brewery with them.

They sold the pub to Patrick Mulligan, who plans no changes except one: the name. He can't keep on calling it O'Hanlon's, he says, when it isn't. He's thinking about changing it – possibly to Mulligan's. There's a nice little early 19th-century charcoal cartoon of a man named Mulligan in the National Portrait Gallery which Patrick thinks would make a good pub sign.

A speciality of the house, by the way, is Guinness. Not the pasteurised Guinness brewed at Park Royal in West London, but the genuine stuff, brewed in Dublin and shipped in by a sympathetic third party in Northern Ireland.

Open: all permitted hours. Food served 12–2.30, 6–9.30. Real ales: selection from O'Hanlon's range plus guests.

Cross Rosebery Avenue and turn right. Turn left at the western end of Exmouth Market and follow Pine Street, through Catherine Griffiths Court, and into Northampton Road. Cross Bowling Green Lane, turn right into Roberts Place, then down the steps into Clerkenwell Close.

House of Detention

Underneath a school on Clerkenwell Green are the foundations of the same House of Detention broken open by Gordon Rioters in 1780 and blown up by Fenians in 1867. When you consider how keen people were to get out, it's ironic that they now pay to get in. The prison kitchen, laundry and some cells survive and have proved a popular attraction since they were opened to the public a few years ago.

Open 10–6.

THREE KINGS
7 Clerkenwell Close

Now here's a delight. The rather bizarre exterior might put you off a bit – I stood outside for a few minutes screwing up my courage before I went in the first time, I admit. I half-expected – more than half-expected – to find some sort of S&M den, with rubber-clad regulars who wouldn't just stop and stare at a stranger, but would tie him up and do unspeakable things to him as well.

Needless to say, it's nothing like that. Landlord John Eichler clearly has a taste for the unusual: the colour-scheme is a bold red and yellow; there are odd little bas-reliefs and dioramas of brightly-coloured papier-mâché dotting the walls; and the enormous rhino head over the fireplace is not stuffed but sculpted, and was a Christmas present. But the Three Kings is not just an unusual pub; it's a welcoming and cheerful one too, with good food, good beer, and a roaring fire; and the regulars aren't the least bit weird.

When John took over the Three Kings around 15 years ago, it was a perfectly ordinary street-corner local which had been pretty much untouched since the 1950s – the brewery windows date it to before 1958, when Mann Crossman & Paulin was swallowed up by Watney's. Unfortunately the local working-class custom the pub had always depended on had pretty much dried up, and it had stood empty for a while.

John, who had run the Hope & Anchor in Islington, one of London's top rock pubs, for 14 years, decided that the best way to revive the pub's fortunes was to reconnect with the new local community, which was mainly one of craftspeople and artists. He got involved with the local festival, held every July; he exhibits work by local artists and photographers; and many of the stranger bits and pieces on display

come from the workshops housed in what used to be the London County Council Depository just around the corner, which was converted in 1975.

Take a closer look at the name board outside over the door: every one of the letters has been made at a different workshop, so the "I" in Kings is the spine of a book, from a bookbinder; and the "G" is a leather cushion, from a leatherworker's shop. You can have hours of fun guessing which letter came from which craft studio – or you can just ask John.

Take a closer look, too, at the hanging sign. It's made of papier mâché, and the Three Kings are Henry VIII, King Kong, and Elvis.

OPEN 12–11 MONDAY–FRIDAY, 7.30–11 SATURDAY. CLOSED SUNDAY. FOOD SERVED 12–3.30 MONDAY–FRIDAY. REAL ALES: MORLAND OLD SPECKLED HEN, FULLER'S LONDON PRIDE, YOUNG'S BITTER.

Continue down Clerkenwell Close to Clerkenwell Green.

THE CROWN TAVERN
43 CLERKENWELL GREEN

You could scarcely imagine a greater contrast than that between the Three Kings and the Crown. It would be an understatement to describe the Three Kings as quirky and individualistic; but the Crown is the complete opposite – a self-conscious heritage pub, dressed up in plush neo-Edwardian finery by a brewery architect using a supplier's catalogue of chintzy print wallpaper and discreet carpets and upholstery.

It's still rather a splendid pub. Established in 1641 and completely rebuilt in 1815, it's a handsome classical building with a late-

Victorian fascia of wood and emerald-green tiles tacked on. Inside, it's broken up into smartly-furnished alcoves and niches, all hung about with sepia photos and old prints. Not much of the old interior is left, though: there's a dark Lincrusta ceiling, and there are stubs of turn-of-the-century partitions; but alas, all the original glass is long gone.

Also long gone is the huge collection of clocks which gave the Crown its old nickname, the Clock House – very apt, in London's old watchmaking district. Only one is left, hanging in a side-room: a big black japanned affair, it claims to have been the very clock that hung in Rye House in Hertfordshire, where (allegedly) a Whiggish plot was hatched to assassinate Charles II. It was almost all made up, but it led to the execution of Algernon Sidney and Lord Russell and the suicide in jail of the Earl of Essex. Someone at some time has painted "Ye Conspirators' Clock" in gold on a japanned plaque, although how this rates as a seal of authenticity I do not know. Nor do I know how important this clock (if this was indeed the clock) was to the conspiracy (if there was indeed a conspiracy).

As well as its clocks, the Crown was known for its dances. Upstairs is the Apollo Room, which in Victorian days hosted concerts and dances. A bill from 1841 for a programme of songs and quadrilles promises "a variety of dancing during which no delay is experienced". Also on display are a pair of tickets, found under some floorboards, to a Grand Bohemian Concert given on 23 March 1896 for the benefit of the widow of Thomas Byford, "who dropped down dead while going to work, leaving her totally unprovided for".

A very nice barmaid showed me a section of ancient brick-lined tunnel hung with little stalactites, uncovered when the cellars were cleared out and said to connect the Sessions House across the green, once a court-house but now a Masonic hall, to the old prison, and supposedly used for escorting convicts back to jail without risk of a rescue attempt. "A likely story" was my first reaction – but then there are mysterious vaults and sections of tunnel all over Clerkenwell, and they must have been used for something.

OPEN: 11-11 MONDAY–FRIDAY, 12–11 SATURDAY. CLOSED SUNDAY. FOOD SERVED 12–3 MONDAY-FRIDAY, 12-4 SATURDAY. REAL ALES: TETLEY, ADNAM'S BITTER, DRAUGHT BASS, FULLER'S LONDON PRIDE.

Turn right out of the pub.

Marx Memorial Library

If any single place could be said to embody the Clerkenwell spirit, it's this. Built as Welsh Dissenters' school in 1737, it was divided into craft workshops when the school moved to bigger premises in 1771. One wing of the building was a pub, the Northumberland Arms, while the other was a working men's coffee house. From 1872 the middle bit was the home of the London Patriotic Society, a radical reform club closely associated with John Stuart Mill and Karl Marx's daughter Eleanor.

In 1892 the building was taken over by the Twentieth Century Press, set up by the Social Democratic Federation to print its journal, *Justice,* and other Socialist and Trade Union publications. A backer was William Morris, who promised to pay the rent if the TCP ever found itself strapped for cash. Lenin, in exile in London in 1902–3, edited his revolutionary magazine *Iskra*, the Spark, in a back room.

In 1933, the 50th anniversary of Marx's death, the Marx Memorial Library was opened here in a rare combined effort by the London Labour movement's various constituent parts. The Socialist-heroic fresco in the lecture room was painted in 1934 and is stirringly entitled "Worker of the Future Clearing Away the Chaos of Capitalism".

The building was saved from demolition in 1966 after a campaign supported by that least likely of reds, John Betjeman; was listed in 1967; and was restored with a Lottery grant in 1998–9. It is a private subscription library, and not really open to the public, but they might let you look at Lenin's office if you ask nicely.

Cross the Green and return to Farringdon via Farringdon Lane and Turnmill Street.

FINISH: Farringdon.

CHELSEA
"LONG-HAIRED CHELSEA"

LENGTH OF WALK: FOUR MILES

UNTIL the 18th century, Chelsea was not much more than a remote Thames-side village whose only notable resident had been Thomas More, Henry VIII's Chancellor, executed in 1535 for refusing to recognise Henry as head of the Church. Indeed, so far was Chelsea from London that it was regarded as a safe haven for City-dwellers escaping outbreaks of plague: during one such, in 1625, a parishioner of St Dunstan-in-the-West, Fleet Street – Izaak Walton – attended a service at Chelsea Old Church conducted by the Rector of St Dunstan-in-the-West, Fleet Street – John Donne.

Throughout the 17th and much of the 18th centuries, Chelsea remained a rural retreat. Charles II bought Nell Gwynne a country home on a little lane which is now the King's Road, and chose a riverside plot for a hostel for old soldiers, later to be matched by another for old sea dogs way down the river at Greenwich. Charles did not live to see the building of the Royal Hospital, which was designed by Wren in 1692; but there is a statue of him in Roman dress to remind the world that the hospital was his idea. It still houses 400 red-coated military pensioners. (Its entrance is in West Road; the Chapel and Great Hall are open free of charge Monday–Saturday 10–12 and 2–4. The National Army Museum is next door in Royal Hospital Road.)xxxx

The botanist and antiquarian Sir Hans Sloane retired to the peace of

Chelsea from the hurly-burly of Bloomsbury, spending his last years in Henry VIII's old manor house, which was demolished after his death in 1753. His country estate wasn't built on until 20 years later when Hans Town – Hans Place, Cadogan Place, Sloane Street and Sloane Square – was developed, and even in the 1890s a writer could reminisce that sixty years since, Brompton, Chelsea, Pimlico and Knightsbridge were comparatively uncovered by streets.

In 1742 there came a development which had Londoners trooping out to Chelsea in their thousands, when a consortium of businessmen got together £36,000 to create Ranelagh Gardens. London at the time, cramped and malodorous as it was, was surrounded by dozens of open-air resorts of one sort or another: some of them, like Hampstead and Highgate, based on spas; others in the form of pleasure gardens large and small. Ranelagh Gardens, with its famous Rotunda, its balloon ascents, and its fireworks, was the biggest of them all. George II himself was a regular attender at its twice-weekly entertainments or ridottos; Horace Walpole described it thus: "There is a vast amphitheatre, finely gilt, painted and illuminated, into which everybody that loves eating, drinking, staring, or crowding is admitted for twelvepence." In 1744 he recorded: "Ranelagh has totally beaten Vauxhall. Nobody goes anywhere else ... the company is universal, from the Duke of Rutland to children out of the Foundling Hospital, from my lady Townshend to the Kitten [a famous courtesan]."

Ranelagh was more expensive than Vauxhall, its nearest competitor; its season was longer, it was less rowdy, and the Rotunda, where people of fashion paraded while leading musicians (including Mozart as a child prodigy in 1764) played, was one of the wonders of the age. Gibbon said it was the most convenient place for courtships of every kind. But Vauxhall had the last laugh: the Rotunda closed in 1803 and was demolished in 1805, whereas Vauxhall lasted until 1859. Ranelagh Gardens was never built over, though: it is now home to the Chelsea Flower Show, held every May since 1913.

Perhaps because of the presence of Ranelagh Gardens, or perhaps because it was still a haven from the pressures of London, Chelsea began to attract a small literary coterie in the mid-18th century: Dean Swift lived in Cheyne Walk where Crosby Hall now stands, while Smollett lived not far away in Lawrence Street from 1750–62, where he wrote *Peregrine Pickle* and *Sir Launcelot Greaves* and was visited by Goldsmith, Dr Johnson and Lawrence Sterne. Meanwhile a coffee house in Cheyne Walk, established by Sloane's valet John Salter and exotically entitled

Salteros, attracted the custom of Goldsmith and Sterne as well as Addison and Fanny Burney. (Salter inherited Sloane's huge collection of antiquities and curios and, probably not knowing what to do with it, donated it to the nation, thus founding the British Museum. Salteros lasted until the 1860s.)

But it wasn't until the 19th century that cheap but characterful Chelsea really hit its literary stride, and the roll-call of writers and painters who chose to settle in the somewhat raffish suburb runs from Thomas Carlyle, who arrived for a short tenancy in 1834 and stayed until his death nearly half a century later, to Dylan Thomas, who had only two brief spells in Chelsea in the 1930s and 40s but left plenty of ripples.

Perhaps the most amazing of menageries – both of authors and of animals – was that kept by Dante Gabriel Rosetti from 1862–82 in Queen's House, 16 Cheyne Walk. Swinburne and George Meredith were both inmates – briefly – as were a raven, a jackdaw, owls, lizards, an opossum that slept on Rosetti's bedside table, a racoon that slept in a drawer, a kangaroo, a zebra, an armadillo, a donkey, and a wombat which ate a guest's hat, prompting Rosetti to exclaim: "Poor wombat! It's so indigestible!" There was also – and God knows where he kept it – a white bull; dormice he didn't realise had died until they started to smell; and peacocks which annoyed the neighbours. Swinburne used to slide naked down the banisters to breakfast and once had a nude wrestling match with another guest – did D H Lawrence, one wonders, know about this? He was chucked out of this prototypical hippy commune in 1863 after pushing William Morris into a dresser full of precious china, which all broke.

Although Chelsea has long had a powerful attraction for writers, they all seem to have had a rotten time here. George Eliot, for example, moved into number 4 Cheyne Walk in 1880 with a husband 20 years her junior. They planned to winter here and spend the next summer by the sea, but she died of a kidney infection three weeks later. George Bernard Shaw lived in Netherton Grove from 1876–82, and wrote five novels. He couldn't get a single one of them published. Henry James moved into Carlyle Mansions in 1913, having previously lived in Lawrence Street, and declared it "just the thing for me". (He it was who coined the title of this chapter.) A few months later, he was dead. The young John Betjeman lived at "poky, dark, and cramped" 53 Old Church Street from 1917–24 – the "slummy end", he said, from which he escaped to explore Metroland. He returned to Chelsea as an old man, moving from Smithfield to Radnor Walk in 1977. He moved again in 1984, to

Cornwall, and died the same year.

But Chelsea's saddest literary tragedy has to be that of Oscar Wilde, who lived at 44 Tite Street in 1881 in a house remodelled by the Aesthetic architect Edward Godwin, and after marrying Constance Lloyd in 1884 lived at 34 Tite Street – which again, was remodelled by Godwin – until 1895. Here he wrote *The Happy Prince* (1888), *The Portrait of Dorian Gray* (1890), *Lady Windermere's Fan* (1892), and *The Importance of Being Earnest* (1895). After his ruin, a mob looted his house, and what was left had to be sold to pay his court costs. In 1914 the borough voted to remove him from a mural in the town hall on the grounds of his homosexuality (the mural included the adulterers George Eliot and Henry VIII), and as late as the 1950s, bigots unsuccessfully tried to stop the London County Council putting a blue plaque up on his old home.

START: SOUTH KENSINGTON TUBE

Take the Pelham Street exit and turn left down Pelham Street. Cross Fulham Road into Draycott Avenue and take the third left.

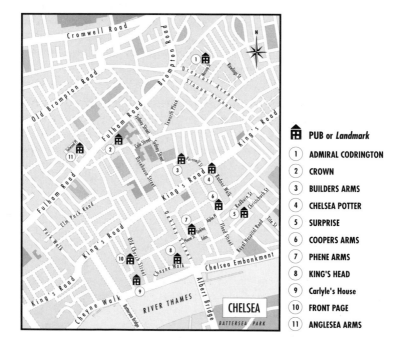

🏠 PUB or *Landmark*

(1) ADMIRAL CODRINGTON
(2) CROWN
(3) BUILDERS ARMS
(4) CHELSEA POTTER
(5) SURPRISE
(6) COOPERS ARMS
(7) PHENE ARMS
(8) KING'S HEAD
(9) Carlyle's House
(10) FRONT PAGE
(11) ANGLESEA ARMS

140

ADMIRAL CODRINGTON

17 MOSSOP STREET

Chelsea, as you are about to discover, is not an area for hoary old alehouses or magnificently unspoilt gin-palaces. It is an area for very smart modern pubs with anaesthetised interiors, almost all of them painted a restful yellow. The Admiral Codrington is the first of many we will encounter.

Mossop Street stands on what used to be an area of market gardens which was all built over in or around 1855, when the eponymous Admiral Sir Edward Codrington died. He had been the Captain of the Orion at Trafalgar, accepting the surrender of the French battleship Intrepide and befriending her captain, who spent his term as a prisoner of war rather more comfortably than his crew as Codrington's house guest. The high point of the admiral's career was his command of the combined British, French and Russian fleets which defeated the Turks at Navarino in 1827, paving the way for the liberation and independence of Greece.

The pub's exterior, with its graceful bow windows, appears to date from about 1900, but the interior is totally contemporary – so much so that even the Sloanes who used to flock here in the early 1980s (including one Lady Diana Spencer) probably wouldn't recognise the place. The colour scheme is, as we have observed, a tasteful, soothing yellow; the floorboards are all stripped and polished, as is the pine dado. There is a cheerful open fire with expensive-looking sofas ranged beside it, and the barman gives you your change on a little silver dish. The old courtyard has been roofed over with glass to form a stunningly chic dining-room. All in all, not really a place for a light and bitter and a knees-up round the old joanna.

OPEN 11.30–11 MONDAY–SATURDAY, 12–10.30 SUNDAY.
BAR FOOD 12–2.30 MONDAY–FRIDAY, 12–3.30 SATURDAY AND SUNDAY.
RESTAURANT OPEN LUNCHTIME AND EVENING.
REAL ALES: BODDINGTON'S, CHARLES WELLS BOMBARDIER.

Return to Draycott Avenue. Cross, and take Ixworth Place next to the old Harrod's warehouse. Turn right into Cale Street, Cross Sydney Street, and turn right up Dovehouse Street.

CROWN
153 DOVEHOUSE STREET

This pleasant little street-corner pub opposite the Royal Marsden Hospital just off the Fulham Road has been in existence since 1863, when it was built as one of the last unlicensed beerhouses before the repeal of the Beer Act in 1869.

It remained a beer-only house, too, for far longer than it needed to: it only got a full licence in 1953. In the dark days of keg, the stubborn tenant of the Crown was true to the pub's roots: he remained one of the few publicans in the area to stick by cask-conditioned ale, however hard the brewery reps tried to persuade him to defect to keg.

The interior of the Crown isn't actually painted yellow; instead, it's an elegant cream, with a pale-green ceiling. But it does have a stripped and polished floor, and the traditional frosted pub windows have been replaced by clear glass.

In fact, the more clear glass I see in pub windows, the more I realise that the opaque alternative is a strong definer of traditional pub character. It not only prevents the outside world from being tempted by the depravity within; it also creates an enclosed, inward-looking space – you don't watch the world go by from inside a traditional pub; you face the bar with your back to the outside, and engage with the other patrons. The quality of the light is different, too: in a continental café, where only a large sheet of clear plate glass divides inside from outside, the light is bright, direct, an intrusion of the outside. In a traditional pub the light is filtered and diffused. A traditional pub is cut off and protected from the outside world, and its etched and frosted windows are its curtain-walls.

Enough of this. The Crown is stripped-out, pared-down, and the cleanest pub in Chelsea, according to one of its regulars. (He may be right, but it would face some pretty stiff competition.) It has recently been extended into its courtyard, creating a new bar which is also stripped-out, pared-down, cream-and-pale green. It's actually rather nice.

OPEN ALL PERMITTED HOURS. FOOD 12–3, 6–9 MONDAY–FRIDAY, 12–4 SUNDAY. REAL ALES: ADNAM'S BITTER, FULLER'S LONDON PRIDE.

Return down Dovehouse Street. Turn left into Britten Street, cross Sydney Street and continue along Britten Street.

BUILDERS ARMS
13 BRITTEN STREET

Another pub that has soared upmarket in recent years, the Builders Arms claims (as its name suggests) to have originated as a canteen/hostel for workers building the beautifully-proportioned St Luke's Church – the Cathedral of Chelsea – almost opposite, which was started in 1820 and finished in 1824. (They also tell you that there's an underground passage linking church and pub, but as one who has heard this story dozens of times and remains resolutely sceptical about it, I have to say I don't believe it). Others say that this story isn't true, and that the pub was built in 1840 as a tap for Matthews & Cannings Anchor Brewery, which was sold to Whitbread in 1899 and closed in 1907 to become a bottling plant.

Whatever its roots, the Builders Arms has far outgrown them now. Until recently it was a two-bar locals' pub, with darts and dominoes and fish and chip suppers and murals of Old Battersea Bridge and Britten Street in the 19th century. All that's gone now, and it's a Chelsea yellow pub; very elegant, with a long lounge bar complete with pale pine panels and stripped polished floorboards on one side and a posh dining-room, broken up into intimate little rooms with bookcases and scrubbed pine tables, on the other.

If you like the Chelsea yellow style – and the civilised denizens of this rather superior residential area clearly do – then this is about as good as it gets. Shame about the murals, though.

OPEN ALL PERMITTED HOURS. FOOD SERVED MONDAY–SATURDAY 12–2.30 AND 7–9.45; SUNDAY 12–3, 7–9. REAL ALES: ADNAM'S BITTER, FULLER'S LONDON PRIDE.

Turn right out of the pub. Follow Burnsall Street into Kings Road.

CHELSEA POTTER

119 KINGS ROAD

A landmark on the King's Road of the Swinging 60s, the Chelsea Potter was a favourite hangout of the far-out. If they ever came back, they wouldn't know it now.

Named in honour of the great artist in ceramics, William de Morgan, who lived in Old Church Street and founded the Chelsea Arts Pottery in 1872, this is a plain early Victorian pub of brown London brick with workaday square sash windows. But it is marked out by its enormous ground-floor bay, which sticks out into the pavement as if it was trying to trip up potential customers and is painted bright red, in case you were going to miss it.

The clear glazing of the little square lights in the bay is a clue to what you're going to find inside: when Mick Jagger and others knew it, it would have been broken up into two or three little bars, but in 1994 the refurbishers moved in and stripped the whole lot out – including any frosted window-glass which might have kept the sunlight out.

So, what you're left with is another of those big, airy, light-filled bars. But the designers were smart enough to leave those original features which helped their scheme along – notably mirrors: in the rather sober pine bar-back there's one which is flanked by Egyptian pilasters carved like fish scales; alongside the bar is one of those rather elegant painted Chinoiserie riverbank scenes; and marooned at the back of a little dais there's a set mounted in what looks like a section of bar-back, with a frieze of pastoral scenes carved above it. OPEN ALL PERMITTED HOURS. FOOD SERVED 11–5.30 MONDAY–SATURDAY, 12–5.30 SUNDAY. REAL ALES: COURAGE BEST AND DIRECTORS.

Follow Radnor Walk beside the pub, passing John Betjeman's old house, number 29. Turn left into Redburn Street, then right into Tite Street and left into Christchurch Street.

THE SURPRISE
6 CHRISTCHURCH TERRACE

It would be hard to imagine anywhere more land-locked and less
Carolean than this quiet little residential enclave off Flood Street.
Nevertheless this handsome mid-Victorian pub is named after the
frigate which whisked Charles II from the Dorset harbour of Bridport
to exile in France after his dramatic flight from defeat by Oliver
Cromwell at the Battle of Worcester, 1651.

The landlord says it's only been called the Surprise since the 1970s.
He doesn't know why it was changed or what from; but don't let it

worry you, because this is the first really unaltered pub we've come across so far, and it bears not a trace of Chelsea yellow. Perhaps that's the surprise?

Instead, it's done out in the Olde English or mock antique style of around 1900, with a surviving partition screening off a public bar with a nice cast-iron fireplace, blackened pine-plank bar-front and dados, bare oak floorboards, and high ceilings covered in dark pressed paper. There's also a third room, a separate little snug at the back.

One comparatively recent addition is a painted frieze round the bar gantry with Chelsea pensioners, Regency street scenes, Nell Gwynne, old Battersea Bridge and so on. It was painted by an artist named Fenella Barker in 1973 and is very much of its time.

OPEN 12–11 (10.30 SUNDAY). BAR SNACKS SERVED ALL DAY.
REAL ALES: DRAUGHT BASS, FULLER'S LONDON PRIDE, ADNAM'S BITTER.

Turn left out of the pub along Christchurch Street, turn left again at the end, then immediately right into Robinson Street and right again into Flood Street.

COOPERS ARMS

87 FLOOD STREET

Another Chelsea yellow pub, the Coopers Arms was first recorded in 1846, when Flood Street was Queen Street. The pub was rebuilt in 1874 at about the time Queen Street was renamed after one Luke Thomas Flood of Cheyne Walk, who on his death in 1868 had left £3,000 to the parish.

In 1990 Young's took it over and decided to transform it from a mid-Victorian relic into a contemporary pub for the Chelsea of today, which meant tearing out almost anything old including a number of little booths and resiting the bar from the middle to create plenty of space, putting in clear window-glass, and – of course – painting anything that didn't move yellow.

It's actually not a bad job. A limited and carefully chosen amount of bric-à-brac has been brought in to liven up what would otherwise be an awful lot of yellow: there's a stuffed wild boar's head, a factory time-clock, the biggest grandmother clock in the world (a 24-hour one, to boot – actually it was originally a railway station clock) and, in the upstairs function room, a 17-foot draughtsman's table bought from a shipyard in Jarrow.

The main point of interest, though, is that a certain Denis and Margaret Thatcher used to live at number 19 up the road. Did Denis used to pop In for the odd sly one? They're not saying.

OPEN ALL PERMITTED HOURS. FOOD 12.30–3, 6–10 (NOT SUNDAY EVENINGS). REAL ALE: YOUNG'S RANGE.

Cross Flood Street into Alpha Place.
Carry on into Oakley Gardens and Phene Street.

PHENE ARMS

PHENE STREET

Every time you walk down a tree-lined London street – or Paris street, or Berlin street, or anywhere street, for that matter – you should thank Dr John Samuel Phene (pronounced Feeney), because the blindingly obvious idea of lining streets with trees originated with him.

A local landowner who lived in a curio-packed house nearby, Dr Phene built two or three streets in the neighbourhood, including the one that bears his name – along with the pub that bears his name - in the early 1850s.

The trees that Dr Phene thought most suitable for lining streets with were acacias – evidently a personal favourite, as there are a couple of ancient specimens in the pub's pleasant garden, but a bad choice, because they're too twisty and bushy to give adequate shade and can grow to obstruct the pavement. But Prince Albert liked the idea, and had the streets of South Kensington or Albertopolis lined with elms, planes and poplars. And as ideas that Prince Albert liked had a tendency to spread, we soon all had pleasant shady streets to amble down.

Dr Phene lived for another 60 years after developing this corner of Chelsea, and so must have had the pleasure very many times in his long life of walking down streets which were, thanks to him, pleasantly shady. He also lived to see his pub bought by Watney's, which in the 1950s or 60s moved in and transformed it, taking out many (but not all) of the original features and replacing them with brass lamps, spindly cast-iron, red plush, and a crow-stepped brick fireplace. Actually it's all rather fun, in a retro sort of way; and it helps that the Phene is a friendly and welcoming locals' local, with good food and good beer. And if you've got to have 60s kitsch anywhere, you've got to have it in Chelsea.

OPEN ALL PERMITTED HOURS. FOOD SERVED 12–3 (12–4 SATURDAY AND SUNDAY), 6–10. REAL ALES: ADNAM'S BITTER, FULLER'S LONDON PRIDE, COURAGE DIRECTORS, MORLAND OLD SPECKLED HEN.

At the end of Phene Street turn left into Oakley Street, then right into Cheyne Walk.

THE KING'S HEAD & EIGHT BELLS
CHEYNE WALK

Dwarfed by neighbouring Carlyle Mansions (in which Henry James, T S Eliot and Ian Fleming all lived), the King's Head & Eight Bells is a pleasant early Victorian pub which used to be on the riverfront and had its own landing, called Feather Stairs, until someone built an embankment outside and put the A3212 on top of it.

A lively games pub, with sports on the TV and a round pool table (a space-saving invention of the 1980s) and giant Jenga and lots of Australians, the King's Head doesn't seem like a favoured haunt of artists and writers. But it was.

Turner, who lived hereabouts at about the time it was built, is credited with discovering it, and he was followed through the saloon-bar doors by painters including Whistler and Augustus John (who was having an affair with Ian Fleming's mother).

149

Writers, too, used the King's Head & Eight Bells, among them Dylan Thomas. He had two spells in Chelsea: in 1934–5 he lived in Redcliffe Street amid "poems, butter eggs and mashed potatoes" with the artist Alfred Janes. One drunken night in the King's Head he explained to a female admirer that the secret to being a poet was to be "drunk, tubercular, and fat", although history doesn't record him as being tubercular. In his second stint in Chelsea, as a resident of Manresa Street from 1942–4, he used to come down to the pub to taunt the local bohemians, whom he called the Cheyne Gang, play shove-ha'penny, and pick fights with American soldiers.

Those days are gone now. What's left is a comfortable one-bar pub with bits and pieces of original glasswork which survived a thorough going-over in the 1960s and a very smart no-smoking dining-room at the back.

The name, incidentally, poses no problem: it merely records the conflation of the licences of two older pubs, probably when the new one was built.

OPEN ALL PERMITTED HOURS. FOOD SERVED 12–2.45, 6–9.45 MONDAY–SATURDAY, 12.30–3.30, 7–9.30 SUNDAY. REAL ALES: TETLEY BITTER, FULLER'S LONDON PRIDE, MARSTON'S PEDIGREE, GUEST ALE.

Turn right out of the pub and right again up Old Church Street.

CARLYLE'S HOUSE

The essayist Thomas Carlyle moved to a tall Jacobean house, 24 Cheyne Row, in 1834 because although it was "unfashionable; also ... unhealthy", it was cheap and had a view of the Thames. Chopin and Dickens were among his guests here over the years, but Carlyle always said he hated the "black jumble" of encroaching suburbs and the "acrid putrescence" of the neighbourhood. In the attic he wrote his magnum opus, the history of the French Revolution. He then loaned the completed (and only) manuscript to John Stuart Mill, whose maid lit a fire with it. By that time Carlyle had thoroughly lost interest in the subject and had actually destroyed all his notes: Mill paid him £200 compensation to reconstruct the work. A museum since 1896, the house is open to the public from 11–5 April-October. Call 0207 352 7087 for details.

THE FRONT PAGE
35 OLD CHURCH STREET

This is it. This is the pub where the Chelsea yellow style had its beginnings. When Rupert Fowler and Chris Phillips bought it in 1986 it was the plain old Black Lion. There had been a Black Lion on the spot for 300 years but this one was just a big, not particularly special 1870s Black Lion with sash windows and a big coach lantern.

The new owners set about changing all that, mainly by banishing darkness. They gave it a sexy new name, opened it all out, made the most of the big windows, buffed up the Edwardian-looking panelling till it shone, and painted everything that wasn't panelled a nice soothing yellow.

Clearly it worked. The Front Page became hot news overnight, attracting not not only Chelsea arts set but also Hollywood stars such as Dustin Hoffman who used the rehearsal studios at the Old Church's former parish hall. Not only has every pub in the area with any social aspirations now gone down the yellow route, but Messrs Fowler and Phillips now own eight pubs, including the Lord's Tavern in St John's Wood.

OPEN ALL PERMITTED HOURS. FOOD 12–3, 6–10 MONDAY–SATURDAY, 12–6 SUNDAY. REAL ALES: CHARLES WELLS BOMBARDIER, THEAKSTON XB, BRAKSPEAR'S BITTER.

Turn left out of the pub and continue up Old Church Street.
Cross Fulham Road into Selwood Terrace.

ANGLESEA ARMS
15 SELWOOD TERRACE

This must be the only street in London with two names: it's Selwood
Terrace on the side where the Anglesea Arms is, but Neville Terrace if
you live across the road. It was Salad Lane, and fringed with market
gardens, until 1830 when the adjoining landowners started building
houses on it: this side belonged to a Mr Selwood, and so he called it
after himself.

He called the pub, however, after the Napoleonic War general
Henry Paget, Marquess of Anglesey, who was riding next to the Duke
of Wellington – an easy mark for the French gunners with his white
horse and big nose – when a cannonball hit him. "By God, sir," he said

to Wellington, "I think I've lost my leg." "By God, sir," replied the Iron Duke, looking down, "I do believe you have." Paget had the leg pickled and took it home to show guests. It was buried with him when he died nearly 40 years later, so an awful lot of guests must have seen it.

The pub was brand new when Dickens lived at number 11 courting Catherine Hogarth, who lived nearby and whose father was Dickens's boss at the *Evening Chronicle*. Charles and Catherine were married on 2 April 1836 at St Luke's in Sydney Street – a mistake, since he really preferred her sister Mary, who died suddenly the following year; and the unhappy couple were messily divorced 14 years later.

The Anglesea has mutated since then into a smart but homely pub, as comfortable as the drawing-room of a good-sized Edwardian rectory or country house, and not unlike it in atmosphere. There is wooden panelling, there is an open fire, there are prints and oil paintings on the walls, there are sofas and armchairs as well as more traditional pub furniture.

This was a bastion of real ale in the dark days when keg was sweeping all before it, and a rare patron of small independent brewers. Which was ironic, because it belonged to Lady Joseph, wife of Sir Maxwell Joseph, the property tycoon who took over the respectable brewing company of Watney, Combe, Reid and turned it into the all-devouring monster that all lovers of traditional pubs and good ale came to hate and fear.

Well, Watney's is gone, sold out and asset-stripped. Even the name no longer exists. But the Anglesea is still there, still in the same ownership, and still supporting small independent brewers. One recent change, though, is that the old snug bar down some stairs at the back, known as the Cubby, has gone; in its place is a handsome and fairly formal dining-room, all dark panelling and rustic prints.

OPEN ALL PERMITTED HOURS. FOOD SERVED 12–3, 6.30–10 MONDAY–FRIDAY, 12–10 SATURDAY, 12–9 SUNDAY.
REAL ALES: ADNAM'S BITTER AND BROADSIDE, BRAKSPEAR'S SPECIAL, FULLER'S LONDON PRIDE, GUEST ALE.

Turn left out of the pub and continue up Neville Terrace.
Turn right into Brompton Road.

FINISH: SOUTH KENSINGTON.

GREENWICH
SCIENCE & THE SEA

LENGTH OF WALK: THREE MILES

LONG a royal manor, Greenwich had its first proper palace built by Henry V's brother, the Duke of Gloucester, in the the early 15th century. In its pleasant and healthful spot, far upwind of the City's stench, it soon became a royal favourite. Henry VIII was born there, and christened in St Alphege's church, and both his daughters, Mary and Elizabeth, were born there too.

James I also loved the place, and in 1616 commissioned Inigo Jones to build a new palace, standing slightly back from the river and looking out over the Thames to the wooded hills of Essex beyond, for his wife Anne of Denmark. The house wasn't finished until 10 years after James's death, but it was loved just as much by his son, Charles I, and Charles's queen Henrietta Maria. The Queen's House is today all that is left of the royal complex that so pleased kings and queens for over two centuries, for under Cromwell the old palace was so neglected – in fact part of it was used as a bakery, making ship's biscuits – that all Charles II could do after his restoration in 1660 was have it pulled down.

Charles never got round to replacing the palace, but didn't lose interest in the site either. In 1675 he commissioned the ubiquitous Wren to build the Royal Observatory and its Octagon Room, where the first astronomer royal, John Flamsteed, worked until his death in

1719. With its naval connections and its observatory, Greenwich became a powerhouse of geographical and astronomical research: the Greenwich Meridian was acknowledged by a conference in Washington in 1884, and GMT was accepted as the universal measurement of standard time. Perhaps it's for this reason, rather than its place in British royal and naval history, that Greenwich has been a World Heritage Site since 1997.

It was William III who commissioned the building of the Naval Hospital in 1692, with Wren as the original architect (although the designs had to be completed by Vanbrugh) and a park landscaped by André Le Nôtre, who also laid out the formal gardens of the Palace of Versailles. Much of the work was funded by public subscription: John Evelyn put money towards it and wrote in his diary of the laying of the foundation stone on 30 June 1696. Dr Johnson, strolling in the park more than half a century later, called it "too magnificent a place for charity".

The whole was designed in two parts, so that the river view from the Queen's House should not be interrupted. The work was long and painstaking: the Chapel was not completed until 1742 and was gutted by fire in 1779, to be rebuilt in the rococo style with marble pillars which are actually synthetic Coade stone. The centrepiece, though, is the Painted Hall: the ceiling, James Thornhill's masterpiece, shows William & Mary triumphing over Louis XIV. On the western wall of the Upper Hall Thornhill painted a small self-portrait of himself into his picture of George I and his family: the artist is in the bottom right-hand corner, pointing at the King. This was intended as the hospital's dining-room, but proved too small, and was unused until 1806, when Nelson's body lay in state here following its long journey home from the battle of Trafalgar.

The Naval Hospital was removed to Portsmouth in 1879, and the Hospital buildings were turned into the Naval College. The Queen's House became the National Maritime Museum, with an entrance in Romney Road. (Its Neptune Court was glassed over before the British Museum was.) The Royal Navy turned the College over to Greenwich University in 1998, whose undergraduates now enjoy the grandest educational facility outside Oxford and Cambridge; but the Chapel and the Painted Hall are still open to the public.

The Observatory and its park, the Hospital, the Maritime Museum, the Cutty Sark, the covered market – these all combine to make

Greenwich an immensely popular resort for a day out from the grime of London. And this is no recent phenomenon: Londoners have historically enjoyed nothing better than a day trip to whatever green spot was in reach, and Greenwich has long been a favourite – hence its thick cluster of taverns, inns and coffee houses – or, as we should say today, pubs, bars and restaurants. The best way to arrive, naturally, is by river, and pleasure cruisers complete with commentary and bar depart from Charing Cross Pier throughout the day; so this walk starts and ends at Greenwich Pier. Should you not have time for a cruise, however, Greenwich is now connected with the outside world by the Dockland Light Railway. Use the Greenwich Maritime–Cutty Sark station rather than Greenwich Station itself.

START: GREENWICH PIER

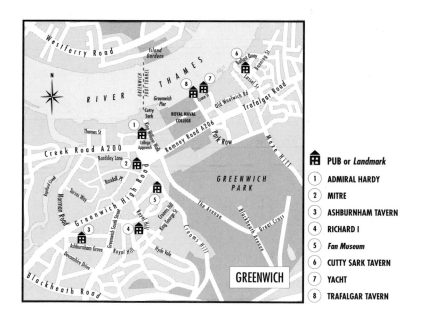

CUTTY SARK

Launched in 1869, the Cutty Sark was the fastest of the tea clippers which plied between London and the East Indies via the Cape of Good Hope, and even though steam power and the Suez Canal by that time were eclipsing these graceful vessels, it continued in harness until 1922. It was brought to Greenwich restored in the early 1950s and moved into its specially-built dry dock in 1957. Among its many delights is the world's largest collection of figureheads.

Had you arrived at this spot some time earlier – before the Luftwaffe did, actually – you would have found not a ship, but the Ship, Greenwich's principal inn and competitor with the Trafalgar Tavern in the great days of whitebait dinners. Dickens, who loved Greenwich, used it for two scenes in *Our Mutual Friend:* in a little room overlooking the river, Bella Wilfer dined with her father and found everything "delightful"; and her wedding breakfast was held at the Ship after she was married to John Rokesmith at St Alphege's in the presence of the Boffins and a grim old pensioner with two wooden legs.

Near the Cutty Sark is a much smaller but equally renowned vessel, Gipsy Moth IV, the tiny yacht in which Francis Chichester made his 226-day solo round-the-world voyage in 1966–7, when he was already 62. He was afterwards knighted by Elizabeth II with the same sword Elizabeth I had knighted Francis Drake after his round-the-world voyage nearly 400 years earlier.

Walk straight on from the Cutty Sark, and College Approach is to your right.

ADMIRAL HARDY
COLLEGE APPROACH

College Approach is a dignified late-Georgian avenue leading up to the gates of the College, whose centrepiece is the formal stone frontage of the Admiral Hardy with its deep, narrow sash windows.

Named after the Captain of the Victory at Trafalgar (the same Hardy from whom Nelson received his dying kiss) the tavern was built in 1830, when Hardy was Governor of the Hospital, and its exterior has changed not a jot since his day. Inside, though, it's a different story. A complete refit in 2000, when the pub changed hands, saw the old island bar torn out and a new one built against one wall. You can see

how the interior used to be divided up from the position of the three fireplaces – one of them, in fact, is behind the new bar.

Such a drastic transformation must have enraged many conservationists, but in many ways the new single-bar is truer to the pub's Georgian roots. Large common rooms, divided by high-backed settles rather than formal partitions, were quite usual then, and the fashion for slicing the pub up into private little compartments only came along much later.

The new management at the Admiral Hardy – the same partnership which runs the Trafalgar Tavern – have helped their case by doing an exceptionally good job. One end is comfy, with leather sofas and armchairs, a couple of nautical oil-paintings (almost the only naval theming the pub now has, unusually in Greenwich) and a decoratively painted cast-iron fireplace. The other end is more pubby, with polished wooden panelling on the walls, bare floorboards, and an unadorned fireplace. It's all very civilised and upmarket.

An unusual feature of the Admiral Hardy is that it has its own food shop, so if you liked your dinner you can take the identical ingredients home with you and have a go at recreating it. The idea came to the new owners because the florists shop at the rear – the pub's back door opens into the covered market – fell vacant at just the right time. It's now a high-class fishmonger, grocer and delicatessen.

Open all permitted hours. Food served 12–9 Monday–Thursday and 12–4.30 Friday–Sunday. Real ales: Ruddles County, Shepherd Neame Spitfire.

Leave the pub by the back door into the covered market. Leave the market by the Nelson Road exit in the opposite corner. Turn right in Nelson Road and follow the road round to the left past St Alphege's Church.

Mitre
291 Greenwich High Road

The Mitre is another dignified Georgian pub, of brick this time, rather than the Admiral Hardy's stone, but with the same classical symmetry and deep formal first-floor sash windows.

It was built in 1827 on the site of a coffee house of the same name which had been destroyed by fire; and was and remains a proper inn rather than just a tavern. Today it describes itself as a hotel and has 16 letting bedrooms (all en suite) and a conference suite in what was originally the Assembly Room.

On the ground floor, the several rooms – coffee room, parlour, bar, snugs – have long ago been opened out to form one big bar. However, you can still see from the traces of dividing walls how it must once have looked, and while the rear is all very comfortable with buttoned leather upholstery and carpeted floors – very much the hotel lounge, in fact – the front part has been left with a less formal, more pubby character. There's also a totally separate bar, which currently has an Irish theme although not overwhelmingly so, which opens only in the evenings.

OPEN ALL PERMITTED HOURS. BAR FOOD SERVED 12–3 MONDAY–FRIDAY; CARVERY OPEN 12–5 SATURDAY AND SUNDAY. REAL ALES: COURAGE BEST, FULLER'S LONDON PRIDE.

Turn right out of the pub and follow Greenwich High Road. Turn left into Egerton Drive, then second left into Ashburnham Grove.

THE ASHBURNHAM ARMS
ASHBURNHAM GROVE

It is always good to encounter on these walks at least one pub which is neither architecturally grand nor especially historic but is exceptionally good at being a pub, and the Ashburnham Arms is certainly that.

This quarter of Greenwich is composed of charming early Victorian streets and terraces of small brown-brick cottages and villas, not originally in the least upmarket but now, thanks to the towering presence of Canary Wharf just across the water, worth (literally, in the case of the larger houses) millions. The Ashburnham Arms was built in about 1850 to serve the artisans, clerks, and tradespeoples with whom the cottages and villas were filling up.

Outside as plain and brown-brick as its plain brown-brick neighbours, inside it's a fairly plush pub, all pine-plank dado, carpets and red velvet upholstery, arranged in one good-sized L-shaped bar with an intimate little snug – favoured spot for the young canoodling couples of the parish, says the landlord – leading through to a spacious, airy conservatory and a popular beer-garden beyond. At one time, it was divided into six bars and a jug-and-bottle, which seems incredible for a building of its size. But all that went at some time after the war when the pub belonged to Charrington's, which ripped out everything including the partitions, all the fireplaces but one, and the old bar; replaced the original ground-floor sashes with the rather incongruous Olde English leaded affairs which survive today; and covered the walls in hardboard cladding.

Shepherd Neame, which bought the pub in 1975, got rid of Charrington's worst excesses to create a really comfortable and welcoming local which has become famous not just in the area but, in ale-loving circles, nationally for the quality of its beer. It's been in the Campaign for Real Ale's *Good Beer Guide* for as long as anyone can remember, and justifiably so; and the landlord frequently finds himself serving parties on beer trips from distant parts of the country.

OPEN 6–11 MONDAY, 12–3, 6–11 TUESDAY-SATURDAY, 12–3, 6–10.30 SUNDAY. FOOD SERVED LUNCHTIME TUESDAY–SUNDAY AND TUESDAY & FRIDAY EVENINGS. REAL ALES: SHEPHERD NEAME RANGE INCLUDING SEASONAL SPECIALS.

Turn left out of the pub. Cross South Street into Royal Hill opposite.

RICHARD I
52 ROYAL HILL

The brown brick Victorian terraces which make up so much of 19th-century London can look terribly dowdy unless, as in Hampstead, as in Dulwich, as here, they have a hill to wind over. Royal Hill is a beautiful and quiet residential corner of Greenwich, and the utterly charming Richard I is the centre of it.

Originally it was a pair of 18th-century cottages, one of which was a pub owned by Tolly Cobbold of Ipswich, while the other was a shop. The present handsome double front, with its matching bay windows

and engraved glass doors, was inserted when Tolly bought the shop and knocked the two buildings together in the early 1920s. Its official name was the Old House, but it was known as the Tolly long after Young's bought it and renamed it in 1974. (Why the Richard I, incidentally? What connection did the Lionheart have with Greenwich?)

The pub still has its two bars, one a basic public with pine-plank walls and bare floorboards, the other a much larger and more comfortable saloon with a boarded pine ceiling held up by a cast-iron column, boxed-in joists and Anaglypta-covered walls. There's also a big beer garden where barbecues are held in summer, and with enormous gas heaters so you can continue to sit out long after the evenings have turned chilly.

The Observatory next door, incidentally, used to be the humble Fox & Hounds. It has been considerably smartened up recently to appeal to the wealthy and stylish Canary Wharf-ites who now live in Royal Hill, but the Richard I needs no such treatment.

OPEN ALL PERMITTED HOURS. FOOD SERVED 12–2, 6–10
MONDAY–SATURDAY; 12–3, 6-9.30 SUNDAY. REAL ALES: YOUNG'S RANGE.

Turn left out of pub, continue down Royal Hill, then turn right into Burney Street.

FAN MUSEUM

At 12 Croom's Hill there is another museum, less well-known than the Maritime Museum and utterly unconnected with Britain's glorious history of ruling the waves: the Fan Museum started as a private collection but grew so large that it took up two fine Georgian town houses and had to be opened to the public. And what it has is fans: thousands of them, from all over the world, dating back to the 17th century. It opens 12–5 (closed Monday) and has to be seen, if only because it's so unroyal and unnautical.

Cross Croom's Hill into Nevada Road. Turn left into King William Walk (entrance to Greenwich Park and Observatory is on your right). Turn right into Romney Road, passing entrances to Queen's House & Maritime Museum on your right and Painted Hall and Chapel on your left. Turn left into Park Row, then right into Old Woolwich Road and left into Lassells Road.

CUTTY SARK TAVERN
BALLAST QUAY

If, as you trudge the dreary length of Old Woolwich Road, shudder in the shadow of Greenwich Power Station, and waver at the unpromising corner of Lassells Road, trust me. Ballast Quay is worth the journey.

Tucked away like an island of civilisation amid the industrial wasteland of the Greenwich Marshes, it's a single row of elegant late 18th- and early 19th-century houses – one of them being the harbour-master's house of 1840 – with its own little riverside terrace just across a narrow cobbled way.

In the middle of it all is a big old pub with an equally big old bow window looking out over the Thames. Built in 1805 on the site of a much older pub, it was the Union Tavern until the Cutty Sark moved into its purpose-built dry dock whereupon, sensing the popularity this new attraction would bring, the pub's owners promptly changed its name. Not that the Cutty Sark Tavern is anywhere near the Cutty Sark – in fact the most you can say is that they're both in Greenwich.

Inside, it's the most curious mishmash of bits and pieces you ever did see. The ground-floor bar is dominated by an enormous formal staircase, plonked down apparently at random, and leading up to a comfortable lounge; but there's nothing formal about the bar itself.

Although all knocked into one (by the look of it) some time in the 1970s, it remains a chaotic jumble of nooks and crannies, some floored with stone, others with bare boards; some walled with black oak, others with bare brick; with odd traces of Victorian glass here, bits of ships timber there, and everywhere brass lamps and lanterns of nautical descent which shine with an indescribably kitsch flicker effect. In fact the whole place is an unmissable museum of kitsch, with more nauticalia than all the antique shops of Greenwich put together. The chairs made out of barrels are a fine example: they look great, but don't sit on one if you can avoid it.

OPEN ALL PERMITTED HOURS. FOOD SERVED TO 9 PM. REAL ALES: DRAUGHT BASS, FULLER'S LONDON PRIDE, MORLAND OLD SPECKLED HEN, GUEST.

Turn left out of the pub and follow Thames Path, passing Trinity Hospital, founded in 1616 by Henry Howard, Earl of Northampton, for 21 retired gentlemen of Greenwich.

YACHT
CRANE STREET

It's a surprise, when you enter the Yacht, to discover what an enormous, rambling pub it is. Judging from its unassuming Crane Street frontage, you would expect to find a small old-fashioned tavern, maybe even with an original layout of two or three dark little rooms still intact.

And if you had entered the Yacht before the Blitz, that is exactly what you would have found – as Charles II is reputed to have done; for it was a well-known riverside watering hole as far back as his reign, and if he did not use it himself, courtiers (or their servants) visiting the Queen's House only a short stagger away are bound to have done.

The bomb that blew the old Yacht apart also destroyed a renowned

garden, for when they rebuilt it in 1950 they decided they needed a much bigger pub; and so today's Yacht covers the whole site, with a glassed-in gallery overlooking the Thames where patrons can watch the river rolling by beneath them in comfort, whatever the weather.

Bits and pieces of the old Yacht survive, and the general effect is one of antiquity, with odd nooks and corners, gas-effect lamps, wooden rails and panels, and a clutter of prints and photographs of old Greenwich. But the overall impression is curiously day-tripperish: it's somehow rather like a harbour-front pub in a fairly upmarket seaside resort like Whitby or Padstow. So it's perfectly fitting that the kitchen's speciality should be fish and chips.

OPEN ALL PERMITTED HOURS. FOOD SERVED ALL DAY EXCEPT 4–6 SUNDAY. REAL ALES: THEAKSTON BEST AND OLD PECULIER.

Turn right out of pub.

TRAFALGAR TAVERN
PARK ROW

More like a small stately home than a mere pub, the great bow-fronted Trafalgar gazes down serenely on the Thames as if lost in thought. And it is entirely apt that it should resemble a stately home, for when it was built in 1837 it was intended as a place of resort for the highest in the land.

Whitebait – the fry of herring, doused in flour and deep-fried whole – was a local speciality when Greenwich was little more than a fishing village. It was in season from May to August, just when London was at its least bearable, and from the early years of the 19th century it became enormously popular to take a cruise up the river of a summer's evening to enjoy a whitebait supper in Greenwich. The fashion is supposed to have been started by a member of Pitt's cabinet who had a house in Greenwich and would entertain his colleagues in government to an evening's respite from the city's heat; and the whitebait suppers became grand political occasions, with Tories and Liberals holding rival events.

The arrival of steam launches soon after can have done nothing but help the fashion spread; and as the Ship was doing so well out of the trade, the owners of the Old George – the Commissioners of Greenwich Hospital – decided to go one better by pulling down the 150-year-old inn and building an entirely new pleasure-palace for the well-heeled seekers after whitebait on the site instead.

To do the work, they used their own architect, Joseph Kay, Surveyor of the Hospital (whose brother John just happened to be a successful wine merchant); and the resulting tavern – renamed to commemorate the lying-in-state of Nelson's corpse in the Hospital's Painted Hall on its return, preserved in a barrel of brandy, in 1806 after Trafalgar – was an instant hit.

While the Ship was the venue for Tory whitebait dinners, the Liberals held theirs in the Trafalgar's grand saloon, now the Nelson Room, and capable of holding 250 diners under its eight chandeliers; Gladstone, when in office, used to arrive in a Royal Navy barge.

Not that whitebait dinners were exclusively political affairs: Harrison Ainsworth gave a whitebait supper as a publication party for Mervyn Clitheroe in 1851; a Doré engraving of 1872 shows the Ship crowded with hundreds of revellers; while an article on the subject in *All Year Round*, the magazine Charles Dickens published in the 1860s, reveals what class of people they attracted: "After dinner, by men of the present generation and where ladies are present, claret is generally drunk; but at the great feeds of the City companies, at the testimonial presentation dinners, at the gatherings of eccentrically named clubs – institutions with a superstructure of indulgence springing from a substratum of charity – nothing but East India Brown Sherry and sound port."

Refrigeration did for whitebait suppers in the 1890s: in 1892 a commentator noted that the parties had greatly decreased in numbers and importance now that whitebait could be procured as fresh in the London shops. The Trafalgar lost its Baedeker listing in 1900; the Ship went broke and closed in 1908; and the outbreak of war dealt the Trafalgar its final blow: it, too, closed in 1915. For a while it was a seamen's mission, then a working man's club; it was almost demolished in the '30s, but another war saved its bacon.

Finally, in 1965 it was reopened following a magnificent, and award-

winning, restoration project carried out by Watney's, of all people. Today it is as aristocratic as ever it was, with a suite of lavish grand saloons ranged along the river dripping with decorative moulded plaster, ornate fireplaces, fine oak panelling and all the other embellishments of a late Georgian mansion. Nonetheless, it's still a pub, with proper beer at pub prices, bar food, and friendly bar staff.

If you fancy a touch of grandeur and you can't afford Claridge's, come to the Trafalgar. And yes, whitebait is still on the menu.

OPEN 11.30–11 MONDAY–SATURDAY, 12–10.30 SUNDAY. FOOD SERVED 12–4 MONDAY, 12–10 TUESDAY–SATURDAY, 12–5 SUNDAY. REAL ALES: COURAGE BEST AND DIRECTORS, GUEST ALE FROM FLAGSHIP BREWERY.

Turn left up Park Row, then right through the Naval College Gates. Turn right at far end.

FINISH: GREENWICH PIER.

HAMPSTEAD
"LOVELY-BROWED HAMPSTEAD"

LENGTH OF WALK: THREE MILES

LONDONERS have always been preoccupied with getting out of London – for exercise, for fresh air, for sunlight, for open space, even for clean water, none of which they could be sure of getting in their cramped and dirty city. That's why the capital is ringed round with resorts of all kinds: spas, parks, pleasure gardens, some as close as Sadler's Wells, others as far off as Greenwich. But Hampstead was the best of them all, the one that had everything.

Well into the 19th century Hampstead was still a separate village, with open fields, mainly hay meadows, feeding London's huge population of horses, dividing it from Camden Town. Its 800 acres of Heath were a realm of greenery bigger than the Square Mile itself; its highest point, although a mere 440 feet above sea level, was a good stiff walk for a city dweller who might never normally climb anything higher than a few flights of stairs; and its springs gave pure water, a rare commodity in the polluted city.

Hampstead was a noted spa from the late 17th century, if not an entirely reputable one: one observer commented: "Its nearness to London brings so many loose women in vamped-up clothes to catch the apprentices that modest company are ashamed to appear there." Defoe saw "more gallantry than modesty" at the spa, adding: "Ladies who value their reputation have of late avoided the wells and walks at

173

Hampstead;" and in Samuel Richardson's *Clarissa* (1748), the Upper Flask Tavern (now buried beneath Queen Mary's Hospital) is the scene of the rape of the heroine and "a place where second-rate persons are to be found, often in a swinish condition". It was a reputation that lingered: Dickens, writing about the Gordon Riots in *Barnaby Rudge*, said the Hampstead of 1780 had been so beset by robbers that few would venture there by night alone and unarmed.

Yet Hampstead's natural advantages shone through: as Robert Louis Stevenson put it: "Hampstead is the most delightful place for air and scenery near London." The Romantics in particular came to love it for the beauty of its setting: it was Leigh Hunt, who lived in the Vale of Health from 1815–1821 after his release from gaol for libelling the Prince Regent, who described it as "lovely-browed Hampstead". He wrote several sonnets about it, including the lines:

...A steeple issuing from a leafy rise
with farms, fields in front, and sloping green,
Dear Hampstead, is thy southern face serene.

Hunt is perhaps not so well known now as formerly, but with his network of acquaintances he played a pivotal role in the Romantic movement, entertaining Hazlitt and Charles Lamb and introducing Keats to Shelley.

Keats, however, remains the bard of Hampstead. Much of his tragically short adult life was spent here, first in Well Walk, then in Wentworth Place (now Keats Grove). He met Wordsworth on the Heath in 1817, and Coleridge in 1819, recalling the latter's talk as "far above singing ... about nightingales, poetry, poetical sensation, metaphysics, different genera and species of dreams, a dream accompanied by a sense of touch, a single and a double touch, a dream related."

While living in Wentworth Place, Keats wrote both *Ode to a Nightingale* and *On Melancholy*; he also fell in love with the girl next door, the 18-year-old Fanny Brawne, and got engaged to her. But it was also then that he discovered his tuberculosis, knowing the fatal symptoms all too well, thanks to his two years as a medical student at Guy's Hospital. The Shelleys urged him to seek a cure abroad, but too late: he died in Rome in 1821.

Blake, too, loved Hampstead, frequently visiting the painter John Linnell and his family at Wyldes Farm, now Old Wyldes, in the North

End. Linnell's son-in-law Samuel Palmer recalled: "The aged composer of the *Songs of Innocence* was a great favourite with the children, who revelled in the poems and in his stories of the lovely spiritual things and beings which seemed to him so real and so near... Here Blake might often be found standing at the door to enjoy the summer air, playing with the children, or listening to the simple songs sung by the hostess." Palmer also wrote of cold winter nights, when Blake was wrapped up in a shawl by Mrs Linnell and sent on his homeward way with a servant, lantern in hand, lighting him across the Heath.

Dickens knew Hampstead and the Heath well. He, like Blake, sought a haven at Wyldes Farm with his wife Catherine in 1837 following the death of her sister. The Spaniards (sadly, rather off our beaten track on this walk) features in both *Barnaby Rudge* and *The Pickwick Papers,* and may have been the spot he had in mind when he wrote to his best friend John Forster: "You don't feel disposed, do you, to muffle yourself up and start off with me for a good brisk walk over Hampstead Heath? I know of a good 'ous where we can have a red-hot chop for dinner and a glass of good wine." (Alternatively, it was Jack Straw's Castle – no longer, alas, worth a visit.)

The Heath figures briefly in *Oliver Twist*, too, but not the safe and invigorating Heath of Dickens's walks with John Forster and Wilkie Collins: perhaps recalling the highwayman Jack Sheppard's escape from Newgate and arrest on Finchley Common in 1724, Dickens has Bill Sikes, in flight from Nancy's murder, walking up to Highgate, crossing Caen Wood, and emerging on Hampstead Heath. "Traversing the hollow by the Vale of Health, he mounted the opposite bank, and crossing the road which joins the villages of Hampstead and Highgate, made along the remaining portion of the Heath to the fields at North End, in one of which he laid himself down under a hedge and slept."

Eventually, in the 1880s and 90s, London finally engulfed Hampstead, filling the village with working-class housing. Still, it continued to attract authors who, in many cases, felt they had to be in London but didn't really want to be of it. D H Lawrence and his wife Frieda, for instance, lived in Byron Villas for a few months in 1915, when *The Rainbow* was published. Here they rubbed noses with Aldous Huxley, Bertrand Russell and E M Forster (who described Hampstead, rather patronisingly, as an "artistic and thoughtful little suburb") among others. But Lawrence wasn't happy, writing: "I am so sick in body and soul that if I don't go away I shall die." The sight of a

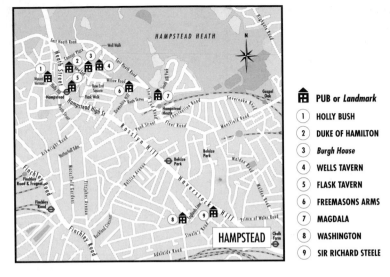

PUB or *Landmark*	
1	HOLLY BUSH
2	DUKE OF HAMILTON
3	*Burgh House*
4	WELLS TAVERN
5	FLASK TAVERN
6	FREEMASONS ARMS
7	MAGDALA
8	WASHINGTON
9	SIR RICHARD STEELE

Zeppelin passing over, and the shocking thought that its crew might well be friends of Frieda's, prompted the couple to flee to Cornwall; but Lawrence was soon back, visiting Katherine Mansfield and her husband (and Lawrence's old friend) John Middleton Murry, and satirising them as Gerald and Gudrun in *Women in Love*.

The list of writers great and not so great who spent periods sometimes of months, sometimes of years, sometimes contentedly, sometimes not, in 'Appy 'Ampstead rolls on, testimony to its semi-rural charm, its inspirational character, and the fact that it was only a few stops down the Northern Line to the great publishing houses of Bedford Square. Edgar Wallace, Stella Gibbons, Compton McKenzie, Daphne du Maurier, Kingsley Amis, J B Priestley, Edwin Muir, Aldous Huxley, John Galsworthy, H G Wells, Stephen Spender, Lytton Strachey, Agatha Christie – all of them have emoted and dominated dinner parties here.

Not all of them loved Hampstead: George Orwell found Willoughby Road depressing enough to use it as the setting for Gordon Comstock's lodgings in *Keep the Aspidistra Flying*. But according to John Braine, writing in *These Golden Days* of sitting outside a High Street café: "I wouldn't be anywhere else. The High Street is a live street, the main street of a village and yet metropolitan, a place where all the action is."

Turn right out of the station and cross Heath Street. Holly Mount is directly opposite; follow it uphill and round to the right.

HOLLY BUSH
22 HOLLY MOUNT

One of Hampstead's landmark pubs, the Holly Bush had been neglected and run down in the late 1990s as the brewery which owned it, fiercely opposed by the local community, tried and failed to get permission to extend it and turn it into yet another chic café-bar. It would have been an outrage had they succeeded, for the Holly Bush has a character entirely its own.

It was originally the stable block to the artist George Romney's

house, and is said to have been built in the 1640s. In 1807, shortly after Romney moved to the Lake District, his house became the local Assembly Rooms, and the old stables were converted into kitchens and servants' quarters. Later still, the Assembly Rooms were taken over by the Literary & Scientific Society, and the stables were sold separately as a tavern – the Holly Bush.

The pub's unassuming exterior merges well into the jumble of houses that fill the surrounding narrow streets of the Mount; but step inside and its true character is revealed. It is a perfectly preserved working-class alehouse of the 1860s, very spartan, all high-backed settles, bare floorboards, matchboard-clad walls and smoke-stained dark ceilings; but with bits and pieces of 1890s ornamentation – such as the two big booths, one at each end – grafted on with a sparing hand. This mixture of styles creates an atmosphere which perfectly suits the historical character of Hampstead, as a largely proletarian quarter speckled with bourgeois artists and writers.

Rescued from its uncertain state by new owners and a lessee prepared to spend some money on it, the Holly Bush looks set for a brighter future. The front bar has been left untouched, except that some of the 1890s features such as the snob-screen, which were shuffled about in a 1960s refurbishment, have been restored to their original position. But a large room upstairs which was a dining-room a century ago is a dining-room once more, specialising in that one-time worker's staple, oysters, and other seafood. Oh, and there are new loos.

OPEN 12–11 MONDAY-SATURDAY, 12–10,30 SUNDAY. FOOD SERVED ALL DAY. REAL ALES: ADNAM'S BITTER AND BROADSIDE, FULLER'S LONDON PRIDE, BENSKIN'S BITTER.

From the pub carry straight on and go down a set of steps to your left. Cross Heath Street, turn left, then right into New End.

DUKE OF HAMILTON
23–25 NEW END

One's first impression on entering this fairly large early Victorian back-street local is of brightness and cheerfulness. It's not a grand pub, but it's an exceptionally comfortable one in an Edwardian-parlour sort of way, with carpets rather than bare boards, upholstered benches rather than wooden ones, and plenty of light and colour rather than the common all-wood look which can get very dingy if it's allowed to.

There aren't many original features left: the bar-back has some nice engraved glass, and there are fireplaces at each end which show by their location how the pub was once divided, and by their character (one is marble, the other is modestly tiled) which end was the saloon and which the public.

What the Duke of Hamilton has, if it has little of historical or architectural interest, is the warm, cheering atmosphere which can only be generated by a popular and respected landlord and a friendly crowd at the bar. It has excellent beer, too: it' been a regular entry in the *Good Beer Guide* for years, and was local Pub of the Year not so long ago. (It also used to have Oliver Reed as a regular: his picture hangs on the wall.)

The little theatre next door used to be the morgue for the former hospital (now flats) across the road. Coroner's inquests were often held in the pub.

OPEN 12–11 (10.30 SUNDAY). BAR SNACKS 12–2.
REAL ALES: FULLER'S LONDON PRIDE, ESP, AND SEASONAL SPECIAL;
GUEST ALE; TRADITIONAL DRAUGHT CIDER.

Turn left out of the pub and walk straight down New End into New End Square.

HAMPSTEAD MUSEUM

Hampstead's Museum is sited in a Queen Anne mansion, Burgh House, which in the 1720s was home to William Gibbons, a doctor who did much to promote the curative properties of the spa's waters.

OPEN WEDNESDAY–SUNDAY NOON–5; CALL 0207 431 0144 FOR DETAILS.

Turn left into Well Walk.

WELLS TAVERN
WELL WALK

"Gone are the wells and the dandies, but the Wells Tavern lives on", wrote Louis Stanley in the 1950s; but not, it seems likely, for much longer.

The Wells Tavern was built in 1837 on the site of two much older houses. One of them had been an alehouse known at different times as the Green Man and the Whitestone Tavern (after Whitestone Pond at the top of the hill). The other was a postman's cottage in which John Keats and his brothers briefly lodged in 1817–18.

By that time, Hampstead's days as a vogueish spa with its "good music and dancing all day" were pretty much over, and this was a well-to-do upper middle-class street, lined with elms and limes, whose residents included John Constable and Tennyson's mother.

The Wells Tavern, as can be guessed from its sober, not to say dignified, exterior was intended to attract the servants and tradesmen dependent upon the street's respectable inhabitants. It would most certainly not have offered the doubtless improper "accommodation for water-drinkers of both sexes" which earlier spa taverns had proudly proclaimed. Inside, if it was typical, it would have been divided into strictly segregated bars and parlours in which house servants need not have mixed with outdoors men such as grooms and gardeners. But all this is guesswork, for although comfortable and pleasant enough, and evidently popular with a good local crowd, the pub has had every original feature gradually refurbished out of it over the years.

Now its owner, a local charitable trust, has decreed that to maximise its revenues it must sell the landlord's flat above the pub separately as a private flat. This will mean two things: that the manager must live off the premises, which always seems to have a depersonalising effect on a pub; and that the trade kitchen must be moved downstairs, which locals fear will swallow up so much space that the resulting pub will no longer be viable. So visit the Wells Tavern while you may, and raise a glass to Keats.

OPEN ALL PERMITTED HOURS. FOOD SERVED 12–5. REAL ALES: GREENE KING IPA, ADNAM'S BITTER, FULLER'S LONDON PRIDE.

Return along Well Walk and carry straight on into Flask Walk.

FLASK TAVERN
FLASK WALK

The Flask is another working-class boozer which, like the Holly Bush, has been apotheosised by lovers both of Hampstead and of Victorian pubs.

It's not to be confused with the former Upper Flask, though. This was the inn where the whiggish Kit-Kat club – Addison, Steele, Pope, Vanbrugh and Congreve were members – met in the shade of a mulberry tree. Dr Johnson stayed at the Upper Flask while writing *The Vanity of Human Wishes* and described the Kit-Kat (named after a mutton pie) as the best club that ever existed. It's also where Lovelace

rapes Clarissa in Samuel Richardson's novel.

During the Upper Flask's heyday, the pub we now know as the Flask was called the Thatched House; after it was pulled down and rebuilt in 1874 it was renamed the Lower Flask, contracting to its present form when the Upper Flask was demolished to make way for Queen Mary's Hospital.

Like the Holly Bush, it's a no-frills two-room boozer but with the odd ornamental flourish inserted a few years later to update it. There is decorative tilework on the facade, and a tiled dado in the public bar; and one wonders whether the regulars of the 1880s complained

about the division of the bars by the acid-etched glass partition with its sentimental oleographs as loudly as modern conservationists object to such transformations as have afflicted the King of Bohemia in the High Street?

In 1990 the pub was extended by the addition of a back bar and a conservatory-dining-room, which remain an object lesson to developers in how to add new to old without jarring.

OPEN ALL PERMITTED HOURS. FOOD SERVED 12–3 AND 6–8.30 TUESDAY–FRIDAY; 12–4 AND 6–8.30 SATURDAY; 12-4 SUNDAY AND MONDAY. REAL ALES: YOUNG'S RANGE.

Turn left out of the pub and then left again down Hampstead High Street and Rosslyn Hill. Turn left into Downshire Hill.

FREEMASONS ARMS
DOWNSHIRE HILL

The southern slopes of Hampstead are a very different proposition from the tangled, narrow knot of lanes and alleys in the old village. Here we are in a quarter of broad leafy avenues lined with elegant bow-fronted Regency villas with wrought-iron railings and balconies and Gothic windows; and as one might expect, the handsome, spacious Freemasons is no humble working-class local.

The present pub was actually built from scratch in the 1930s, its

early 19th-century predecessor – described in 1919 as "a smallish box of a building covered with creeper" – having been found structurally unsound, thanks to a tributary of the Fleet flowing under it, and demolished. But the architects, builders and fitters of the new Freemasons did a worthy job which puts much of the pub design of the period (and, indeed, of today) to shame.

Outside, its clean lines and Regency windows complement its neighbours perfectly; and while inside it's actually a single big T-shaped room – railway-compartment bars, elaborately glazed partitions, and private booths having by then gone right out of fashion – there's nothing remotely barn-like about it.

Its three separate spaces are defined by subtly different gradations of decor ranging from moderately plain to moderately elaborate (there are no extremes of anything at the Freemasons) broken up by glazed pine screens, but with elegantly pale panelling and a rather

incongruous quarry-tiled floor creating a unity.

Its food and wine offerings are appropriately upmarket for its *Daily Telegraph*-reading clientele, but the Freemasons hasn't forgotten that it's a pub: children are ostentatiously welcomed; the ale is well-kept; and there's even a skittle-alley – not just a common-or-garden skittle-alley, mind (there is nothing common-or-garden at the Freemasons), but a London skittle-alley, where heavy cheeses of lignum vitae are not rolled at the hornbeam pins but hurled at them.

OPEN 12–11 (10.30 SUNDAY). FOOD SERVED 12–10.
REAL ALES: TETLEY BITTER, DRAUGHT BASS.

Turn left out of the pub and right into South End Road. Keats's House is to the right in Keats Grove.

KEATS'S HOUSE

Keats lived in Wentworth Place (now Keats Grove) from 1818–1820, where he wrote *Ode To A Nightingale* and met his fiancée Fanny Brawne.

OPEN 10–1, 2–6 MONDAY–FRIDAY; 10–1, 2–5 SATURDAY, 10–1 SUNDAY
APRIL–OCTOBER. OTHERWISE 2–5.

Return to South End Road; turn right and then left into South Hill Park.

MAGDALA
2A SOUTH HILL PARK

Robert Napier is an unfortunate fellow. A hero of the Indian Mutiny and other Imperialist adventures, he was famous enough in his day to be awarded a statue in Trafalgar Square. Now the Mayor of London suggests its removal to free the plinth for some more memorable subject, on the grounds that he's never heard of him.

If the suggestion is taken up, Napier will still have his memorial here, however, for Magdala was an Ethiopian fort he destroyed in 1868 (he got raised to the peerage for it, too, as Lord Napier of Magdala). But why, other than because it was there and there were no other wars on at the time? Few can remember, and it's probably no good asking the Mayor. Nonetheless, his victory is memorialised by a singularly hideous ceramic landscape (presumably of Magdala) in the lobby.

The Magdala — a big and rather gaunt pub, with little decoration other than the green marble columns dividing the upper-story Venetian windows — is far more famous as the scene on Easter Sunday 1955 of the shooting by Ruth Ellis of her abusive and faithless lover, David Blakeley, as he came out of the pub. The mitigating facts — that she had a small son, that she was being treated for depression, that Blakeley had beaten her badly enough to cause a miscarriage, that she had been egged on by another admirer who actually gave her the gun to do the shooting with — were not even allowed to delay her ascension to the scaffold: her hanging followed with indecent haste just three months after the crime, and was the last hanging of a woman in Britain.

The Magdala used to celebrate the episode: odd bits of damage to the pub's tiled fascia were pointed out, rather questionably, as bullet holes, and framed copies of her death warrant and death certificate were displayed indoors, along with another of her last letter from Holloway and a glamour shot from her days as a night-club hostess.

A recently-installed management decided, along no doubt with many others, that all this was distasteful, even ghoulish: the event was too recent and the injustice too great to be used as a marketing device, and all the memorabilia save one small notice recounting the bare facts of the case were swept away.

Instead, the Magdala was reinvented as a rather smart, understated, two-room pub, very cool and light and airy, with pale panelled walls and pictures of old Hampstead. There's a calm and uncluttered lounge bar, and a bigger room with French windows opening on to a pleasant garden. In the rather unlovely surroundings of south Hampstead, the Magdala is something of an oasis.

Open all permitted hours. Food served 12–3, 6.30–10 Monday–Friday; 12–10 Saturday; 12–9.30 Sunday.
Real ales: Greene King IPA, Fuller's London Pride.

Cross South End Square and turn right up Pond Street, then left down Haverstock Hill. Cross Haverstock Hill and turn right into England's Lane.

THE WASHINGTON
ENGLAND'S LANE

England's Lane provides a calm haven from the mad traffic of Haverstock Hill, with its south side lined with flats of about 1910 (including a sub-Lutyens cottage in which Arthur Rackham lived), and its north side consisting of a couple of rather grand Italianate parades of the 1860s. At the far end of the second of these is the stately Washington, originally a hotel, with its fascia of rusticated quoins, huge sash windows, and black marble columns with fancy gold-painted capitals.

If the pub's exterior is of the classically-minded mid-19th century, its interior is triumphantly 1890s. Actually it can be fairly accurately dated, since the gilded and brilliant-cut glazing in the doorway uses a staining process introduced by the firm of Walter Gibbs in 1891. There are mirrors of engraved glass, and another painted with a riverbank scene; there is a partition of pitch-pine and acid-etched glass screening the public bar; there is a curious canopy around the elaborate bar with panels of brilliant-cut glass in it (and, sadly, with some of its supports rather brutally sawn away); there is a magnificent plaster ceiling painted dark green, with equally ornate cornices picked out in cream; there are heavy drapes framing the big sash windows.

Oddly, some of these elements seem to have been jumbled about during some previous refurbishment, so although it's all the right stuff, some of it appears to be in the wrong place. You could spend hours working out how it's all meant to fit together.

By the strangest coincidence, the present landlord, a gentleman named Tidy, discovered after moving into the Washington that he is descended from the builder who originally developed the surrounding streets, which were once known as Tidytown. The Washington is named, according to a local researcher, not after George Washington at all but after the Sussex village the developer originally came from.

OPEN 10–1 MONDAY–FRIDAY; 12–10.30 SUNDAY. FOOD 10–10 MONDAY–FRIDAY, 12–10 SUNDAY. REAL ALES: IND COOPE BURTON ALE, DRAUGHT BASS, GREENE KING IPA, ADNAM'S BITTER, FULLER'S LONDON PRIDE.

Return to Haverstock Hill and turn right.

SIR RICHARD STEELE
HAVERSTOCK HILL

What a fantastic pub to end the walk with! Big and plain from outside, the interior of this 1870s street-corner pub is a treasure-trove of bric-à-brac – and not the kind of warehouse stuff sold by weight to give a spurious sense of age to yet another Victorian-pastiche refurbishment, either, but the real McCoy, collected over the years – some of it donated by customers – and placed with wit and aplomb.

The place is festooned with prints, photographs, drawings, paintings (including some oils worth valuing and restoring), stone busts, typewriters, mincers, irons, sewing machines, clocks, toys, enamel advertisements, railway signs, mirrors, bottles, books by the thousand – even a child's dogcart hanging from the ceiling over a fireplace, with a plaster hand trailing languidly over its side. This is bric-à-brac with attitude.

Now look at the ceiling. It's not just the dark pressed-paper you'd expect, but a Renaissance pastiche of heroic proportions, skilfully and laboriously painted by an enterprising young artist who worked at it for over three months, erecting his scaffolding once the regulars had departed and toiling on through the night until their return. Many of them are actually in it, as are several of the politicians who were in the news at the time (it was an election year).

It all gives style and humour to a pub which would probably have been scraped out and given a standard pattern-book refurbishment if it had been owned by some big brewery or pub company, rather than by a private individual with a well-developed sense of the bizarre. (The lead-light windows with their single band of pale green stained glass indicate that this was once a Charrington's house, but luckily they sold it before they ruined it.)

And the pub itself deserves the attention that has been lavished on it: originally built principally as a concert room, it's named after the journalist and playwright Sir Richard Steele (1672–1729), whose house was nearby (Steeles Lane is the next street). The enormous public bar was clearly divided into as many as three or four rooms back in the 1890s, from when many of the surviving decorative features date, but when it was all opened out in the 1960s or 70s two cosy little snugs were fortunately left at the back.

Steele, who was born in Dublin, was an ex-soldier who married into a fortune, was widowed, was knighted, blew the fortune, married again, and was widowed again. Both a moraliser and a spendthrift, he co-founded both the *Tatler* and the *Spectator* with Addison and ended his life hiding from his creditors in Carmarthen, his second wife's home town. A fixture of coffee-house society in the reigns of Queen Anne and George I, he was later rather unfairly described by Dr Johnson as "the most agreeable rake that ever trod the realms of indulgence". Although the fantastic stained-glass window to Steele in a corner of the pub, dating to about 1900, makes him out to be rather more saintly than he was, he was a serious journalist and a leading intellectual of his day.

Recently, a skull thought to be his has been discovered in Carmarthen. The landlady is planning to make an offer for it.

OPEN ALL PERMITTED HOURS. NO FOOD. REAL ALES: MORLAND OLD SPECKLED HEN, FLOWER'S ORIGINAL, GREENE KING IPA, ADNAM'S BITTER.

Turn right out of the pub and continue down Haverstock Hill.

FINISH: CHALK FARM TUBE

SOHO
DIRTILY PLEASANT

LENGTH OF WALK: ONE-AND-A-HALF MILES

A FRIEND who used to work on Titbits magazine once told me that it was house style always to refer to Soho as "London's glittering West End". The aim was to evoke all the glamour of West End theatre, the film industry in Wardour Street, and the nightclubs and restaurants that went with them; but to most people, Soho meant sex. The Windmill Theatre with its non-stop nude revue (never review) was the evil epicentre, trailing its muddy swirl of dirty bookshops, seedy strip-clubs, and little neon lights in upstairs windows saying "model".

"The devious, vicious, dirtily-pleasant exoticism of Soho" was H G Wells's description; a pithier summary could not be imagined. It's certainly devious and vicious, as anything that involves gangsters, prostitutes and drugs must be. But the dirtiness of it is pleasant, too, in a very British way. It's smutty rather than hard-core; naughty rather than depraved. In fact, it's rather like 1960s school food: stodgy, not at all spicy, and appealing only to the very, very hungry.

As for the exoticism – well, thereby hangs the story of Soho.

In medieval times the area was crown land, mostly used for hunting. But after the Restoration a needy Charles II saw a way of turning this conveniently-sited property into a source of cash by granting leases: some to courtiers who wanted mansions within easy reach of Westminster, others to entrepreneurs who saw a potential for humbler development. Among the former was Charles's bastard son, the Duke of Monmouth, who built a grand house on the south side of today's Soho Square. It was the latter class, however, which set the tone. After the Great Fire there was huge demand among City merchants for newer, more spacious homes, and as quickly as the grand mansions had gone up they began to be pulled down to make way for much denser housing. The builders of the new Soho ranged from large-scale developers like Colonel Panton, who built Coventry Street, Rupert Street, Whitcomb Street, Oxendon Street and Panton Street, to small men like John Meard, a carpenter who built Meard Street in 1692.

In 1685 Louis XIV revoked the religious freedom of French Protestants, and within three years 14,000 had fled to London, many settling in Spitalfields but others arriving in the building site that was Soho. It was on this that Soho's reputation for "exoticism" was founded, for the first wave of continental migrants was followed by many others, like the refugees from the Ottoman-controlled Balkans who gave Greek Street its name. Much of Soho remained well-heeled throughout the 18th century, but the influx of penniless Europeans saw most of the fine houses slide into multiple occupancy, being carved up into ever smaller units: the final divorce between affluent Mayfair and shabby Soho came in 1825 when Nash chose to build Regent Street along the line of Swallow Street, which he saw as "a boundary and complete separation between the streets and squares occupied by the nobility and gentry, and the narrower streets and meaner houses occupied by mechanics".

Among the steady stream of Europeans arriving in Soho there came, in 1849–50, 1,000-odd refugees from the failed revolutions of 1848. Among them was Karl Marx, who rented "an old hovel – two evil frightful rooms" at 28 Dean Street from 1850–56. There he lived on handouts from Engels while writing *Das Kapital* and impregnating both his wife and their maid. The collapse of the Paris Commune in 1872 brought Verlaine and Rimbaud to Soho too, to shared lodgings in Old Compton Street.

As immigrants often do, many of Soho's foreigners turned to the catering trade – Kettner's in Romilly Street was founded by Napoleon III's chef in 1867 – and a cosmopolitan social life based largely on French and Italian restaurants, and on the growing number of theatres around Leicester Square, began to develop. G K Chesterton, Hilaire Belloc, John Masefield, Joseph Conrad, John Galsworthy, and Ford Madox Ford formed a regular coterie at the Mont Blanc restaurant in Gerrard Street;

while Oscar Wilde would entertain young men upstairs at Kettner's, where the Prince of Wales and Lily Langtry also had their trysts.

The film business moved into Wardour Street in the 1920s. Nightclubs followed, with 150 of them in Soho in the 1920s and '30s. This brash, hedonistic demi-monde proved the ideal milieu for London's vice industry. Cocaine was very much part of the Soho interwar scene, and prostitution was also growing: prostitutes had largely been moved off the streets of theatre-land before the First World War, and the founders of the Soho sex industry were the ex-Haymarket girls who started operating out of upstairs apartments in the 1920s. Often – and here we return to Soho's "exoticism" – they pretended to be French. Often they actually were French – or Belgian, or Italian, or Spanish; victims of a trade in young women orchestrated by the local vice gang, the Sicilian Messina Brothers.

After the war, Soho became notorious for its self-regarding coterie of young Bohemian writers and artists, many of them as celebrated for their intake as their output. Undoubted geniuses like Francis Bacon and Dylan Thomas attracted lesser geniuses who won fame by glamorising them, and who were in turn glamorised by lesser talents still – journalists. It was a wasting asset, and when the seedy '70s came along Soho found it had precious few geniuses left and a sex industry which, thanks to heroin, had become seamier and seamier – still dirty, but no longer pleasant.

A slump in property prices and tougher regulation stemmed directly from this downward spiral and, in time, halted it. A new wave of restaurateurs moved in, lured both by cheap premises and Soho's cachet, to be followed in the '90s by a tide of style bars. The vice industry is still there, if less so than formerly. The exotic is still there, too – the Gay Hussar, a dwindling number of French patisseries such as Maison Bertaux in Greek Street and Patisserie Valerie in Old Compton Street, the Huguenot Church in Soho Square, a dense and vibrant Chinatown around Lisle Street. The film industry and the nightclubs are also still there – and so are some wonderful pubs.

START: LEICESTER SQUARE TUBE STATION

Use Exit 2. Turn left up Charing Cross Road and immediately left again into Little Newport Street, then right up Newport Court, left into Gerrard Street, and right into Macclesfield Street.

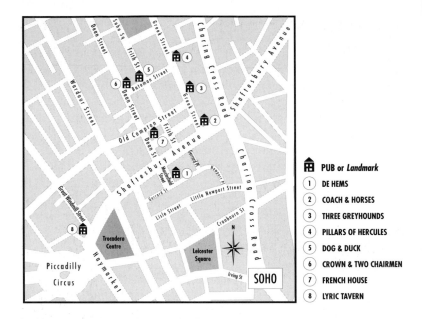

PUB or *Landmark*
1. DE HEMS
2. COACH & HORSES
3. THREE GREYHOUNDS
4. PILLARS OF HERCULES
5. DOG & DUCK
6. CROWN & TWO CHAIRMEN
7. FRENCH HOUSE
8. LYRIC TAVERN

DE HEMS
11 MACCLESFIELD STREET

De Hems, like the French House which we will visit later in this tour, is a fine illustration of Soho's old appeal to emigrés.

It stands on the site of a coaching inn called the Horse & Dolphin, built in 1685 on a plot leased to Charles Gerrard, Lord Macclesfield. The name survives in Horse & Dolphin Yard, but the inn itself was pulled down in 1890 by a private entrepreneur named Crimmen, who commissioned the great pub architects Savile & Martin to build its replacement, named the Macclesfield.

Soon after, the pub was bought by a retired Dutch sea captain called De Hem, who reinvented it as an oyster bar, charging a shilling and fourpence ha'penny for a dozen oysters, brown bread and butter and a glass of stout. Instead of throwing away the shells, he covered the walls with 300,000 of them in a nacreous grotto which probably looked as hideous as it sounds. These were later transferred to the restaurant upstairs which became known as the Shell Room, and were finally consigned to the skip in the 1950s.

De Hems, as the Macclesfield became known, rapidly became a

rendezvous not only for the Dutch community but also for a literary set, one of whose number, George R Simms, penned the following.

When oysters to September yield
And grace the grottoed Macclesfield,
I will be there, my dear De Hem,
To wish you well and sample them.

De Hem died after World War I, but the Macclesfield retained its Dutch links and became a rendezvous for refugees from the Netherlands in World War II. Its name was formally changed to De Hems in 1959, and in the 1980s it was redesigned along the lines of a Dutch or Flemish "brown bar" or city beerhouse. There's a good range of Dutch and Belgian beers in bottle and on tap, with imported Oranjeboom lager from Breda rather than the British-brewed version, and strong Abbey beers such as Chimay and Orval for the unwary (or the knowledgeable). A number of Dutch items such as Bitterballen (meatballs), Frikkadelle sausages, and Bittergarnitur – a kind of Dutch tapas – appear on the menu. There is also a range of Dutch genevers, very different from English gin and drunk short and very cold, like schnapps.

For all that, the building itself retains its identity as an 1890s London pub, with its dark wood panelling, its tiled cast-iron fireplace, its marble bar-top, and its high Lincrusta ceiling.

OPEN 12–12 MONDAY–SATURDAY, 12–10.30 SUNDAY. FOOD ALL DAY.
NO REAL ALE. DUTCH AND BELGIAN BEER SELECTION.

Turn right out of the pub, cross Shaftesbury Avenue,
and turn left up Greek Street.

THE COACH & HORSES
29 GREEK STREET

The Coach & Horses has become Soho's, if not London's, best-known pub thanks to its superlatively grouchy landlord Norman Balon – catchphrase: "F*** off, you're barred" – and a clientele of boozy journalists of the old school.

The rather plain street-corner pub dates to 1847, but before that there had been a posting house of the same name on the site for over a century, nicknamed the Iron House because of its unusual wrought-iron railings.

As a simple beerhouse, the Coach might have escaped media notice for good had it not attracted the custom of renowned Soho drinkers such as Francis Bacon, the cartoonist Michael Heath, and the journalist Jeffrey Bernard, "Low Life" in the *Spectator*, whose frequent absences owing to alcohol were explained by a terse "Jeffrey Bernard is unwell". Bernard died in 1997, but he was outlived by Keith Waterhouse's dramatisation of his later years – entitled, naturally, *Jeffrey Bernard Is Unwell* – in which he was played by an actor who knew a thing or two about booze, Peter O'Toole.

The satirical magazine *Private Eye,* which is based round the corner in Carlisle Street, holds its fortnightly lunches upstairs, and it is said to be Norman Balon's joke to ambush literary demigods such as

Germaine Greer and Melvyn Bragg on their way upstairs by suddenly yelling at the top of his voice: "Oi - where d'you think you're going!?"

(Actually, there's another side to Norman: for many years he chaired the local Licensed Victuallers Association, ably representing fellow landlords in disputes with their breweries and tirelessly raising funds for charity. But he'd probably rather you didn't know that.)

Worth a visit whether there are any drunken journos slumped over the bar or not, the Coach is a pleasantly airy but simple beerhouse, divided into three by turn-of-the-century pale deal partitions.

OPEN ALL PERMITTED HOURS. NO FOOD. REAL ALES: IND COOPE BURTON ALE, MARSTON'S PEDIGREE, FULLER'S LONDON PRIDE.

Turn right out of the pub and continue along Greek Street.

THREE GREYHOUNDS
25 GREEK STREET

On the face of it a straightforward Olde English pub of 1910 or thereabouts, the mock-Tudor exterior of the Three Greyhounds with its fake timbering, leaded casements, small gables and big lanterns hides a mystery: where is Roxy Beaujolais?

According to Angus McGill, the London *Evening Standard*'s pub guru, Miss Beaujolais took over this unassuming street corner pub in 1992 and set about transforming it, bringing "glamour, oysters, cocktails, interesting snacks, cosmopolitan customers" and white curtains which she ran up herself, as well as some stuffed piranhas which one of the cosmopolitan customers apparently half-inched.

Well, there's no trace of oysters or white curtains now, and the surprisingly tiny bar betrays no sign that they were ever there. Instead, the Three Greyhounds has reverted to type: its stone-flagged floor, wooden settles, pleasant fireplace, rough-plastered walls and spurious beams overhead could have been there for years. The only incongruous hints of modernity are a couple of cast-iron garden seats doing duty as benches, and they don't exactly sound like Roxy Beaujolais' style.

OPEN 12–11 MONDAY–SATURDAY, 3–10.30 SUNDAY. FOOD SERVED 12–3. REAL ALES: ADNAM'S BITTER, FULLER'S LONDON PRIDE, DRAUGHT BASS, TETLEY.

Turn right out of the pub and continue along Greek Street.

PILLARS OF HERCULES
7 GREEK STREET

Like the Three Greyhounds, the Pillars is an Olde English pub of 1910 or thereabouts, with fake half-timbering in spades.

Inside, it retains much of its original layout and many original features: there's a fine bar-back with twisted columns and a little clock; there are wood-panelled walls and bare floorboards; there are alcoves with glass screens; and there's a tiny snug to one side of the front door. It's all very dim and cosy in a mock-Dickensian way – but

it wasn't a bit like that when Dickens actually knew it.

Before the present pub was built, there had been an earlier Pillars of Hercules on the site since 1733, and Dickens included it in *A Tale Of Two Cities* (1859). Dr Manette's house is based on the House of St Barnabas in Soho at 1 Greek Street, now a women's hostel; and Manette Street alongside the pub is named in the character's honour.

Francis Thompson, the cricket-loving but opium-addicted poet, was rescued, destitute, dead drunk, and collapsed in the doorway of the Pillars of Hercules one night in 1888 by Wilfred Meynell, editor of *Merry England*. When the two discovered they were both Catholics – a kind of freemasonry so soon after the Emancipation – Meynell compounded his act of charity by publishing Thompson's work. Thompson had been sleeping rough underneath the arches at Charing Cross, later writing in *The Kingdom of Heaven* of "Jacob's Ladder, pitched between Heaven and Charing Cross".

More recently Martin Amis, Julian Barnes and Ian McEwan were regulars.

OPEN ALL PERMITTED HOURS. FOOD SERVED ALL DAY. REAL ALES: COURAGE DIRECTORS, THEAKSTON BEST, MARSTON'S PEDIGREE, TWO GUEST ALES.

Cross Greek Street and turn left. Turn right into Bateman Street.

DOG & DUCK
FRITH STREET

One of the most exquisite small 1890s pub interiors in London is to be found behind the workaday yellow brick and black marble facade of the Dog & Duck.

This was one of the earliest residential streets to be laid out in Soho, and stands in the grounds of the mansion built by the Duke of Monmouth, which was acquired by Lord Bateman shortly after the Duke's execution. (The house itself was demolished in 1773.)

A pub of this name, recalling Soho's past as a royal hunting ground, was recorded in 1743, and Mozart, Constable and Dante Gabriel

Rosetti may all have drunk in it, or at least passed its doors, since they all lived or stayed at one time or another in Frith Street.

The original pub was pulled down in 1897 and rebuilt by the architect Francis Chambers, who smothered the interior in ceramic tiles, many of them bearing a dog-and-duck motif, and decorative mirrors, including a huge one in a tiled surround surmounting the marble fireplace at one end of the tiny bar.

It's nothing like Orwell's fictional *Moon Under Water,* yet Orwell was a regular and was evidently fond of it, for here he celebrated the news that the American Book of the Month Club had chosen *The* as its top title. The landlord of the Dog & Duck had "mysteriously acquired a cache of real absinthe", and although sugar was rationed he allowed Orwell and his friends to drink it the traditional way, with water dripped slowly on to it through a sugar cube.

OPEN 12–1 MONDAY–FRIDAY, 5–11 SATURDAY, 6–10.30 SUNDAY. NO FOOD. REAL ALES: FULLER'S LONDON PRIDE, TIMOTHY TAYLOR LANDLORD, ADNAM'S BROADSIDE, TETLEY, DRAUGHT BASS, SHEPHERD NEAME SPITFIRE.

Cross Frith Street and continue along Bateman Street.

204

THE CROWN & TWO CHAIRMEN

31 DEAN STREET

I hate to pooh-pooh a good story, but I simply can't believe the supposed derivation of the Crown & Two Chairmen's name.

The story goes that Sir James Thornhill lived opposite, and when Queen Anne dropped by to have her portrait painted at his studio, her sedan-chair carriers waited for her in the pub that then stood on this site. It's the sort of story that can neither be proved nor disproved, but stinks of the apocryphal.

For a start, there are other pubs called the Two Chairmen – it's a

fairly straightforward sort of a name for a servants' tavern, of which there were plenty. Secondly, would the Queen have called on Thornhill? He did paint her, we know: his portrait of her hangs in the House of Commons. But wouldn't he have called on her? And thirdly, combination names like this are normally evidence that at some point in the past two licences have been combined – an explanation which I, being an old spoilsport, prefer.

Don't let that put you off the Crown & Two Chairmen, though: it's a plain but cosy pub, with bare boards and flagstones, heavy beams and a snug wood-panelled side bar.

One story that is true is that Thackeray and the illustrator G A Sala first met here, at a time when the landlord, Dicky Moreland, was renowned for his antique costume of top-boots and pigtail. Thackeray, recalled Sala, treated the clientele to a rendition of The Mahogany Tree. Karl Marx may have drunk here: he lived in two squalid rooms above Quo Vadis next door in the 1850s.

OPEN 12–11 MONDAY–SATURDAY, 2PM–10.30 SUNDAY. FOOD SERVED 12–3 MONDAY–SATURDAY. REAL ALES: YOUNG'S BITTER, TETLEY, ADNAM'S BITTER, FULLER'S LONDON PRIDE.

Turn left out of the pub

FRENCH HOUSE
DEAN STREET

More evidence of H G Wells's "exoticism" is provided by the famous French House which – despite the circuitous route of this walk – is actually within sight of De Hems.

Until 1900 or thereabouts, this was a perfectly unexceptional pub, the York Minster, probably dating from the 1840s or 50s. Then it was taken over by a German grocer and wine-shipper, a Herr Schmitt, under whose name it traded until 1914, when Germans became suddenly unpopular. No-one knows what happened to Schmitt, but he sold it to a Belgian, Victor Berlemont, who had worked in the kitchen of Escoffier himself. When Herr Schmitt got fed up with bricks through his windows Berlemont was working in the next-door restaurant and presumably made him an offer he couldn't refuse.

Maison Berlemont, as the York Minster was renamed, was an instant hit both with the large local Francophone population and with the swarms of refugees arriving from Belgium. By 1918 Victor had built up such a reputation that in the 1920s and 30s the restaurant became a magnet for foreign stars, especially French ones, visiting the West End. The walls are lined with framed photographs of visitors such as Maurice Chevalier and the boxer Georges Carpentier.

The French connection continued during the war, when French officers made a beeline for the one place they'd heard of. Among them was Charles de Gaulle: here he assembled a nucleus of like-minded officers who refused to accept defeat; here his ringing declaration "A Tous Les Français" rejecting Vichy, was penned (a copy still hangs in the bar); here the Free French government and army were founded.

The flying bomb which virtually destroyed St Anne's Church opposite also took out the pub's Victorian frontage, including the rather pretty shopfront the Berlemonts had inherited from Herr Schmitt. The cost of rebuilding forced Victor to sell out to a brewery (and the rebuilding the sale financed, it has to be said, was rather niggardly); but, sensibly, the new owners allowed his son Gaston – born in the pub in 1914 – to take over the reins when Victor retired.

Under Gaston the pub – now officially the York Minster again, but known to all as the French Pub – became, along with such raffish venues as Muriel Belcher's Colony Room just up the street, one of the garrisons of the Soho Bohos. There were great names such as Brendan Behan, Dylan Thomas (who left the only typescript of *Under Milk Wood* under a bench one drunken night; fortunately Gaston rescued it for him), Francis Bacon, Nina Hamnett and Dan Farson as well as a whole host of lesser-known artists, writers and journalists who found in the French Pub, in Gaston, and in a number of long-serving staff, a home from home and a second family.

When Gaston retired aged 75 on Bastille Day 1989, no-one knew what would happen to the French Pub. It was even rumoured that the brewery had sold it to the porn king, Paul Raymond. Sensibly (and few breweries hold a record for doing the right thing twice in a row), the brewery let it to a couple of journalists who were already regulars and who changed as little as they could. They refurbished the restaurant and loos and, apart from one rather mystifying alteration, left it at that.

The mystifying bit was an official change of name from the York

Minster. True, nobody used it, and there was one occasion of genuine confusion when a consignment of wine addressed to the York Minster, Dean Street, was delivered to the Dean of York Minster, who very sportingly sent it on to the correct address. But why choose a new name – the French House – which was never, and still is never, uttered by anybody? The French Pub it always was and it always will be.

OPEN 12–11 MONDAY SATURDAY, 12–10.30 SUNDAY. RESTAURANT OPEN 12–3, 6.30–MIDNIGHT MONDAY–SATURDAY. NO REAL ALE.

Turn left out of the pub and right into Old Compton Street.
Cross into Brewer Street and turn left into Great Windmill Street.

LYRIC TAVERN
37 GREAT WINDMILL STREET

To reach the last stop on our tour of Soho we have hurried through Brewer Street, the tacky core of the peep-show and sex-shop trade; and it's a relief to arrive at a reassuringly ordinary pub where both vice and all those self-laudatory Bohemian drunks are securely shut outside.

Not one but two pubs, the Windmill and the Ham (after Ham Yard next door) stood on the site in 1739. A hundred and fifty years later the two were knocked into one but, to avoid confusion, it kept both names and was the Windmill & Ham for a very brief period. In 1892 the old buildings were pulled down and an entirely new pub was built in their place. At the same time the Lyric theatre was a-building opposite, and the new pub took the same name (although the landlord swears that the pub was called the Lyric before the theatre was; and as the theatre undoubtedly took longer to build than the pub, he may be right).

The Lyric has changed little since. It has a nicely-carved wooden bow-fronted fascia, whose lobby has a quarry-tile floor and green-tiled walls; and inside there is a single big bar with wooden panelling, etched glass, and dark pressed-paper ceiling, with an open fire to warm it.

The same cannot be said of the theatre. It changed its name soon after World War I to become the notorious Windmill with its naked *poses plastiques* (because the Lord Chamberlain would only allow nudes provided they didn't move), its topless fan-dancers (whose whirling fans occasionally slipped, to the thrill of the audience), and its daring revues whose proud boast was that throughout the war, "we never closed".

OPEN ALL PERMITTED HOURS. SANDWICHES SERVED ALL DAY.
REAL ALES: COURAGE BEST AND DIRECTORS.

Continue down Great Windmill Street and turn left into Shaftesbury Avenue. Turn right into Charing Cross Road.

FINISH: LEICESTER SQUARE TUBE STATION

OXFORD STREET
AVOIDING OXFORD STREET

LENGTH OF WALK: ONE-AND-THREE-QUARTER MILES

WHY do we flock to Oxford Street? Oxford Circus and Tottenham Court Road are among London's busiest tube stations, and the pavements between them are almost too crowded to walk on; yet what is there in Oxford Street but, in the words of the Lonely Planet Guide, a "gauntlet of permanent closing-down sales and slimy shop-front salespeople who draw people in by offering dubious bargains"?

But the streets on either side are filled with fascination, and this walk aims to explore them while spending as little time as possible – one short stretch, in fact – in Oxford Street itself.

It was a coach road in the 18th century; but it wasn't called Oxford Street because it led to Oxford but because the man who first developed the area, starting in 1717 with Cavendish Square, was the Earl of Oxford. Before then it was Tyburn Way, and it may sober today's shoppers and tourists to reflect that between 1196 and 1783 more than 12,000 unfortunates passed this way en route from Newgate to Tyburn. The two-hour journey gave rise to the expression "gone west".

At the time, it was "a deep hollow road, full of sloughs; with here and there a ragged house, the lurking-place of cut-throats"; but with fashionable housing springing up on either side, Oxford Street gradually became fashionable itself. The Pantheon, literally a pleasure-dome, was opened in 1772 and quickly became a major attraction: Dr Johnson

ruled it inferior to the Ranelagh pleasure-gardens in Chelsea; but to Boswell's comment that there was not half a guinea's pleasure to be had in seeing it, he replied that there was "half a guinea's worth of inferiority to other people in not having seen it". It burnt down 20 years later.

Thomas De Quincey, writing of his time as a penniless 17-year-old runaway in the Oxford Street of 1802, describes gazing northward up avenues that ended in fields and woods; and indeed northward development proved slow. It was still mostly open land when William Blake used to go on long country walks from his home in Soho in the 1770s and 80s, and Fitzroy Square and its surrounding quarter were not built (by the Duke of Grafton, an illegitimate descendant of Charles II) until around 1800.

It's often said that this area had no name until the term Fitzrovia was coined in 1940 by Tom Driberg, then writing the William Hickey column in the Daily Express. This isn't strictly true: De Quincey describes it simply as Marylebone; and until the 1920s it remained a smart residential area. In the interwar years, though, business started encroaching, and fine houses were one by one turned into offices until today there can hardly be any residents in the entire district bounded by Regent Street, Tottenham Court Road, Oxford Street and Goodge Street.

The building of Broadcasting House in Portland Place in 1932 was the genesis of Fitzrovia's Bohemian reputation: the BBC was a meal-ticket for the likes of Orwell, Dylan Thomas and Louis MacNiece, and much of its fees found their way over the counters of local pubs. Thomas in particular was apt to spend his money before he'd earned it: on one occasion he fell asleep, dead drunk, two minutes before he was due live on air; on another he interrupted his own broadcast, saying: "Someone's boring me. I think it's me."

Oxford Street was in the 19th century a busy through-route edged with slum courts and alleys described by Hyppolite Taine in 1860 as "stifling lanes encrusted with human exhalations". It wasn't until the 1880s and 90s that the grand frontages that now line its length were built; and indeed Oxford Street, above the tacky shopfronts, is still a gallery of the best in late Victorian architecture. It had by then become a smart shopping street, "London's High Street"; the arrival in 1909 of Selfridge's, founded by a man who had already retired after a successful career with Marshall Field's department store in Chicago, set the seal on its reputation. Alas, it's a reputation that hasn't endured.

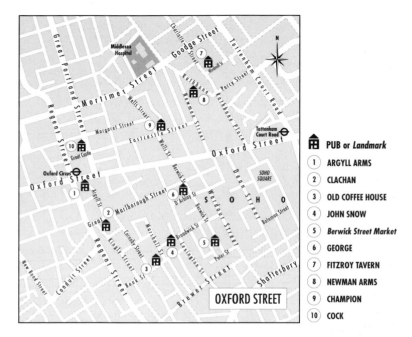

🏠	**PUB or** *Landmark*
①	ARGYLL ARMS
②	CLACHAN
③	OLD COFFEE HOUSE
④	JOHN SNOW
⑤	*Berwick Street Market*
⑥	GEORGE
⑦	FITZROY TAVERN
⑧	NEWMAN ARMS
⑨	CHAMPION
⑩	COCK

START: Oxford Circus Tube Station

Exit 6 into Argyll Street.

The Argyll Arms
18 Argyll Street

The Argyll Arms has without doubt the finest pub glass in London.

A big pub of the 1860s, it replaced a tavern known to have occupied the site in 1743 and named after one of Marlborough's generals, whose town house stood where the London Palladium is today.

In around 1895 the owner, a Mr Bratt, commissioned the designer Robert Sawyer to remodel the interior in keeping with the new vogue for privacy. This was not mere snobbishness: in the larger bars of the past it had been (as now) almost impossible either to hold a conversation or to avoid a brawl; and in those days the great unwashed really were unwashed. There was a strong demand for drinking places which were quiet, safe and discreet, and the solution was to break the

pub up into as many separate compartments as possible.

Sawyer's layout is on a plan which was not then unusual. A side-passage gives on to a front bar and two small "railway-compartment" private bars, divided by partitions but sharing the same counter. At the back, the passage opens into a big saloon.

It's the quality of the acid-etched and brilliant-cut glazing in the screens and mirrors which sets the Argyll apart. Classical and floral motifs writhe in luxuriant profusion over vast surfaces in a breathtaking display of bravura. The light is caught and refracted from thousands of edges, creating an illusion of space and air in what is actually a series of small rooms. The whole is enriched by shining mahogany and ornately moulded plaster; and although the term "gin palace" properly belongs to an earlier style of pub, the Argyll can truly be called a palace.

OPEN 11–11 MONDAY–SATURDAY, 12–9 SUNDAY. FOOD SERVED 11.30–4. REAL ALES: GREENE KING IPA, TETLEY, ADNAM'S BITTER.

Turn right down Argyll Street; cross Great Marlborough Street into Kingly Street.

THE CLACHAN
34 KINGLY STREET

When the Regent Street department store founded in 1875 by Arthur Liberty expanded in 1924, it built itself a huge mock-Tudor extension in Great Marlborough Street, separated from the main buildings by Kingly Street.

Part of the new site comprised a rather grand pub built in 1898, the Bricklayers Arms. For 60 years, owning a pub did not faze the management of Liberty; but eventually someone must have started wondering what a department store with an international reputation for printed fabrics was doing in the licensed trade. So in 1983, the Bricklayers was sold to Allied, which promptly enrolled the old pub into its battalion of Nicholson's Inns - ie, pubs of special historical or architectural interest marked down for the heritage treatment. And the first thing it did, by way of preserving the Bricklayers Arms's heritage, was to rename it the Clachan. Nobody knows why.

Still, it has to be said that the Clachan's fabric was well worth preserving and has been very competently preserved.

Its towering exterior, which stubbornly refuses to be overawed by Liberty's looming bulk, is of mellow brick with huge ornately carved stone window-cases, a marble fascia, elaborate dormers, and a hanging turret with a copper cupola.

215

Inside, two bars wrap round an island counter with much of its carved bar-back, including a small clock in a fancy pediment, intact. The decor is Edwardian-comfy rather than Victorian-stern, with subdued green wallpaper and carpets under a dark red fancy plaster ceiling supported on cast-iron columns. There are enough old prints and framed sepia photographs to stock a small shop, and up a few steps at the back is a cosy alcove for intimate drinking. All in all, a truly great place to take a breather from Regent Street shopping.

OPEN 11–11 MONDAY-FRIDAY, 11.30–11 SATURDAY. CLOSED SUNDAY. FOOD 12–4, 5.30–8. REAL ALES: GREENE KING IPA, TIMOTHY TAYLOR'S LANDLORD, FULLER'S LONDON PRIDE, GUEST ALES. ADDLESTONE'S CASK-CONDITIONED CIDER.

Turn left down Fouberts Place and right into Carnaby Street.

CARNABY STREET

Resist the temptation, as you stroll through this historic but wholly unexceptional, and indeed thoroughly tacky, pedestrianised shopping street, to murmur that Carnaby Street is Not What It Was in the '60s. After all, if you can remember how it was in the 60s, as the saying goes, you weren't really there.

Turn left into Beak Street.

OLD COFFEE HOUSE
49 BEAK STREET

Say the magic words "coffee house" and everybody starts thinking about Addison, Steele, Pope, Dryden and so on. This is not one of the first-generation coffee houses, despite what it says about itself, for the coffee houses of the late 17th and early 18th centuries where politicians and scandalmongers went about their daily doings were a dead duck by the time this building came on the scene in 1800 or thereabouts. But there were two subsequent generations of coffee houses, both connected with temperance movements, and this one could belong to either of them.

The second generation sprang up in the 1820s as an antidote to the first gin palaces, which sold liquor and nothing else. The new coffee houses, by contrast, supplied food for working men's bodies and, often, free newspapers for their minds. Many of them became the headquarters of serious and high-minded organisations aimed at the improvement of the working classes — co-operatives, trade unions, and friendly societies.

The third generation came 40 years later and were effectively temperance pubs, mirroring the real thing in every detail except one. Instead of booze they sold tea, hot chocolate, coffee, and alcohol substitutes such as Winterine and Anti-Burton.

Temperance pubs lasted for many years, but eventually the movement burnt itself out thanks to an irresistible temptation to preach. Many of the premises, by cruel irony, were ideal for conversion to pubs, and it's in this category that Marc Girouard in his authoritative *Victorian Pubs* places the Old Coffee House.

Whatever its origins, the Old Coffee House is an almost unique survival of its era in a street which Dickens knew as "a bygone tumbledown street with two irregular rows of tall, meagre houses" — although the pub itself is neither tall nor meagre, being a perfectly plain building with, as its one concession to decoration, a little pediment over the central window in the first-floor frontage.

Inside, it's far from plain: in fact it's the original bric-à-brac pub, with stuffed fish and birds, mounted stags' heads, brass jugs and musical instruments, old enamel advertising plaques for things like Melox dog food, World War 1 recruitment posters, a cello, a brass hot-towel dispenser from an Edwardian barber's shop, the ship's drum from HMS Chatham and God knows what else besides screwed to every square foot of wall or hanging from the ceiling.

The Old Coffee House also has the honour of being one of the few central London pubs to belong to a micro brewery: it's owned by Brian Brodie, who also owns the Sweet William Brewery in Bow.

OPEN 11–11 MONDAY–SATURDAY, 12–3 AND 7–10.30 SUNDAY. FOOD SERVED 12–3 MONDAY–SATURDAY. REAL ALES: SWEET WILLIAM BRODIE'S BITTER AND BRODIE'S BEST, MARSTON'S PEDIGREE, COURAGE DIRECTORS.

Turn left out of the pub, then left up Marshall Street and right into Broadwick Street.

John Snow
39 Broadwick Street

First licensed in 1721 as the Newcastle-upon-Tyne, this was the visionary poet and painter William Blake's local.

Blake was born in 1757 at the corner of Marshall Street, where his father was a hosier, and lived there until he was 25 when he was apprenticed to an engraver. He had been educated at home by his mother, who thought he was too sensitive for school. Sensitive or not, he was certainly a little strange: he once said he saw God's face pressed against the window, and when he told his father he had seen a tree filled with angels, that practical man's response was a sound thrashing. After his father died in 1784, Blake set up his own engraver's shop at number 27; when it failed he moved to a Poland Street, where he wrote *Songs of Innocence* and *The Marriage of Heaven and Hell*. He finally moved away, to Lambeth, in 1793.

The great man commemorated in the name of the pub was of a rather more practical bent. In the 1850s cholera was raging in London: the 1854 outbreak claimed 500 lives in 10 days. The received wisdom was that it was an airborne disease created by the miasma that rose from sewage. A local doctor, John Snow, thought otherwise: he believed it was waterborne, and with difficulty persuaded the parish to let him examine the Broad Street pump (still to be seen in its original position at the corner of Lexington Street). When it was found to be contaminated with sewage from the cesspool in the cellar at number 40, Snow was vindicated and became something of a local hero. Alas, he died only four years later; but in 1954 the owners of the pub decided to mark the centenary of his discovery by renaming the pub after him. Not that he would recognise it: it was completely rebuilt in 1867 and is today a gaunt yellow-brick pub with a very plain wooden fascia, divided into three bars by wooden partitions, and comfortably done out with leather banquettes, dirty-gold pressed paper wall-coverings, and heavy drapes over etched sash windows.

Open 11.30–11 Monday–Friday, 12–11 Saturday, 1 pm–10.30 Sunday. Food served 12–9. No real ale.

From Broadwick St. turn left into Berwick St., right into D'Arblay Street.

GEORGE
D'ARBLAY STREET

This handsome street-corner local with its pink brick and stucco bands has something of a split personality. The unusual gilded hanging signs undoubtedly represent George II. They even carry his regnant dates, 1727–60. But the plaque on the wall just as undoubtedly portrays George IV. So which George does the pub celebrate?

The answer may lie in the rebuilding date prominently displayed outside: 1897. At the time, many wags were drawing satirical parallels between Albert Edward, Prince of Wales, and his great uncle. Both had to wait years before the death of a stubbornly long-lived parent gave them belated accession. Both were distinctly corpulent. Both were celebrated for their appetites – for drink, for food, for a wager, and especially for women. Both were involved in public scandal. It may be that the dedication of the pub to one Prince of Wales was a joke at the expense of another. But why, then, does George II appear on the hanging signs? They look to me of a rather later date than the stucco plaque, and I wonder if they were put up when Albert Edward had become Edward VII, in retraction of the original lese majesté?

Inside you will find no such ambiguity: it's a plain London boozer, with a single small bar, bare floorboards, a dark pressed-paper ceiling, and a number of big mirrors, one of which is truly remarkable. This advertises Meux ales and bears a beautifully-painted riverbank scene complete with heron, carp, reeds and kingfisher all in the most vivid colours.

OPEN 11–11 MONDAY–FRIDAY, 12–11 SATURDAY, 2 PM–10.30 SUNDAY. SANDWICHES SERVED 11–3. REAL ALES: TETLEY BITTER, WADWORTH 6X.

Turn left up Wardour Street and right into Oxford Street. Cross Oxford Street and turn left up Rathbone Place. Fork right into Charlotte Street.

FITZROY TAVERN
16 CHARLOTTE STREET

If ever there was a pub that traded on past glories, it's the Fitz.

A big corner pub of pink brick, with scallop-shell friezes over its windows and terracotta and black marble dressings, it was one of 21 designed by the architect W M Brutton in his annus mirabilis, 1897. (He designed 65 in all).

In 1919 it was taken over by an immigrant, Judah "Pop" Kleinfeld, and under his kindly guidance it proved a magnet for the near-destitute artists then starving in the garrets of Cleveland Street. Augustus John was the best-known of the painters who made the Fitzroy their second home, and with him came the Queen of Bohemia, the artists' model Nina Hamnett, who entitled her autobiography *The Laughing Torso* and used to extort her drinking-money by rattling a collecting-tin under the noses of strangers until they paid up. She also, rather grotesquely, lionised another regular, Albert Pierrepoint, the hangman.

The presence of the BBC at Broadcasting House not far away drew a second, younger set of more literary Bohemians; while a third group consisted of left-wing politicians and journalists including Tom Driberg and, perhaps surprisingly given his serious reputation, the young Hugh Gaitskell.

The Kleinfeld dynasty lasted until 1956, for Pop Kleinfeld passed control of the pub to his daughter Annie and her husband Charles Allchild. But by the time the Allchilds left the Bohemians had already gone, for they had become so well-known that the pub had turned into something of a tourist attraction and – being shy creatures who hated nothing so much as an audience – the literary shrinking violets drifted away to other, more discreet, drinking dens.

Today there are pictures of John, Hamnett, Louis MacNiece, Dylan Thomas, Driberg and others plastered all over the walls of the pub, along with scraps of their verse, their witty epithets, and so on. All that's missing is a modern generation of them. But don't let that put you off: the Fitz is a fine pub in its own right, with several drinking areas round a big island bar, all done out in Edwardian-comfy style: leather banquettes, carpeted floors, warm red wallpaper, and pine dados and panelling.

OPEN ALL PERMITTED HOURS. FOOD 12–2.30, 6.30–9.30 (EXCEPT FRIDAY EVENING). NO REAL ALE.

Cross Charlotte Street and take Percy Passage.

NEWMAN ARMS
23 RATHBONE STREET

Surely the smallest pub in Fitzrovia, everything about the Newman Arms is utterly charming – except its tartan wallpaper, that is. A tiny little chocolate-box of a place, it's perversely popular and can get very crowded.

Dating from 1863, it was one of the last pubs in the district to have a beer-only licence and was a favourite of George Orwell's. In fact he used it twice in his novels: in *Keep The Aspidistra Flying*, it's the pub where the penniless poet Comstock argues about socialism with his wealthy friend, Ravelston; and in *Nineteen Eighty-Four* it's the pub where Winston Smith questions an elderly prole about life before the revolution, but comes away only with the information that beer used to be served in pints, and that while a litre is too big, a half-litre is too small.

The pub is also the point of departure for Christopher Pettit's 1991 short story *Newman Arms*, in which he sets out to examine swinging London by revisiting film locations: Newman Passage was the scene of the first murder in Michael Powell's mould-breaking *Peeping Tom*.

Although the pub's one bar is tiny, it also has an acclaimed upstairs restaurant, the Pie Room.

OPEN 11.30–11 MONDAY-FRIDAY. BAR SNACKS LUNCHTIME. PIE ROOM OPEN 12–3, 6-9 MONDAY–FRIDAY (EXCEPT FRIDAY EVENING).
REAL ALES: DRAUGHT BASS, FULLER'S LONDON PRIDE.

Take Newman Passage beside the pub. Turn left into Newman Street and right into Eastcastle Street.

CHAMPION
13 WELLS STREET

Sam Smith's, the Yorkshire brewer, which seems to have nearly cornered the market in historic and characterful London taverns, is not only very good at brewing beer, but also very good at decorating pubs – and in the Champion, it has excelled itself.

The large, late Victorian pub stands on the site of a booth where in the early 18th century Tom Figgs, the first prizefighter to be recognised as national champion, trained tyros – many of them well-born young bucks – in fighting with cudgels, staves, and broadswords, as well as in the arts of the ring. The same Figgs visited Jack Sheppard in the condemned cell at Newgate and attended him on his way to Tyburn, drinking a last glass of wine with him at the City of Oxford in Oxford Street on 16 November 1724.

Like many Victorian pubs, the Champion became grubbily run-down in the years of austerity after World War II, when both funds and materials were in short supply. It was the subject of a highly-praised restoration in the 1950s, which contemporary writers lauded to the skies. "The result recaptures the true atmosphere of the public house and creates a permanent exhibition of London public house design," gushed Louis Stanley, while the rather racier Denzil Batchelor, a sports writer by trade, said the pub had been "as beautifully reconstructed as the arena of a chariot-race in a billion-dollar film".

But the effects of such restorations soon wear off if they are not maintained, and by the 1980s, when Sam Smith's bought the yellow-brick Champion with its modest wooden fascia, it was once again sadly down-at-heel.

So Sam's first did it up, reintroducing the pine partitions to the single bar and sprucing up the linoleum floor and dark pressed-paper ceiling, and then did it proud, commissioning the York-based artist Anne Sotheran to produce a set of stunning stained-glass windows on the theme of champions.

The combination of the brewery's imagination and the artist's inspiration makes the Champions interior a truly unique space. Sitting in it is like sitting inside a jewel. The windows are a vivid gallery of champions in all fields, some obvious – W G Grace, Fred Archer, Bob Fitzsimmons; some no longer famous – the turn-of-the-century golfer Young Thomas Morris and his contemporary at tennis William Renshaw; some totally unconnected with sport – David Livingstone, Florence Nightingale. The most recent is Captain Bertie Dwyer, a pioneer of tobogganing, who died only in 1967.

Literally hundreds of millions are spent every year in refurbishing old pubs and creating new ones. But where are the owners and designers who have the vision and daring to create what Sam's and Anne Sotheran did at the Champion nearly 20 years ago?

OPEN ALL PERMITTED HOURS. FOOD SERVED 12–2.30, 5.30–8.30
MONDAY–FRIDAY (EXCEPT FRIDAY EVENING). NO REAL ALE.

Cross Wells Street and continue along Eastcastle Street.
Cross Market Place into Castle Street.

COCK
27 GREAT PORTLAND STREET

Another truly great Sam Smith's house, the Cock is a glowing
example of how a pub should be restored and maintained.

It helps that it's such a splendid pub to start with. Another from
the great 1897 vintage, its exterior is of pink brick dressed with stone
string-courses and window surrounds, with a brown marble fascia, an
intricate terracotta frieze above the first-floor windows, a corner
turret with copper cupola, and a set of four huge coach lamps, which
had gone missing when Sam's bought the pub in the 80s and had to
be reconstructed from old photos.

Inside, it is truly glorious, from the polychrome quarry-tile floor
right up to the deep red Lincrusta ceiling, which has cream plaster
roses round the lights. A long bar is divided into three by dark
wooden partitions, and the carved bar-back appears to be original.
There is plenty of dark wood panelling, and even a single surviving set
of louvred etched-glass snob-screens. Dark green leather banquettes
line the walls, lit by shiny brass lamps mounted on the windowsills.

The place is always heaving at lunchtime, but it's not all
businessmen: a gaggle of ancient regulars props up one end of the bar,
and it's good to see that the cheery bar staff pay them as much
attention as they do the higher-spending suits.

OPEN 11.30–11 MONDAY–SATURDAY, 12–10.30 SUNDAY. COLD BAR
MEALS 12–7. DINING-ROOM OPEN 12–3, 6.30–8.30 MONDAY–SATURDAY.
REAL ALE: SAM SMITH'S OBB.

Continue along Castle Street and turn left into Regent Street.

FINISH: OXFORD CIRCUS

ST GILES'S

THE ROOKERY

LENGTH OF WALK: TWO MILES

IF any one London street could be chosen to typify urban nightmare, New Oxford Street would be it. A maelstrom of traffic enclosed by haggard concrete cliffs, it is a nowhere place, to be passed through and forgotten as quickly as possible. So why have I brought you here?

Well, partly because this short walk begins and ends at two of London's most spectacular Victorian pubs; but also because this is a place where, for more than a century, the width of a single street divided the mansions of some of the capital's wealthiest inhabitants from the squalid, overcrowded tenements of its very poorest.

St Giles's has always been one of those in-between places which nobody seems to want. Its church was founded in 1101 as a leper hospital, intended to isolate the city's outcasts. Gradually a village grew up around it, but it was a pariah village to which the taint of its origin still clung. Literally lawless, it continued to fill up with London's outcasts long after the twisted bones of the lepers who first settled it had turned to dust. Slowly it grew; and as it grew, it festered.

It festered because it became overcrowded, and it became overcrowded because the Dukes of Bedford, who owned the land to the north which became Bloomsbury, prevented it from expanding. Instead, while St Giles's became more and more packed with migrants, its courts and tenements divided and subdivided to house them, the

229

empty land was earmarked for luxury development. Bedford House was built in what is now Bloomsbury Square in 1661 and Montagu House, now the British Museum, in 1683; and throughout the 18th century streets of substantial houses gradually grew up around them.

Meanwhile conditions in the ghetto became ever more desperate. In the mid-18th century one in four of its houses was a gin shop − every street here was a Hogarthian Gin Lane − while the rest were squalid lodging houses interspersed with coiners' dens and brothels. The six acres enclosed by Great Russell Street and St Giles's High Street were the most densely-packed of all, impenetrable to the forces of law and order and known either as the Rookery or the Holy Land.

The Holy Land was a secure base from which pickpockets, prostitutes, footpads, card-sharpers and professional beggars could exploit the rich pickings of the West End. The rookery protected its own with armed mobs easily the equal of any raiding parties sent by the law and with a labyrinth of escape routes linking cellars, attics and courtyards. In 1731 the rich of burgeoning Bloomsbury had to build themselves a new parish church, St George's, because the old one, St Giles-in-the-Fields all of 500 yards away across the Rookery, was no longer accessible to them.

In 1780 the slums boiled over into Bloomsbury, roused to anti-Catholic hysteria by Lord Gordon. The house of Lord Mansfield, the Lord Chief Justice, in Bloomsbury Square was burned down in week-long riots described by Boswell as "the most horrid scenes of outrage that ever disgraced a civilised country". The hangings that followed are described by Dickens in Barnaby Rudge. Public hangings were, indeed, almost the only recourse available to the authorities of the 18th century; and to cow the masses of the Holy Land, St Giles's High Street formed part of the pageant of tumbrels travelling from Newgate to Tyburn. It was customary for the cart to stop at a pub to allow the condemned man a last drink. As Jonathan Swift wrote:

As clever Tom Clinch, while the rabble was bawling,
Rode stately through Holborn to die at his calling,
He stopped at the George for a bottle of sack
And promised to pay for it when he came back.

Only after the foundation of the Metropolitan Police in 1829 were serious efforts made to clean up the rookery; and even in the 1840s it took a strong party of armed plainclothes officers, with back-up at the ready and a fleet of cabs waiting on the edge of the ghetto, to arrest a team of coiners.

Charles Knight described the Holy Land as "a dense mass of houses through which narrow and tortuous lanes curve and wind. Whoever ventures here finds the streets thronged with loiterers and sees through half-glazed windows rooms crowded to suffocation. The stagnant gutters in the middle of the lanes, the filth choking up the dark passages which open upon the highways, all these scarce leave so dispiriting an impression as the condition of the houses. Walls the colour of bleached soot, doors falling from their hinges, door-posts worm-eaten, windows where shivered panes of glass alternate with wisps of straw bespeak the last and frailest shelter that can be interposed between man and the elements." Shortly after these words were written, the Rookery was brutally broken up when New Oxford Street was driven through the heart of it as part of a new arterial system linking west and central London with the docks. The planners gave no thought to rehousing the displaced slum-dwellers; it merely meant that the remaining slums became even more crowded.

Dickens, touring the reduced but still festering Rookery in 1850, wrote: "How many people may there be in London who, if we had brought them blindfold to this street, would know it for a not remote part of the city in which their lives are passed? How many, who amidst this compound of sickening smells, these heaps of filth, these tumbling houses with all their vile contents slimily overflowing into the black road, would believe that they breathe this air?" He described several lodging houses and their inmates, including refugees from the Irish potato famine, pavement artists, match-sellers, begging-letter writers and decayed ex-servants "in various conditions of dirt and raggedness", adding: "Thus we make our New Oxford Streets and our other new streets, never asking where the wretches whom we clear out crowd."

New Oxford Street became the new front line, with the north side enjoying rapid improvement. It soon became associated with bookselling and publishing – the bookshops are still there, although the publishing houses mostly moved out over a decade ago. In Bloomsbury Street were the offices of the Adelphi Magazine, where George Orwell began his writing career. He and his colleagues were regulars at the New Oxford Street branch of Express Dairies, on which he modelled the Chestnut Tree Café, the haunt of painters and musicians – and of Winston Smith after his sojourn in Room 101 in 1984. It is now (make of this what you will) a McDonald's.

Further south, the old slums too began to crumble under the combined assault of the police and local authorities. After the building of Shaftesbury Avenue in 1886, commerce slowly began to take over – a process hastened by the Blitz, after which many evacuees never returned; and by the 1950s every trace of what was once the most appalling slum in central London had vanished.

START: TOTTENHAM COURT ROAD TUBE STATION

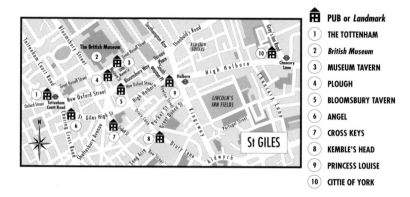

🏠	PUB or *Landmark*
1	THE TOTTENHAM
2	*British Museum*
3	MUSEUM TAVERN
4	PLOUGH
5	BLOOMSBURY TAVERN
6	ANGEL
7	CROSS KEYS
8	KEMBLE'S HEAD
9	PRINCESS LOUISE
10	CITTIE OF YORK

THE TOTTENHAM
6 OXFORD STREET

Opposite Tottenham Court Road tube is the Tottenham, the last pub in Oxford Street. In 1855 there were 38; by 1955 there were but eight; and now there is only the Tottenham. Luckily, the Tottenham is one of London's most magnificent palaces of High Victorian pub architecture and pub fitting.

Originally it was the Flying Horse and belonged, along with the Horse Shoe just across Tottenham Court Road, to Charles Best, who was one of a number of entrepreneurs in late Victorian London who bought and sold pubs with bewildering speed, feverishly rebuilding and refitting them in ever greater degrees of ornate lavishness. In 1890, Best sold both the Horse Shoe and Flying Horse to the largest private pub-owning partnership of them all, the Baker Brothers.

William and Richard Baker fitted the mould perfectly, buying, rebuilding, and selling an ever-changing portfolio of pubs, music halls and hotels. The biggest brewers and distillers of the day backed them heavily: Nicholson's, the gin distiller, bankrolled their purchase of the Horse Shoe and the Flying Horse to the tune of £40,000, and senior representatives of the whisky distillers Buchanan and the Burton brewer Bass attended the Horse Shoe's grand reopening.

The Baker Brothers turned the Horse Shoe into one of the biggest, most opulent pubs in London, a warren of snugs, parlours, and dining-rooms to suit every taste and pocket. Today it stands forlorn next to the Dominion Theatre, broken up into shops, burger bars and offices, with not a shred of its past greatness evident.

The much smaller Tottenham, by contrast, is still a wonderful testament to the skill of the pub fitters of the time. Its elegant brick exterior, with its stone bands, arched windows and fancy Flemish gable, was rebuilt by the leading pub architects Saville & Martin, for the then massive sum of £12,120.

Inside the lush single bar are glorious examples of the work of three of the best firms of craftsmen in the trade. The multicoloured mirrors in their mahogany surrounds are particularly fine: they were by Jones & Firmin of Blackfriars, which revived a forgotten 18th-century technique to popularise polychromatic mirrors. Above is a course of acanthus-decorated tiles by Millington, Wisdom & Co of Shaftesbury Avenue, and between are three painted panels of fashionably curvaceous, bosomy ladies representing the Seasons – there appears never to have been a fourth – by Felix de Jong, a leading decorative artist in the world of music hall. His work is still to be seen at the Hackney Empire.

The Tottenham may be grand, but it is not particularly large. Indeed, it appears never to have been subdivided into separate bars, unless the rear area was originally partitioned off for billiards, as its colourful octagonal skylight suggests. In the callow, gimcrack environment of Oxford Street, however, it's refreshing to find this monument to an era of genuine and manifestly joyful craftsmanship.

OPEN 11–11 MON–SAT, 12–10.30 SUN. FOOD SERVED 12–3 AND 5–8.
REAL ALES: DRAUGHT BASS, TETLEY BITTER, FULLER'S LONDON PRIDE.

Cross Tottenham Court Road and turn left, then right into Great Russell Street.

BRITISH MUSEUM

Montagu House was built in 1683 and served for over 70 years as the London home of the Earls of Montagu, but in 1759 its fortunes changed dramatically.

The inn sign of the Museum Tavern commemorates Sir Hans Sloane, the physician, botanist, antiquary and collector, who had a herb garden in what is now Bloomsbury Place. On his death in 1753 his huge collection of books and artefacts was left to the nation, and the Government raised money through a lottery to buy Montagu House to keep it in, along with the Harleian and Cottonian collections. In 1759 this became the British Museum.

When in 1823 it was also required to house George III's library, it was obvious that the old house was no longer big enough. Starting in 1838, it was progressively demolished while the new British Museum, designed in the neo-classical style by Robert Smirke, gradually went up in its place. The building took nine years, but the new museum was still only open by appointment. A vocal campaign in the 1850s led to its being opened every day to the public for the benefit of the "middle and operative classes"; and in 1857 the circular Reading Room was added, almost filling Smirke's courtyard.

Recently, following the transfer of the British Library to a grand new home in St Pancras, the Museum has been transformed again, with a glass dome covering the courtyard and a new portico being built – famously, in the wrong stone.

MUSEUM TAVERN
49 GREAT RUSSELL STREET

The Museum Tavern was first recorded as the Dog & Duck in 1723, when the district was an odd mixture of grand mansions, market gardens, and marshy fields where a peculiarly nauseating form of duck-hunting was pursued. A duck would be pinioned – that is, it had its feathers trimmed so it couldn't fly – and then let loose in a pond. As it flapped across the water in a vain effort to take off, a dog would be thrown in after it. That the outcome was never in doubt didn't hinder the sport's popularity, and pub landlords were among its keenest promoters.

Before the British Museum opened, the Dog & Duck was a small

tavern used by the servants of the surrounding mansions. Now it found its fortune, and in 1762 its name was changed to the British Museum Tavern. In 1798 the landlord, William Reeves, rebuilt it completely; and the 1841 census recorded that it had seven maidservants living in.

In 1845 it was taken over by an ambitious Devonian, Richard Maddren, who was active in the campaign to open the British Museum to the public, hosting meetings in an upstairs room. In 1854 he signed a new lease, not just on the pub but also on the buildings adjoining it in Great Russell Street and what was then Queen Street. In 1855 Queen Street was rebuilt as Museum Street, with its upper end redesigned in a modestly ornate classical style by William Finch Hill as the two identical facades which survive today.

Inside there was a coffee room separated by a passageway from three bars radiating from a semicircular servery. There was also a small parlour for the landlord's favourites. This was the layout which Karl Marx would have known if he actually frequented the pub during his breaks from work in the British Museum Reading Room, although

there is no record of his doing so. Whether Marx knew the pub or not, Conan Doyle did: it's the model for the Alpha Inn in *The Case of the Blue Carbuncle*.

Maddren was succeeded in 1858 by George Blizzard, who shortened the name to its present form and whose son in 1889 commissioned the architects Wilson & Long to further subdivide the pub into five bars by means of partitions incorporating, unusually for the period, a good deal of stained glass. The present bar counter and back-fitting are theirs, as is a mirror advertising Watney's Imperial Stout by Samuel Trenner & Sons. This scheme survived until 1935, when it was turned back into three bars. In the 1960s they were all sadly knocked into one, but a couple of Wilson & Long's stained-glass panels can still be seen in the food servery.

OPEN 11–11 MONDAY–SATURDAY, 12–10.30 SUN. FOOD SERVED 11 AM–10 PM. REAL ALES: COURAGE DIRECTORS, GREENE KING ABBOT, CHARLES WELLS BOMBARDIER, THEAKSTON BEST & OLD PECULIER.

Cross Museum Street and turn left.

PLOUGH
27 MUSEUM STREET

The Plough was one of the many taverns that sprang up in this part of Bloomsbury in the mid-18th century: in what used to be Queen Street, Peter Street, and Bow Street – all subsumed into the newly-named Museum Street following the building of New Oxford Street – there were no fewer than 10 pubs in 1760.

Today's Plough stands on the corner of Little Russell Street on that stretch of Museum Street rebuilt by William Finch Hill in 1855. It is, so to speak, the Museum Tavern's companion piece and shares with it the exterior design of rusticated quoins, smooth render, and arched first-floor windows with charming little oval medallions above.

Of course, it is not nearly so well-known as the Museum Tavern because it is 100 yards further from the Museum. But its interior is far more cheery and welcoming than that of its more famous cousin simply because, during the buildings and rebuildings of recent years, it has retained a two-room layout.

The decor is unremarkable but atmospheric enough, with the statutory wood panelling and low lighting, but the intimate front bar and larger back room create that cosy, cheery bustle which is the hallmark of a well-laid-out pub.

OPEN 11–11 MONDAY–SATURDAY, 12–10.30 SUN. FOOD SERVED 12–7
EVERY DAY. REAL ALES: IND COOPE BURTON ALE, MARSTON'S PEDIGREE,
YOUNG'S BITTER, ADNAM'S BITTER.

Continue down Museum Street; cross New Oxford Street.

BLOOMSBURY TAVERN
236 SHAFTESBURY AVENUE

In the horror that is New Oxford Street, the Bloomsbury Tavern is a
gem of late Victorian pub architecture. In another setting its baronial
exterior might go unremarked, but in this grim brutalist waste whose
architects seem to have viewed ornament as the Antichrist, its jolly
excesses are as welcome as a bottle of Evian in the Kalahari.

The Bloomsbury Tavern was built in 1895, soon after Shaftesbury
Avenue had been blasted through the surviving slums, and at the
height of Gothic-folly extravagance. At ground level there are black
marble pillars, supporting a first-floor Gothic oriel dressed with stone.
The masonry is mostly pink brick, but as well as the oriel there are
stone quoins and also two round stone turrets.

At first, in keeping with the area's genteel pretensions, it was a wine
lodge, and was the last pub in London to have a wine-only licence.
What is surprising is that the interior is so small. The trading space
available in the single L-shaped room – even though, admittedly, there
is another small room upstairs – can never have justified the immense
outlay evident on the exterior: no wonder so many pub builders went
bust in 1899!

Having said that, its interior is very pleasant, wood-panelled and
hung with Spy cartoons and other appropriate bits and pieces. It's said
to be popular with members of the orchestra of the neighbouring
Shaftesbury Theatre, who pop out during intervals to moisten their
embouchures.

OPEN 11–11 MON–SAT; USUALLY CLOSED SUN. FOOD SERVED 11–3, 6–9.
REAL ALES: TETLEY BITTER, BRAKSPEAR BITTER; FULLER'S LONDON PRIDE.

Continue down Shaftesbury Avenue; turn right into St Giles's High Street.

THE ANGEL
61 ST GILES HIGH STREET

The Angel hasn't found its way into many guidebooks recently because, frankly, it's been so awful. Built in 1898, its massive, unadorned frontage of dark glazed brick has always been uninviting; and until a couple of years ago it had a shabby, run-down barn of an interior to match.

Given the pub's history, its melancholy air is not inappropriate, for under its original name, the Bowl, it was one of those pubs which were traditional stopping-places on the via dolorosa from Newgate to Tyburn – a long public ride meant by the authorities as a show of might in the face of the slum-dwellers of the St Giles's Rookery along whose boundaries the procession, whose futility was demonstrated by its frequency, passed.

If the Angel's exterior is still somewhat dour, its interior has been transformed in the three years since Sam Smith, the Yorkshire brewer, bought it from Courage and set about redividing it into three separate bars. Now there is a public bar; a pleasant but still rather bare lounge with an ornate moulded plaster ceiling; and a cosy little snug, all

leather banquettes, at the rear. Sam's has also restored the unusual tilework in the pub's side passage to create a sheltered al fresco drinking area leading to a little yard behind.

OPEN 11–1 MONDAY–FRIDAY; 12–11 SAT; 12–10.30 SUNDAY. FOOD SERVED 12–9. REAL ALE: SAM SMITH'S OBB.

Turn right out of the pub and back along St Giles's High Street, cross Shaftesbury Avenue and turn right again down Endell Street.

CROSS KEYS
31 ENDELL STREET

The northern half of Covent Garden is not the fashionable end; but if it lacks the character of the tourist area round the Piazza and the Royal Opera House a few hundred yards south, it is also far quieter.

The Cross Keys dates to 1848, when Endell Street was created as a relief road to carry north-south traffic to and from Westminster Bridge. It was also a slum clearance measure, and the Cross Keys certainly has the respectable and dignified air of a pub that is going up in the world.

The dense foliage which covers the frontage creates a cottagey feel entirely in keeping with the character of the area. But the facade itself is rather grander than first sight would suggest. The three arches at ground-floor level are all of green marble, with columns supporting gilded capitals. Over the door is a large stone plaque with two chubby cherubs in bas-relief supporting two large crossed keys, and the upper

windows are elegantly arched.

Inside there's a single long, cosy, wood-panelled bar with low-beamed ceilings which is also an absolute riot of bric-à-brac, with brass instruments and vessels of all descriptions hanging from the beams, and the walls almost completely covered in cigarette cards, old prints, stuffed fish, and one or two crazed and grimy Victorian oils which a collector might well look closely at. There's a fine long-case clock in one corner, although the hum of conversation from the local clientele drowns its tick.

The pub belongs to the same small East End brewery, Sweet William, as the Old Coffee House in Beak Street, Soho.

OPEN 11–11 MON–SAT, 12–10.30 SUN. FOOD SERVED 12–2.30.
REAL ALES: COURAGE DIRECTORS, MARSTON'S PEDIGREE, BRODIE'S BITTER.

Continue down Endell Street to Long Acre. Cross the road and turn left.

KEMBLE'S HEAD
LONG ACRE

What better place than the corner of Drury Lane to find this memorial to one of the great figures in Covent Garden's theatrical history?

The Kemble's Head stands on the site of a coffee house once

frequented by John Philip Kemble, the Shakespearean actor-manager who made his London debut playing Hamlet at the Drury Lane Theatre, managed at the time by Richard Brinsley Sheridan. Kemble was noted for his stentorian voice, but it probably helped his career that his sister Mrs Siddons, the greatest actress of her time, also played at the Drury Lane Theatre.

In 1788 Kemble foolishly agreed to manage the theatre – London's oldest, and the place where in 1665 King Charles I watched a young actress named Nell Gwynne make her stage debut in Dryden's *The Indian Queen* - on Sheridan's behalf. By 1791 it became clear that the theatre needed rebuilding. Kemble masterminded the three-year project, which had Henry Holland as architect, and starred with his sister in the grand reopening production of *Macbeth*.

Soon afterwards he fell out with Sheridan, the spendthrift of his age, who used to pocket the takings before Kemble could pay the bills. Being arrested for one of Sheridan's debts was the last straw, and Kemble stormed out in 1796. He was persuaded to return in 1800 for two more unhappy years, but in 1803 went to manage the Theatre Royal Covent Garden (replaced by the Royal Opera House in 1858), taking his sister with him.

In 1808 the Theatre Royal burnt down with the loss of 23 lives, and once again Kemble was called upon to build a new theatre, modelled on the Acropolis. Unfortunately his means of paying for the work – raising the price of seats – enraged the mob, and there was uproar in the theatre every night for two months, dubbed the "old price riots". After 61 nights, Kemble gave in. He retired in 1817 and died five years later.

The pub which bears his name dates from the middle of the 19th century, and before Covent Garden market moved to Vauxhall in the 1970s it had a market licence, like those at Smithfield, allowing it to serve alcohol from 5am for the benefit of the market porters. It is decorated with rather jolly swags of carved stone foliage, with a fancy carved gable above the street corner. Inside it has all been knocked into one plain but comfortable room.

OPEN 11–11 MONDAY–SATURDAY, 12-10.30 SUN. FOOD SERVED TO 10
REAL ALES: COURAGE BEST AND DIRECTORS.

Cross Long Acre and turn right. Turn left up Newton Street and right into High Holborn.

PRINCESS LOUISE
208 HIGH HOLBORN

Decrepitude can be a great preserver. No-one wants to spend money where there's no money to be made, and so often the survivors of change are the disregarded, the neglected, the overlooked. Think of the medieval hill towns of Tuscany — would any still exist if coal had been found in the region?

So it is with the Princess Louise, a frankly drab building at the drab end of High Holborn. If its exterior had been flashier, if its location had been more prominent, its former owner Watney's would doubtless have moved in with sledgehammer and crowbar in hand to rip out the interior and replace it with something more contemporary. But it fell again and again to the bottom of the refurbishment list, and its Victorian fittings survived, gently mouldering beneath a pall of kindly dust.

And what a treasure house it is; and in particular what a monument to the craftsmanship that was taken for granted in the 1890s. No mahogany-stained plywood here, to give a temporary illusion of grandeur; no machine-stamped brass-effect uplighters; no cobbled-together boxing of pipes and ducts. This is a Rolls-Royce of pub-fitting.

The pub was built in 1872, and named after one of Queen Victoria's countless offspring. But the interior dates to a complete remodelling of 1891, undertaken by an architect named Arthur Chitty and a firm called Simpson's, based in nearby St Martin's Lane.

Founded in 1833 as a painter and decorator, by the 1870s Simpson's was undertaking whole contracts, commissioning wallpapers, tiles and mosaics and describing itself as "art workers". As well as pubs and shops, it undertook private contracts and oversaw the creation of many of the Aesthetic movement interiors of the late 19th century. It was the London agent for the Shropshire tilemaker Maw & Co, whose contracts included the grill room at the Victoria & Albert Museum in 1874, the Old Cock at Highbury for the Baker Brothers in 1888, and a number of the historical tableaux which enjoyed a vogue in the 1890s. Sadly, the abstract tilework at the Princess Louise, in bands above and below the mirrors and in the sumptuously coloured fruit and flower motifs of the tablets between, is almost all that survives.

The mirrors, by Richard Morris of Kennington, are equally magnificent. Brilliant-cut and gilded, these are not for preening in. They are lighting effects, there to refract and amplify the glow of the

gas lamps and to create an illusion of space and air in the little snugs which originally radiated from the horseshoe bar.

The partitions which then divided the pub are, alas, long gone, but they and the bar itself – and probably the original furniture, also long gone – were probably by Lascelles & Co of Finsbury, a firm associated with Norman Shaw: Shaw designed furniture for Lascelles from 1875–1885, while Lascelles did the construction work on many of Shaw's buildings.

This, then, is quality stuff; but so far had it fallen from favour by the 1970s that Watney's planned to pull it down to make way for yet another office-block. Outcry ensued, and after a planning wrangle Watney's, rather than go to the trouble and expense of restoring it, sulkily washed its hands of the whole place and sold it. After a thorough restoration and a couple more changes of ownership the pub came into the hands of the Yorkshire brewer Sam Smith's, in whose London estate of outstanding historic pubs it is one of the brightest jewels.

OPEN 11–11 MONDAY–FRIDAY, NOON–11 SAT; CLOSED SUNDAY. FOOD 12–3, 5.30–9. REAL ALE: SAM SMITH'S OLD BREWERY BITTER.

Turn right out of the pub and continue along High Holborn.

CITTIE OF YORK
22 HIGH HOLBORN

The Long Bar at the Cittie of York is an experience no lover of pubs should miss. This is Victorian gothic at its apogee: from the private booths that line one side of the bar up to the raftered roof 30 feet overhead it is an 1890s evocation of a medieval great hall; and with its clerestory windows and carved woodwork it has more of the feel of an Oxford college than a pub.

The Cittie of York is perhaps the finest example of an architectural style known in the 1890s as Mock Antique, which was a reaction against the dazzling glass-and-marble vulgarity of so many pubs of the period. With its frontage of stone mullions and Early English archways, it consciously invokes the ghosts of Chaucer and Shakespeare.

It replaced the Grays Inn Coffee House, built in 1695 on a site where there had been an inn since 1450, and was one of the five-strong Hennekey's chain of wine bars bought by Sam Smith's in 1979.

To reinforce the sense of antiquity, Sam's borrowed the name of a tavern which had once formed part of Staples Inn, the huge half-timbered building slightly further along High Holborn.

It also opened up part of the 17th-century cellar as another bar, and added a third at the front, alongside the long, narrow entrance lobby. This front bar is more intimate and cosier than the Long Bar, and there are portraits of celebrated Holborn residents such as William Morris, Charles Dickens, Dr Johnson, Sir Thomas More, Sir Frances Bacon − and Aimée Browning, daughter of the manager, born in 1992 and the first child ever to be born at the Cittie of York.

But it's the Long Bar which marks the Cittie of York out, not only for its overall grandeur but also for its detail − in particular the huge wine butts mounted on the gantry over the bar, which were in regular use until the Blitz, when they were drained for safety; and the triangular stove of 1815, taken from Gray's Inn, with a grate on each side and an ingenious flue built into the floor beneath.

"Take away the long bar counter and strew the floor with well-trodden rushes," said one architectural critic, "and you might well be going into a 15th-century tavern when you penetrate into that long high-raftered hall."

OPEN: 11.30–11 MONDAY–SATURDAY (LONG BAR), 11.30–3, 5–11 (FRONT BAR), 12–3, 6–11 (CELLAR BAR). FOOD SERVED 12–9. REAL ALE: SAM SMITH'S OLD BREWERY BITTER.

FINISH: CHANCERY LANE TUBE

COVENT GARDEN
LONDON AFTER DARK

LENGTH OF WALK: ONE-AND-A-HALF MILES

"COVENT Garden", wrote Thomas Burke rather longingly in the dark days and darker nights of 1940, "was for a century and a half the heart of London's night-life." Now we no longer have to share our nights with the Luftwaffe, it is the heart of London's night-life once again.

"The Piazza and the side-streets were thick with taverns, coffee houses, vapour baths, and scores of less reputable houses which described themselves as bagnios," wrote Burke in his *English Night Life;* and if the less reputable houses have migrated to the other side of Charing Cross Road and the vapour baths are a thing of the past, Covent Garden is still thick with the modern equivalents of taverns and coffee houses – pubs, bars and restaurants.

At the centre of it all is the Piazza itself, ordered by the Duke of Bedford to grace his new house (which the family abandoned only 30 years later for an even grander one in Bloomsbury), and built by Inigo Jones in 1630 in accordance with Charles I's express desire for a new Palladian quarter which would rival anything in Italy. The scheme included St Paul's Church, the first purpose-built Anglican church in London. Bedford had commissioned "nothing much better than a barn". "Then you shall have the handsomest barn in England," said Jones. In its Tuscan portico Samuel Pepys watched the first Punch & Judy show in England in 1662; in the same portico, over three centuries

later, Shaw had Professor Higgins first clap eyes on Eliza Doolittle.

The Piazza did not start life as a market, but it soon became one; perhaps because street vendors of fruit and vegetables saw the grand square as nothing more than a glorified marketplace, or perhaps because an ancient tradition was mysteriously reasserting itself: Covent Garden was for centuries Westminster Abbey's vegetable patch, after all. The swift evolution of the market – which only moved out in the 1970s – created a quarter that was open for 24 hours a day, for as the last revellers were staggering home from the bagnios, the market porters were taking beer with their breakfast in the taverns. It also attracted street entertainers such as Pepys's Punch & Judy puppeteers, who always appear where there are crowds.

Perhaps it was the quarter's liveliness that persuaded a company of actors seeking a new home after the lean years of Puritan prohibition to look here. The Theatre Royal, Drury Lane, opened in 1663 (and burnt down in 1672, to be rebuilt by Wren), was home to the King's Servants, the first company to be granted a patent by Charles II after the Restoration. It was here in 1665 that the Merry Monarch first saw Nell Gwynne, then only 15 and making her debut in Dryden's *The Indian Queen.*

Thanks to the theatre, Drury Lane and its taverns and coffee houses soon became a magnet for London's literati. Dryden was associated with its early years; Garrick was its star for nearly 30 years from 1747; Colley Cibber, Sheridan and Kemble were among its famous managers; Mrs Siddons and Edmund Kean were its great names in the late 18th and early 19th centuries. In 1809 it burnt down again; Sheridan watched the flames from his chair at the Great Piazza Coffee House. Asked how he could be so calm, he replied: "Can't a fellow enjoy a drink by his own fireside?"

In 1732 a second great theatrical institution, the Royal Opera House, appeared not a stone's throw from Drury Lane. It premiered Goldsmith's *She Stoops To Conquer* in 1773, and in the 1820s Thomas de Quincey, who lived in Tavistock Street, described it as "by much the most pleasant place of public resort in London for passing an evening."

With so many actors and writers concentrated here, Covent Garden was soon the centre of a lively coffee-house society: at Will's in Russell Street, opened in 1671, Dryden had his own chair and held forth for 40 years, attracting, according to Pepys, all the wits of the town and engaging in very witty and pleasing discourse. The wits included Aphra Behn and Dean Swift; Swift also patronised Button's, just down the street, as did Pope and Addison.

There was, of course, low-life as well. According to Burke: "The Piazzas were the nightly walk for women of the town, and it was a regular practice for rich rakes to sit in their coaches and watch the procession until they saw a face that attracted them, when they would make a signal and the lady would join them." Boswell picked up prostitutes in the Strand: on 14 December 1762, he met "a civil nymph with white-thread stockings who tramps along the Strand and will resign her engaging person for a pint of wine and a shilling"; while on 12 April 1763 he picked up a woman in the Strand and took her to a tavern where she "displayed to me all the parts of her enormous carcass."

For all that — and despite the lanes full of coal wharves and warehouses to the south of it, which included Warren's Blacking Factory where the 12-year-old Charles Dickens was forced to work in 1824 when his father was in jail for debt — the Strand was one of the most fashionable streets in 18th-century London. It remained so in the 19th century with the opening of theatres such as the Lyceum, the Adelphi (originally the Sans Pareil), and the Vaudeville; hotels such as — again — the Savoy, managed by César Ritz, with Escoffier himself in the kitchen; and restaurants — notably Romano's, long a London institution and patronised by a group of wags who orbited the rather lugubrious, cynical figure of Phil May.

May once discovered that his dining companion was carrying a surveyor's tape measure. They therefore started measuring the width of the Strand from top to bottom, and Whitehall and Northumberland Avenue too, very solemnly, until a passing policeman arrived. But far from arresting them, and much to their surprise, he held up the traffic to help them do it.

Writing mournfully during the blackout of the *fin-de-siècle* glory days, Burke recalled: "The Strand at that time was the centre of the theatre world. Its business was pleasure, and its nights, when its iron lilies were aflame and the theatres were emptying and the restaurants filling, were nights of carnival ... Its crowd was not of the fashionable world; it was mainly a street of actors, poets, artists, journalists, actresses, and chorus-girls and their young men."

Whether Burke, who was a bit of a snob, would approve of the revellers who throng the bars and restaurants of Covent Garden and the Strand today I don't know. But the 1990s since the market moved out, and the tourists moved in – much to the disgust of Dan Farson, who described Covent Garden as "a tarted-up tourist attraction" – have seen a huge revival in the area's fortunes.

START: CHARING CROSS TUBE

Take Trafalgar Square exit. Walk up east side of Trafalgar Square and into St Martin's Lane.

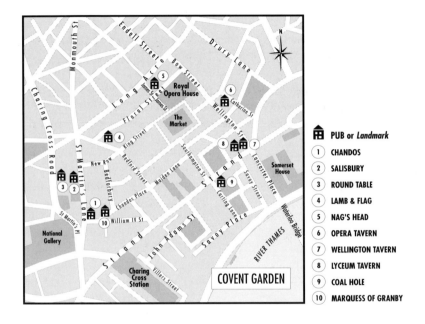

CHANDOS
ST MARTIN'S LANE

Modern pub design tends to be written off either as cheap and gimmicky or horrible pastiche Victorian. The Chandos proves that neither need be true.

A big pub standing virtually on the corner of Trafalgar Square, the Chandos dates back to the 1880s when it replaced an early Georgian tavern on the site. It is named after a contemporary member of the Chandos clan who was a great patron of, among others, Handel.

The interior, however, dates back only to 1984 when Sam Smith's took it over. As you enter the big ground-floor bar, your first impression of the decor is that it's fairly plain but pretty straightforward late Victorian or Edwardian. That first impression is misleading, though: many of the characteristic features of turn-of-the-century pub design are here, but this is no ill-conceived concatenation of Victorian-ish bits and pieces.

Instead the elements have been separated out, stripped down, and used sparingly in flourishes, rather than as the overwhelming mass of ornament favoured a century ago. There is plenty of exposed joinery, and of the finest quality; but it is simple in detail. There are decorative floral tiles, elegantly painted; but only a single band at dado height. There are booths, too, lining one wall; snug, comfortable, and intimate, they are the ideal rendezvous for parties planning a theatre-land excursion.

The final result, first impressions notwithstanding, could not be further from pastiche-Victorian: it's simple, smart, uncluttered, and contemporary – all qualities which are sadly rare in modern pub design.

OPEN ALL PERMITTED HOURS. FOOD SERVED 11–7 MONDAY–THURSDAY, 11–6 FRIDAY–SUNDAY. HOT FOOD IN UPSTAIRS LOUNGE; SANDWICHES IN DOWNSTAIRS BAR. REAL ALE: SAM SMITH'S OLD BREWERY BITTER.

Turn right out of the pub and cross the road.

SALISBURY
ST MARTIN'S LANE

Perhaps the designers of the Chandos turned their back on pastiche Victoriana because they had, in their near-neighbour, one of the finest examples in London of the real thing.

The Salisbury stands on the site once occupied by a raffish tavern called the Coach & Horses. Its landlord in the 1840s and 50s was the great prizefighter Ben Caunt, whose father had been a servant of Lord Byron's; after his death the pub was briefly renamed the Ben Caunt's Head. Caunt had won the national title from the much smaller Bendigo in 1841, and lost it four years later in an 85-round rematch held in fields near Newport Pagnell. The huge crowds who streamed from all over England behaved so appallingly that prizefighting finally

lost what last tatters of high-society patronage it still had; within 20 years it was dead as a mainstream sport.

In 1892 the old tavern was demolished, and in its place sprang up the ornate Salisbury Stores, named after the current Prime Minister, the third Marquis of Salisbury, whose family owned the freehold of the site (Cecil Court nearby bears Salisbury's family name). The "Stores" element indicates that this was not only a pub but also a wine merchant's. However this aspect of its trade did not last long: in 1898 its interior was stripped out and largely refitted, and the fantastic etched and brilliant-cut mirrors, the bronze lamps in the form of nymphs, and the grand mahogany bar-back all date from this project.

With its prominent location and its magnificent decor, the Salisbury quickly became one of the most famously theatrical pubs in the West End. This meant that it had a large gay clientele long before homosexuality was legalised: in 1961 it had a starring role in Joseph Losey's film *Victim*, starring Dirk Bogarde and dealing with the subject of homosexual blackmail.

OPEN ALL PERMITTED HOURS. FOOD SERVED ALL DAY.
REAL ALES: COURAGE BEST & DIRECTORS.

Turn left out of the pub down St Martin's Court.

ROUND TABLE
ST MARTIN'S COURT

Like the Salisbury, the Round Table is a Victorian theatre-land pub with a past rooted in the racier world of prizefighting.

The existing building went up in 1877, when Charing Cross Road was being driven through this rather raffish quarter on the shadowy borderland of the slums of Seven Dials. The original Round Table had been one of the headquarters of "the fancy", the supporters and promoters of bare-knuckle prizefighting. In 1805 three such gentry – Lord Grosvenor, a Colonel Mellish and a Captain Halliday – were promoters of a title bout between the great Jem Belcher and the wonderfully-named Game Chicken. These men had such influence that in 1808 they were able to secure the temporary release from Newgate of Jack Gully – later a successful bookie, owner of three Derby winners, and an MP – to face the Game Chicken.

In 1860 the Round Table – so named to convey the impression that fights arranged there would be fair and just – became the headquarters of an American import, John C Heenan, also known as the Benecia Boy, brought over to challenge the last British prizefighter of any repute, Tom Sayers. The fight ended in a draw, with both men too exhausted to carry on, but Heenan remained in Britain until 1862 when he was doped before a fight and was so badly injured that he never regained his health.

The present Round Table has a curiously bland facade of highly-glazed yellow brick, but standing as it does in a narrow sunless court, it was maybe thought that anything more elaborate would be wasted.

Inside, the decorative scheme of the single downstairs bar dates only from a recent refurbishment, but with its cladding of stained pine planks, its bare floorboards, and its leaded lattice windows with odd scraps of stained glass, it's a reasonable stab at the Olde English style of 1900–10.

OPEN ALL PERMITTED HOURS. FOOD SERVED ALL DAY. REAL ALES: THEAKSTON BEST & OLD PECULIER; GREENE KING IPA; GUEST ALES.

Return to St Martin's Lane. Cross the road and turn left, then right into Garrick Street. Take the second left.

LAMB & FLAG
ROSE LANE

Before Garrick Street was built in 1859, Rose Lane – or Red Rose Street, as it was originally – stretched much further south than it does now, and it had a villainous reputation. "Here might be seen low gambling-houses; floors let out to numerous families with fearful broods of children; sundry variations of the magisterial permission to be "drunk on the premises"; strange, chaotic trades to which no one skilled contribution imparted a distinctive character; and, by way of a moral drawn from the far-off pure air of open fields and farmyards, a London dairy professing to be constantly supplied with fresh butter, cream, and new milk from the country," wrote a contemporary.

Rose Lane was mostly built in the early 17th century, and among its many alehouses and taverns was the Coopers Arms. This was better-known as the Bucket of Blood, a nickname supposedly – although if it's true, the tavern must have been much bigger than it is today – derived from the prizefights held there. Just outside the Bucket of Blood on 19 December 1679 the poet Dryden was set upon and nearly murdered by thugs hired by the Earl of Rochester, who suspected the poet of writing a satirical pamphlet lampooning him. (In fact the anonymous author was the Earl of Mulgrave.)

In the later 19th century the district became a more respectable, artisanal one, and the Lamb & Flag, as the Coopers Arms was rechristened, was rebuilt as a respectable artisanal pub (although it's said to retain much of its 17th-century fabric). Now rather pleasingly scruffy, it still has that same stolid, no-frills atmosphere: the pine plank dado, the hessian wall-coverings, the built-in benches, the dark pressed-paper ceiling, the original parlour fireplace and simply decorated glass screens of its two small bars were not put there to please tourists – although they do so, very much indeed.

OPEN ALL PERMITTED HOURS. HOT FOOD IN UPSTAIRS BAR 12–3 MONDAY–SATURDAY; BAR SNACKS 12–4 MONDAY–SATURDAY. REAL ALES: COURAGE BEST & DIRECTORS, YOUNG'S BITTER.

Take the passage – Lazenby Court – beside the pub and turn right into Floral Street.

NAG'S HEAD
10 JAMES STREET

Standing as it does almost opposite the Royal Opera House and just down the road from the Theatre Royal, you'd expect the Nag's Head to be a shrine to all things theatrical. And so it is, with its walls plastered with playbills and other memorabilia. Until a few years ago, however, this big late Victorian red-brick pub with its turret, its ornate stone dressings and spiked cupola, its marble bar-top and its polychrome quarry-tile floor, was more than just a shrine: it was almost a museum.

Dating back to 1700 and rebuilt in the 1890s, it was originally a hostel for touring opera companies. Later it became popular with porters from Covent Garden Market, and had an early-opening licence until the market moved to Nine Elms. But it was best-known for its priceless collection of Theatre Royal and Royal Opera House playbills going back to the early 19th century and beyond, many of them wrapped round the marble columns in the bar.

One, dated 31 March 1814, advertised Edmund Kean playing Hamlet in a run of 68 nights which supposedly put a staggering 166,742 bums on seats. Another was for his performance in *Romeo & Juliet* the following year, on which a scribbled note recorded opening-night takings of £420.3.6. Others advertised performances by David Garrick, Sir Henry Irving, Mrs Siddons, and the Kembles.

There was also a collection of hundreds of prints and engravings of old Covent Garden, and in the upstairs restaurant (currently closed) a display of original designs for theatre and ballet by Cecil Beaton, Honor Frost, Oliver Messel and Tanya Moisevitch. Denzil Batchelor, writing in the early 1960s, said: "There is no inn in England which has been more carefully and expertly restored to do justice to its fabulous past and exciting present."

What happened to the oldest of the exhibits I don't know: maybe they went missing when Whitbread sold the pub to the Hertford brewer McMullen. Maybe they were casualties of the refurbishment which saw the original layout knocked into one big bar. Maybe they've been transferred to the safe custody of the Theatre Museum in Russell Street nearby. But the brewery is clearly doing its best to build up a new collection, so perhaps in another 150 years the Nag's Head will look as it did 30 years ago.

Continue along Floral Street, then turn right into Bow Street.
Turn left into Russell Street, then immediately right into Catherine Street.

OPERA TAVERN
21 CATHERINE STREET

Immediately opposite the Theatre Royal, the little Opera Tavern has the most startling facade of dark green striated marble, with two tiny gilded wood-framed bay windows incongruously inserted.

Built in 1879, it is the work of the prolific architect George Treacher, who was responsible for dozens of London pubs in different styles between 1872 and 1897, first working on his own, then as a partner in the practice of Treacher & Fisher. Many of Treacher's pubs have long fallen before bomb or bulldozer; but fortunately the Opera Tavern is one of the best of them, a "nice example of vulgar stucco classicism", according to Mark Girouard.

The interior, alas, does not quite live up to the splendour of the facade: as you would guess, its internal partitions have long been removed, and only the bar-back and a single small fireplace survive of the original work. What remains is pleasant enough, if rather plain; but the pub naturally remains a popular rendezvous for theatre-goers.

OPEN 12–11 MONDAY–SATURDAY, 12–9 SUNDAY. FOOD 12–3 AND 6–8. REAL ALES: ADNAM'S BITTER, GREENE KING IPA, DRAUGHT BASS.

Continue down Catherine Street and bear right down the Aldwych.

WELLINGTON TAVERN
351 STRAND

What a curious beast the Wellington is. For a start, it seems from the outside to be truly enormous, with six stories occupying a big site at the corner of the Aldwych facing Waterloo Bridge. But inside its single split-level bar, while capacious enough, is hardly cavernous. This "reverse Tardis" effect is not uncommon in Victorian pubs: I often find myself wondering whether there are secret rooms to account for it, or whether the walls are several feet thick, or whether the apparent size from outside is just a design trick.

Responsibility for the looming and rather gaunt exterior goes to the veteran practice of Bird & Walter, which was founded in the early 1860s and had at least 74 pubs to its credit up to the beginning of the last century. This is one of the last, and was built in 1903 to replace an earlier pub of the same name dating from 1848. There's a fascia of speckled brown marble and a carved stone corner turret with some delightful little gargoyles; but the sheer scale of the building rather overwhelms the details.

The second curious thing is that although many fine interior features survive, the whole is less than the sum of its parts. The carved wooden bar-back and the door lobbies are original, there are high coffered ceilings of grandly sculpted plaster, and a huge marble fireplace at the back is set in a wall entirely covered by plaques of multicoloured marble which were uncovered under layer after layer of wallpaper during restoration in 1988. The walls are liberally covered in Duke of Wellington pictures and memorabilia including a display case of Peninsular War socket bayonets.

And yet, for all its detail, the overall effect is rather bare. Without partitions, the original features are rather dwarfed: they were designed to be seen in the context of at least two rooms, possibly three; some means of breaking up the space – some booths, perhaps – would immeasurably improve the pub's atmosphere.

OPEN ALL PERMITTED HOURS. FOOD SERVED 12–10.
REAL ALES: FULLER'S LONDON PRIDE, DRAUGHT BASS.

Turn right out of the pub.

Lyceum Tavern

354 Strand

The Lyceum Tavern is a very different proposition from its neighbour, the Wellington. Part of the Hennekey's chain founded in 1695 and acquired by Sam Smith's in 1980, it has all the hallmarks of a Sam Smith's refurbishment: calm and uncluttered, with workmanship of the first quality.

Outside, it is an undistinguished building with a homely wooden fascia. Inside, although like so many London pubs it has all been knocked into one, it manages to retain a feeling of intimacy with its wooden panelling and its row of really snug little booths, more like alcoves, built into the length of one wall.

The Lyceum Tavern was among a number of pubs listed in an article in Licensing World in March 1914 on the then-current vogue for "Mock Antique Taverns", characterised by the "cosy nooks, high-backed chairs, oil paintings, and green plush" of the Six Bells in King's Road, Chelsea (now some sort of theme pub), where: "Everything about the place carries one's mind back to the days of yore," and "even the light fittings consist of lanthorns and wrought-iron brackets."

No such excesses are to be seen in today's Lyceum Tavern, yet Sam Smiths has preserved the restrained, rather masculine character sought by the original designer in revulsion against the gaslight-and-glitter gin palaces of the 1890s.

OPEN 11.30-11 MONDAY-SATURDAY, 12-6 SUNDAY. FOOD 12-3.30, 5-8. REAL ALE: SAM SMITHS OLD BREWERY BITTER.

Turn right out of the pub, then cross the Strand.

COAL HOLE
91 STRAND

A precursor of Victorian music hall, the original Coal Hole was a cellar in Fountain Court, off the Strand, run by – and named on account of – one Rhodes, the Singing Collier. It was a "song and supper" club, where regulars including the cartoonists Gillray and Rowlandson were encouraged to entertain each other with comic songs and sentimental ballads.

In late Georgian times, the great Shakespearian actor Edmund Kean established at the Coal Hole one of the last of the informal clubs which had once been so popular. The Wolves' Club was dedicated to providing late-night "supper, song, and good fellowship" for actors who would arrive to begin the night's revels after finishing their various performances.

As well as being a great tragedian, Kean was an alcoholic manic depressive who, at times of great stress, would saddle up after a performance and gallop aimlessly through the night, returning home exhausted after daybreak. According to Thomas Burke: "There [at the Coal Hole] he spent his midnight leisure and squandered his health and genius. When drawing-rooms were waiting to receive him, he turned his back on them and proudly took the chair of the Wolves, whose members he exhorted to have 'a pride that ranked them with the courtier and a philosophy that put them with the peasant'. It was composed almost entirely of men of the theatre, 60 or 70 in number; a fraternity of choice spirits passing the night in harmony and losing in each other's society all their wrongs and worries."

Kean died of drink in 1833 after collapsing on stage.

In the middle of the 19th century, the Coal Hole was run by the porn king of the time. Renton Nicholson, according to Burke, was "a purveyor of the more raffish kind of entertainment, and was more than once in trouble. He kept, one after the other, a number of taverns, and while for a time he made a good thing out of them, he brought them all eventually into disrepute ... He had the Garrick's Head in Bow Street and for a time the Coal Hole, the Cyder Cellar (in Maiden Lane), and Cremorne Gardens, and whatever he touched he soiled. At the three taverns named he carried on his notorious Judge & Jury trials, at which he himself was the judge under the style The Lord Chief Baron. These were mock trials of unsavoury subjects ... Plaintiff, defendant, witnesses and counsel were actors from the minor theatres, and the jury was empanelled from the supper company. The purpose of the trials was to evoke laughs by the indecent nature of the evidence ... These shows drew all the town and numbers of country visitors. All those who attended agreed that they were a scandal and should be stopped; but they seem to have gone more than once."

The Baron also published *The Swell's Night Guide to the Great Metropolis,* listing "the Paphian beauties ... the introducing houses, the French houses"; essentially a directory of prostitutes and brothels, and at the Garrick's Head he staged poses plastiques in which naked women posed against a black backcloth; admission, one shilling.

The Coal Hole was pulled down in the 1880s to make way for the Savoy Theatre and Hotel, but when a huge Olde English tavern, the New Strand Wine Lodge – with an equally enormous wine bar in its cellar – was incorporated into Savoy Buildings in 1904, it evoked memories of the notorious old Coal Hole and quickly acquired its name.

It has, according to Mark Girouard, "more than a touch of Arts & Crafts in its elaborate wrought-iron sign and the frieze of willowy ladies running round the top of the bars ... More significant, perhaps, than its Arts & Crafts trimmings are its leaded windows, black pseudo-oak beams, and gallery." The "willowy ladies" are full-thighed Roman maidens, who are idly harvesting grapes while clad in wispy, revealing shifts totally unsuited to the work. They have been described as being of plaster and even marble, but on close inspection turn out to be no more than pressed paper.

OPEN 11–11 MONDAY-SATURDAY, 12–8 SUNDAY. FOOD SERVED 12–5. REAL ALES: TETLEY BITTER, ADNAM'S BITTER, FULLER'S LONDON PRIDE, MORLAND OLD SPECKLED HEN.

Take Southampton Street immediately opposite the pub. Turn right into Maiden Lane and follow it into Chandos Place.

MARQUESS OF GRANBY
51–52 CHANDOS PLACE

The Marquess of Granby, named after an 18th-century general who set up many of his veterans in pubs, is so thin it seems to be breathing in. It stands on a site crammed up against the side of the Coliseum, so it has a long frontage but almost no depth. Wedge-shaped, it has a snug at each end: one of reasonable size at the thick end and one at the thin end so constricted that two large men and a tray of drinks would find it a squeeze.

In the 17th century a low tavern called the Hole in the Wall occupied the site. It was here in 1669 that the romantic highwayman Claude Duval was arrested. Born in France, he had come to England as a servant in the retinue of Charles II on the Restoration in 1660,

aged only 17. He soon fell into bad company and turned to robbery, particularly haunting the Uxbridge Road or, as it is now, Bayswater Road. During one robbery he persuaded the lady in the coach he was holding up to dance with him to the tune of a flageolet, and gallantly returned £300 of the £400 he had stolen from her. The episode, described by Lord Macaulay and painted in 1859 by William Powell Frith, turned him into a romantic hero, and after his arrest at the Hole in the Wall – heavily armed, but too drunk to fight – there were passionate appeals for clemency. But Charles II would hear none of it, for among Duval's victims had been his Master of Buckhounds. Duval was hanged on 21 January 1670 amid national mourning and a welter of pamphlets and epitaphs.

The present pub dates to the 1860s or thereabouts and is simple, light, and airy. The screens dividing off the two snugs are of a low gothic style that could have come from a nonconformist chapel. The bar-back has twisted wooden columns and a decorative frieze, and there is a cast-iron fireplace with a tiled surround in the larger of the two snugs.

OPEN 12–11 MONDAY–SATURDAY; 12–10.30 SUNDAY. FOOD SERVED 12–5. REAL ALES: ADNAM'S BITTER, TIMOTHY TAYLOR LANDLORD, FULLER'S LONDON PRIDE, GUEST ALES.

Turn right out of the pub into William IV Street, then left down St Martin's Lane.

FINISH: CHARING CROSS TUBE

THE BOROUGH
PRISONERS & PLAYWRIGHTS

LENGTH OF WALK: THREE MILES

THE important thing to remember about Southwark is that it's south of the river. This may seem an obvious, even a silly thing to point out, but what it meant in medieval and Tudor times was that it was nobody's job to run it.

The City of London's writ ran out at the end of London Bridge, so the only authorities in Southwark were the big landowners, mostly religious foundations and institutions such as the diocese of Winchester which were not set up to administer towns and tended to be very bad at it. Unless the townspeople ran the show themselves, with a proper structure of charter, mayor, aldermen, wards, constables, guilds and so forth, anarchy tended to prevail. Southwark became known, derisively at first, as the Borough because that's precisely what it wasn't: it didn't have any of the structures of a proper borough; bad characters could find refuge from authority in it, and all sorts of illegal activities – not just the obvious ones, like prostitution, but more workaday offences like holding unregulated (and untaxed) markets – could be carried on with comparative impunity. (Southwark prostitutes and the brothels they worked in, the "stews", were actually licensed by the Bishops of Winchester, who took a cut of their earnings, until Henry VIII stopped it.)

Many, if not most, English towns and cities had just such

unregulated faubourgs just outside the city walls – criminal blots on the landscape to some, but also full of energy and vitality. The Borough was even more energetic and vital than most, not just because of its size, but because it sat astride the main road between London and the Channel ports. Its main street was lined with inns – the King's Head, the White Hart, the George, the Tabard, the Mermaid, the Angel, the Three Tuns – which, being unregulated, enjoyed a strong competitive advantage over their rivals across the Bridge. The Borough was therefore packed not only with criminals, prostitutes and unlicensed market traders, but also with travellers, native and foreign, great and small, on their way to and from destinations as mundane as Canterbury or as exotic as the Holy Land.

From the middle of the Tudor period, a new profession emerged whose very existence was legally doubtful. For members of this profession, the comparative licence of the Borough offered the possibility of being allowed to pursue their calling in relative peace. They were actors, the inheritors of a diverse set of traditions embracing semi-sacred mystery plays, minstrelsy, the fairground entertainment provided by strolling jugglers, fire-eaters, and mountebanks, and the semi-official office of court jester. In the Borough all these strands came together; and for the first time in British history, drama had a home.

Not, at first, a terribly secure or permanent home. The first purpose-built theatre in the Borough was the Rose, built in 1587 at what is now the corner of Rose Alley and Park Street. It was strongly associated with Marlowe and the actor Edward Alleyn, founder of Dulwich College, who took the lead in the first productions of *Tamburlaine the Great*, *The Jew of Malta*, and *Dr Faustus*. Shakespeare himself was a member of the company at the Rose when he first arrived in London. But less than 20 years later, in 1605, it was closed down and demolished. Even its site was forgotten until its foundations were discovered in 1988.

The largest and longest-lived of the Borough theatres was the Swan, whose site is in Hopton Street. It lasted from 1595 to 1640, but its early years demonstrate the legal twilight in which the theatre lived. Two years after it opened it staged Thomas Nashe's *Isle of Dogs*, which was judged seditious. The cast, which included Ben Jonson, were jailed, and all the playhouses were briefly closed.

The Globe itself, Shakespeare's own theatre, was no more long-lived. It opened in 1599, having been built from the timbers of the first Globe, which had opened in 1576 in another of London's extra-mural faubourgs, Shoreditch. The opening performance was the first production of *Henry V* (which refers to "this wooden O"), followed in the same year by *Julius Caesar*. During the premiere of *Henry VIII* in 1613, prop cannons set fire to it and it burned down. It was rebuilt, but was finally closed and demolished in 1644.

The Hope Theatre at the corner of Bear Gardens and Park Street opened when the Globe burned down; its first performance was the premiere of Jonson's *Bartholomew Fair*. But it was never a success as a theatre: every Tuesday and Thursday, drama gave way to bear-baiting, but within a couple of years the bear-baiting proved the more popular, and the owners gave up on drama altogether. The Hope remained a bear garden until it closed in 1656.

Where you find criminals and prostitutes (and actors), you also expect to find prisons; and the Borough had more than its fair share of them. The Clink, which has left us its name as a synonym for prison, was almost next to the Bishop of Winchester's Palace – there's a rather grizzly museum in the basement of the Victorian warehouse which now occupies the site. The Marshalsea in Borough High Street may have been founded as early as 1300, and another seminal figure in English drama once enjoyed its hospitality as well as Jonson. He was Nicholas Udall, author of the first true English comedy, *Ralph Roister Doister* (1541), and coincidentally headmaster of Eton, who was imprisoned here on charges of theft and buggery.

An earlier inmate of the Marshalsea had been Sir Thomas Malory, the Warwickshire knight who as well as being a brigand and a murderer was also the author of the *Morte d'Arthur*. In fact for a long time historians thought there must have been two Malories, since they could not accept that the chivalrous author could also have been a ruthless armed robber. Walter Raleigh was another occasional occupant of the Marshalsea; but its most famous inmate must have been Charles Dickens's father John, who was jailed here for debt for four months in 1824, when Dickens was only 12. Little Charles lodged at first in Camden Town, but soon moved to Lant Street near the prison, characterising his landlord and landlady there as the kindly Mr and Mrs Garland in *The Old Curiosity Shop*. Then John Dickens's mother died, leaving him enough to pay his debts; but the experience, though brief, left a deep mark on his young son. Much of *Little Dorrit* (1857) is set in the Borough.

Also in the Borough was the King's Bench Prison, established opposite what is now Little Dorrit Court in 1758. An early inmate was Tobias Smollett, who wrote *Launcelot Greaves* while incarcerated in 1761. Yet another was Horsemonger Road Prison, where Leigh Hunt was gaoled in 1813 for calling the Prince Regent "a fat Adonis of 50".

Most of the old Borough was swept away in the 19th century when the development of river traffic and the railways turned it into a hive of industry. Food processors in particular sited their factories here, including Jacobs and Crosse & Blackwell. The first steam-driven flour mill in the world was established near Blackfriars Bridge in the late 18th century, and with Kent & Sussex hops coming up by road and East Anglian barley coming in by river, brewing was a thriving industry. Courage was the biggest Southwark brewery, but there were many others. The massive industrialisation of the Borough spelled the end for its many slum courts and alleys, which was good; it also spelled the end for all of its great coaching inns except one-third of one of them, which was not so good.

Despite the fact that most of its Chaucerian, Shakespearian and Dickensian past has been effectively obliterated, the Borough has in recent years become one of London's busiest tourist areas. This is surely more because of the huge number of individual attractions situated here than for the Borough's intrinsic character. As well as long-established lures such as the London Dungeon, HMS Belfast, and the Old Operating Theatre at Guy's Hospital, there's now the the Britain at War Experience, the Golden Hind replica, the Clink Exhibition, the Bankside Gallery, Vinopolis, and the two big ones - Shakespeare's Globe and Tate Modern. Hopefully, by the time you read this, there will be the Millennium Bridge as well.

And of course, there's always the pubs.

START: LONDON BRIDGE TUBE

Take the Borough High Street exit and turn left.

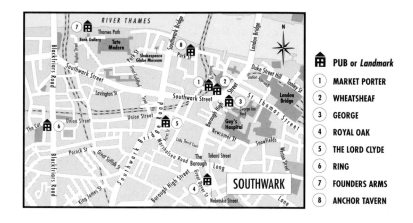

⌂	**PUB** or *Landmark*
①	**MARKET PORTER**
②	**WHEATSHEAF**
③	**GEORGE**
④	**ROYAL OAK**
⑤	**THE LORD CLYDE**
⑥	**RING**
⑦	**FOUNDERS ARMS**
⑧	**ANCHOR TAVERN**

OPERATING THEATRE MUSEUM & HERB GARRET

9A St Thomas Street. Built in 1819 as homes for the hospital apothecary, superintendent, secretary and gatekeeper. The apothecary's herbs were dried in the garret at the top of the tower of St Thomas's Church. The operating theatre was opened in 1821 in a women's surgical ward and was turned into a museum in 1956.

OPEN 10–4. RING 0207 955 4791 FOR FURTHER DETAILS.

Cross Borough High Street.

MARKET PORTER

9 STONEY STREET

Borough Market just across the road may be under threat from Railtrack's plans to flatten much of the area, but at the Market Porter they still hang on to their market licence to allow the porters who work in it their traditional beery breakfast, which you are welcome to share.

There's been a pub on the site since 1638 (called the Harrow until fairly recently); but the existing building dates very defiantly from the late 1890s and is firmly of the Olde English style then coming into vogue as a reaction against the gas-and-glitter gin palaces of the preceding 20 years. There's wood here, lots of it: beams, panels, stub ends of old partitions, carved bar-back and semi-glazed gantry, bare floorboards, the lot. There are small-paned leaded windows, there are bits and pieces of stained glass, there are open fires – everything that the robust and manly English male of circa 1900 could wish for.

There's also ale. This is a pub which has built a reputation on the quality and variety of its ales over a number of years. Its owner co-founded Bishop's Brewery opposite, and although the brewery is now an unconnected business (it brews the house bitter for the George down the road), the Market Porter hasn't forgotten its love affair with ale. Eight are on tap at any one time, mainly from micro breweries, and all are in excellent condition.

OPEN 6–8.30 AM, 11–11 MONDAY–FRIDAY, 12–11 SATURDAY, 12–10.30 SUNDAY. FOOD SERVED 6–8.30 AM MONDAY–FRIDAY, 12–2.30 ALL WEEK. REAL ALES: HARVEY'S BEST, COURAGE BEST, SIX GUEST ALES.

THE WHEATSHEAF
6 STONEY STREET

There was a time when all pine in pubs was treated with a distinctive thick orangey stain and artificially grained. I have drunk in pubs all over Britain where the woodwork was Chivers-coloured, and I always took it for granted and scarcely noticed it. A trip to the Wheatsheaf suddenly made me realise that it was an effect I had not seen for a long, long time.

But that's the kind of pub the Wheatsheaf is. Although it has now given up its early market licence, it's still in some ways much more of a traditional market boozer than the Market Porter three doors down. The aforementioned orange stain is slapped on to the long pine-plank partition that divides the saloon bar (upholstered banquette and open-weave carpet on the posh side, greasy spoon-style tables and chairs on the public) and on every other wooden surface in sight. It's all very 1950s/60s eel-pie-and-mash, except it serves cask beer.

And how! The Market Porter may have eight real ales, but the Wheatsheaf runs it a close second with five, and it holds regular beer festivals too. All in all, these two pubs are a great reason for spending a day in Stoney Street.

But maybe not for much longer. The Wheatsheaf is one of the

buildings earmarked for demolition to improve rail access to London
Bridge. The houses either side are already blighted and empty, and the
roof of Borough Market is scheduled to be sliced off. There has been
virulent opposition, but bodies like Railtrack are hard to stop. If it all
goes ahead – and we should know one way or another by the time
this book comes out – it will be the end of this vibrant corner of Old
London. There must be a better way.

OPEN 11–11 MONDAY–SATURDAY, CLOSED SUNDAY.
FOOD SERVED 12–2.30 MONDAY–FRIDAY.
FIVE CHANGING REAL ALES, MAINLY FROM MICRO BREWERIES.

Return to the High Street. Cross it and turn right.

GEORGE
77 BOROUGH HIGH STREET

You don't need me to tell you that this is one of a very few classic inns of its kind in London – in fact, if you disregard a handful of examples in the outer suburbs, it's the only classic inn of its kind in London.

The George trades heavily on its links with Shakespeare, and indeed it has pre-Tudor roots: it was one of the great inns of Southwark, along with the White Horse on one side (where Mr Pickwick first met Sam Weller), and the Tabard on the other (from which Chaucer's pilgrims departed for Canterbury on that bright April morning). These and the Borough's other inns were central to the bustling life of the faubourg: their courtyards resounded with all the accents of Europe, for they were London's forecourt. They were marketplaces, they were hiring marts, they were ad-hoc theatres, they were international exchanges.

But that is not what you actually see when you peer through the narrow gateway into the George's yard. What you see is, first of all, not Tudor but 17th century, for it was rebuilt from the ground up after a fire in 1676; and secondly, you see almost the last surviving relic in London of what was once an enormous industry: long-distance horse-drawn transport.

We like to think of the 18th century as the coaching era, with post-horns and blunderbusses and enormous complicated overcoats; but the mail-coaches of romantic imagination are only one aspect of a multifarious business on which almost the entire commercial life of the country depended for over a century.

As well as the glamorous mail-coaches (which were only introduced in 1784), there were passenger coach services, some of them fast and efficient, many of them slow, unreliable, and bum-numbingly uncomfortable; there were goods carriers who would also take the poorest passengers; and there were privately-owned coaches, gigs, flies, and broughams, which needed fodder and stabling

for the horses and brandy and beefsteak for the drivers.

The George never joined the first rank of coaching inns, but at its peak 80 regular services used it every week, as well as private travellers in their own vehicles. It was as workaday as Kings Cross or a motorway service station. There were dozens like it at every approach to the capital, many of them household names like the Belle Sauvage; but the arrival of steam trains in the 1830s and 40s sent them into terminal decline. Most of them closed down, and the George very nearly did, dwindling from an inn to a mere tavern – although, touchingly, the landlords always kept a couple of four-posters made up just in case.

The George survived again after 1898, when the Great Northern Railway planned to demolish it to make way for new railway lines and warehouses. Indeed, most of it was demolished: it used to surround the whole yard, whereas now there is only a single range down one side; and there used to be a second yard behind the first, with rows of stabling stretching back under what are now railway arches.

What's left, though, is enough: there's a rambling row of five separate rooms, all black oak, high-backed settles, nicotine-stained plaster, and heavily-beamed ceilings; all is just as your imagination says it should be, and is carefully kept that way by the joint ministrations of the National Trust (the owner) and Whitbread (the tenant). There's history, too: Shakespeare acted from the back of a cart in the yard (perhaps), and Dickens knew the place well and set scenes of *Little Dorrit* in it. There is everything, in short, to satisfy the Dickens definition of "great rambling queer old places with galleries, and passages, and staircases, wide enough and antiquated enough to furnish materials for a hundred ghost stories."

OPEN ALL PERMITTED HOURS. BAR FOOD SERVED 12–3 MONDAY–FRIDAY, 12–4 SATURDAY AND SUNDAY. RESTAURANT OPEN 12–2.30, 6–9.30 MONDAY–SATURDAY. REAL ALES: MORLAND OLD SPECKLED HEN, FLOWER'S ORIGINAL, BODDINGTON'S, GEORGE INN RESTORATION ALE, GUEST.

Turn left out of the yard. Follow the High Street to St George the Martyr (Little Dorrit's Church), and fork left down Tabard Street.

ROYAL OAK
TABARD STREET

Tabard Street is a short walk off the beaten track, but it was not always so. Until the New Kent Road and Great Dover Street were blasted through this southern end of the Borough in the 1870s, Tabard Street, then Kent Street, was part of the main road from London to the Channel and thence the rest of the world.

There was a Royal Oak on the site before the pub you see today, but it and its surroundings had a very different character from the fairly quiet semi-industrial area of modern Tabard Street. It was instead a district of packed and teeming slum courts, hidden behind the facades lining the main road and debouching on to it through narrow and carious mouths: Royal Oak Yard was one such.

There are no memories of those times in today's Tabard Street, with its new housing estates, light industry and recreation grounds. The big brick Royal Oak, with its elaborate stone dressings, has been the very epitome of civilised drinking since the Sussex brewer

Harvey's bought it from Courage in 1997. (Entirely coincidentally, the present bosses of Harvey's, Miles and Anthony Jenner, are the direct descendants of the owners of one of the great Southwark breweries of the 19th century, Jenner's of Southwark Bridge Road, which was sold only in 1938. Jenner's was known as the theatre brewery because one of the family had trod the boards before rejoining the firm and, through his showbiz contacts, managed to put Jenner's beers into virtually every theatre bar in town.)

The interior is cool, clean, and airy, broken up into three comfortable bars by partitions which were made using as much of the original woodwork as possible. It's a bit of a step from the centre of the Borough – but Harvey's beers make the walk well worthwhile.

OPEN 11.30–11 MONDAY–FRIDAY. CLOSED WEEKENDS. FOOD SERVED 12–2.15, 6–9.15. REAL ALES: HARVEY'S RANGE.

Turn right out of the pub and right again up Nebraska Street. Cross Great Dover Road into Marshalsea Road. Follow round to the right and turn right into Ayres Street.

THE LORD CLYDE
AYRES STREET

The Lord Clyde was not originally included on this walk, but it proved impossible to ignore. The profusion of elaborate emerald-green ceramic ornamentation around its doors and windows were a command to enter which could not be disobeyed.

The pub dates back to 1863, the year when Colin Campbell, Lord Clyde, a Scottish carpenter's son who rose to become Commander-in-Chief of the army, died. (There's another pub of the same vintage named after him in Bethwin Road, Camberwell, an example of how developers of the period turned to the headlines to find topical and resonant names for their new pubs.) Campbell, known as "Old Careful" because of his concern for casualties, rose to fame after his victory in the Sikh War of 1849, for which he was made a Commander of the Bath. But he became a hero of the British Empire as one of the leading figures in suppressing the Indian Mutiny in the 1850s, relieving Lucknow and Cawnpore, among other successes.

However the quite astonishing ceramic ornamentation which marks out the exterior of the Lord Clyde dates not to 1863 but to 1913, when the pub was largely rebuilt and the landlord whose name appears in the tilework, E J Bayling, took over. The ground-floor fascia is entirely of green tiles, with the windows mullioned and framed with more green tiles, and one oval window is capped by an elaborate ceramic pediment supported on ornate floral columns. The green is offset by a large name-plaque and cornice of cream tilework.

Inside, the Lord Clyde does not disappoint. It has a large L-shaped bar and a separate parlour behind, all done out in cosy red plush, with a pine-plank dado, printed red wallpaper and a cream pressed-paper ceiling. Various sailing prints recall the river of Colin Campbell's title, although he himself was definitely a landsman, and there are pictures of the regulars of the 1920s, Mr Bayling holding centre-stage, setting off on charabanc trips to the seaside. The quality of its food and ale is proved by the fact that alongside the many locals there is also a strong showing of lawyers from the Crown Court two blocks away.

OPEN 11–11 MONDAY–FRIDAY, 12–4, 8–11 SATURDAY, 12–4, 8–10.30 SUNDAY. FOOD SERVED LUNCHTIME AND EVENING. REAL ALES: GREENE KING IPA, COURAGE BEST, YOUNG'S BITTER & SPECIAL, SHEPHERD NEAME SPITFIRE.

Continue along Marshalsea Road. Turn right into Southwark Bridge Road and left into Union Street. Walk up Union Street to its junction with Blackfriars Road.

THE RING
72 BLACKFRIARS ROAD

It would be all too easy to ignore the Ring as just another Victorian street-corner pub, especially as the corner it stands on is not a particularly prepossessing one. Union Street, along which you approach the pub, is a narrow and dowdy drag of run-down warehouses and blocks of flats, while Blackfriars Road is an endless torrent of traffic. But don't be fooled by its unexceptional looks: the Ring is a monument to an intriguing period in the social history of South London.

Until recently the pub was the more prosaic Railway; the original Ring stood on the opposite corner of the crossroads, on the site at present occupied by a 1950s barracks of an office-block called Orbit House, and was not a pub at all but a major boxing venue.

The Ring, an enormous octagonal building, had been a South London landmark since 1783, when it was built as the Surrey Chapel by the fiery preacher Rowland Hill, who chose the idiosyncratic shape for the same reason that Templar chapels were round: it left the Devil no corners to hide in. In 1803 it was the scene of the inaugural meeting of the National Union of Sunday Schools, but later in the century its congregation moved to a new church and the Surrey Chapel went through a variety of uses before falling into dereliction.

In 1910 it was rented by a former lightweight boxing champion, Dick Burge, and his wife Bella, to become one of the most popular venues for the noble art in London. Dozens of matches were staged there, some between contract men who only fought at that venue, but others involving such great names as Georges Carpentier, Bombardier Billy Wells and Kid Berg. Boxers fought far more frequently then than now, and for far less money; but then they were often desperate men, especially after World War I. The former British cruiser weight champion Harry Reeves, out of work and with no other way of feeding his family, insisted on a fight at the Ring immediately after his discharge from the army, even though he hadn't boxed since 1916 and had an unhealed wound on his leg. He struggled on for four rounds, ring-rusty and handicapped, against a much more agile man, until his wound burst and the fight was stopped. He never fought again.

Dick Burge died in the flu epidemic of 1918, leaving Bella (an adoptive sister of Marie Lloyd and a former music-hall star in her own right) to run the Ring on her own, as Britain's – and perhaps the world's – only woman boxing promoter. Evidently a formidable character, she managed riotous crowds and truculent fighters with matriarchal majesty, preventing one pugilist who'd tried to deck the referee from leaving the ring until he'd said sorry.

Bella sold the Ring in 1940, and it was about to be refurbished and modernised when it was bombed flat, never to rise again. An era was over, but not forgotten: the name of the Railway was changed soon after, and in 1990 the pub was taken over by former Army champion and pro boxer Neville Axford, with 25 fights under his belt.

There's nothing fancy about the Ring: it was stripped of any original features long ago, and today it's a straightforward boozer serving good ale and plain pub grub. But it's still a shrine to the other world of professional boxing of the 1920s and 30s, its walls covered in dozens if not hundreds, of black and white promotional portraits of fierce, eager young men with Brylcreemed hair, faces in various conditions of damage, stripped down to shorts and singlet, posed in the boxer's half-crouch, experienced fists at the ready.

London's past is not all Charles Dickens and Dr Johnson.

OPEN ALL PERMITTED HOURS. FOOD SERVED 12–2 MONDAY–FRIDAY, 12–4 SATURDAY AND SUNDAY. REAL ALES: YOUNG'S BITTER, FULLERS LONDON PRIDE, IND COOPE BURTON ALE.

Turn left out of the pub and walk up Blackfriars Road. Cross the road and, at the southern end of Blackfriars Bridge, turn right down steps signposted Thames Path.

FOUNDERS ARMS
52 HOPTON STREET

You either love brand-new pubs or you hate them. The Founders Arms was built in 1979, and as its two joined brick single-storey octagons incorporate not a shred of mock-Victoriana but are uncompromisingly contemporary, you'll either love it very, very much or hate it very, very much.

The original Founders Arms was actually a few doors away at 56 Hopton Street and dated from the very early 19th century. The name owed nothing to the esteemed founder of Young's Brewery, Charles Allen Young, but refers to the fact that this used to be Founders Wharf, probably because of an iron foundry which stood nearby.

Young's bought the Founders Arms in 1956, but in 1973 it was closed to make way for the local council's Bankside Reach development, of which the Bankside Gallery behind the pub forms a part. A new site was secured, much closer to the Thames than the old one, and a totally new pub in keeping with the modernity of its surroundings was planned.

It was ready for business nearly a year before it could actually open because the surrounding roadways were far from finished. But since the Dean of St Paul's declared it officially open in 1980, it has proved immensely popular – hardly surprising, given its terrific riverfront location. Whether you like its egg-box exterior or not, its interior is very pleasing, with huge picture windows looking over to St Paul's and flooding the pub with light reflected from the river. The decorative scheme of cream-painted walls, parquet flooring round the bar-counter, and pale blue carpets elsewhere make a very cool, airy pub absolutely ideal for sitting and watching the pleasure-boats go by.

OPEN ALL PERMITTED HOURS. FOOD 12–8.30 MONDAY–SATURDAY, 12–7 SUNDAY. REAL ALES: YOUNG'S RANGE.

Continue along Thames Path.

BANKSIDE GALLERY

Headquarters of the Royal Watercolour Society and the Royal Society of Painter–Printmakers.

OPEN 10–8 TUESDAY, 10–5 WEDNESDAY–FRIDAY, 1–5 SATURDAY–SUNDAY. 0207 928 7521 FOR FURTHER DETAILS.

TATE MODERN

Opened in May 2000 in Giles Gilbert Scott's Bankside Power Station, Tate Modern has proved one of the hottest tickets in Millennium London.

OPEN DAILY 10–5.50. 0207 887 8000 FOR FURTHER DETAILS.

GLOBE THEATRE

Although some distance from the original site, which has long been built over, the Globe is as faithful a reconstruction of Shakespeare's wooden O as could be designed. Not just the reconstructed theatre, though, but a complex of buildings including exhibitions of Elizabethan London and of American actor Sam Wanamaker's struggle to realise his dream, first formulated in 1949 but not finally realised until 1997, four years after his death.

OPEN TO VISITORS 10–5; 0207 928 9444 FOR FURTHER DETAILS.

THE ANCHOR TAVERN

34 PARK STREET

What a perfect pub to end our last walk with. The Anchor, with its haphazard maze of little bars and parlours, all black oak boards and beams, tobacco-glazed plaster, high-backed settles and open fires, would be the epitome of the 18th-century tavern even if it weren't replete with stories of Pepys and Dr Johnson.

There's almost certainly been a pub on the site – quaintly known in the past as Deadman's Place thanks to the proximity of a plague pit – since the 16th century, when it was probably the Castle, and certainly since the 1660s when a leading ship's Chandler, Josiah Childs, owned both the tavern and the brewery attached to it. It may even be the "little alehouse on Bankside" from which Pepys watched the Great Fire of London growing and spreading, noting: "All over the Thames with one's face in the wind you were almost burnt with a shower of fire drops" and describing the scene as: "one entire arch of fire above a mile long, the churches, houses, and all on fire at once, a horrid noise

the fire made, and the cracking of houses in their ruin."

In the 18th century the brewery came into the possession of the Thrale family, the great friends of Dr Johnson's declining years, and as a highly successful porter brewery grew to occupy nine acres. Johnson used to stay with the Thrales at their grand home in Park Street, and had a room at the brewery where he wrote *Lives of the English Poets* (1781). He also attended a salon regularly held by Hester Thrale at the Anchor along with Goldsmith, Edmund Burke, David Garrick and (of course) Boswell.

He was one of the executors of Henry Thrale's will, and it was while discussing the sale of the brewery to two bankers called Barclay and Perkins that he remarked, "We are not here to sell a parcel of boilers and vats, but the potentiality of growing rich beyond the dreams of avarice." Three years after Johnson's death, Barclay Perkins was sold to an ambitious young entrepreneur called John Courage who already owned a substantial brewery a mile or so down river in Horselydown. In 1955 the old Thrales brewery was closed and the name itself was transferred, so for the last 30 years of its life (it is now luxury flats), the Courage brewery was known as the Anchor brewery.

There are no more Pepyses or Johnsons in the story of the Anchor. It was completely rebuilt in about 1775, but from then on went steadily downhill along with its neighbourhood. The likes of the Thraleses moved out of Park Street as industry and the railways moved in – the site of the Clink Prison next door to the pub is now buried under railway arches. The Anchor became a plain working man's pub, and luckily for us it was never considered worth modernising. In fact it was so decayed by 1939 that plans were laid for its demolition. Fortunately, the war intervened. Since then it has been propped up here and tweaked there, and recently an attractive little patio has been laid out with tables and chairs on the riverfront itself; so you end this walk and this book just where you want to: in an 18th-century tavern, a pot of ale in your hand, the slow Thames rolling past you, and the ghost of Dr Johnson in the corner of your eye.

OPEN ALL PERMITTED HOURS. BAR FOOD 12–3. RESTAURANT OPEN 12–3, 6–9.30. REAL ALES: MARSTON'S PEDIGREE, COURAGE DIRECTORS, WADWORTH'S 6X.

Continue along Thames Path.

CLINK EXPERIENCE

The Clink, the private prison of the Bishops of Winchester (fragments of their medieval palace are still to be seen next door) was burnt down in the Gordon Riots of 1780, by which time it had already been disused for a century. However it left us the expression "clink" for prison, and (supposedly) "on the fiddle" for fraud, as there was a fiddle on the prison's signboard. The Clink Exhibition in the cellars of a Victorian warehouse at 1 Clink Street.

OPEN 10–6; FURTHER DETAILS ON 0207 378 1558.

GOLDEN HIND REPLICA

Moored in St Mary Overie Dock is a full-size replica of the ship in which Sir Francis Drake circumnavigated the world in 1577–80. You won't believe how tiny it is – and you won't be surprised that Drake went a little bit mad on the voyage.

OPEN 9 – SUNSET. FURTHER DETAILS 0207 403 0123.

SOUTHWARK CATHEDRAL

St Mary Overie (St Mary's over the River) stands on the site of a 7th-century Saxon nunnery which became an Augustinian canonry 500 years later and a cathedral 800 years after that. Being south of the river, it escaped the Great Fire of London and is one of the few genuinely medieval churches in London. It's packed with tombs, including that of Shakespeare's actor brother Edmond, monuments, memorials and ancient church furniture and is well worth a visit.

OPEN 8–6. FURTHER DETAILS: 0207 407 3708.

Cross Borough High Street and return to London Bridge.

FINISH: LONDON BRIDGE TUBE

INDEX